HYPERCONFLICT

Hyperconflict

GLOBALIZATION AND INSECURITY

James H. Mittelman

STANFORD SECURITY STUDIES

An Imprint of Stanford University Press

Stanford, California 2010

Stanford University Press
Stanford, California

Printed in the United States of America on acid-free, archival-quality paper

Library of Congress Cataloging-in-Publication Data

Mittelman, James H.
    Hyperconflict : globalization and insecurity / James H. Mittelman
        p. cm.
    Includes bibliographical references and index.
    ISBN 978-0-8047-6375-2 (cloth : alk. paper) —
    ISBN 978-0-8047-6376-9 (pbk. : alk. paper)

    1. Globalization.   2. International relations.   3. Security, International.
    4. International economic relations.   5. World politics—1989–.   I. Title.

    JZ1318.M57   2010
    303.4—dc22   2009021453

Typeset at Stanford University Press in 10/14 Minion

For Linda
Alexandra, Jordan, and Alicia

CONTENTS

TABLES AND FIGURES

TABLES

FIGURES

ACKNOWLEDGMENTS

A project of this scope benefited from substantial assistance along the way. A visiting professorship at the Institute of International and Malaysian Studies at the National University of Malaysia, resident fellowships at the Helsinki Collegium for Advanced Studies (a most congenial atmosphere in every respect), a travel grant from the American Political Science Association, and overall support from the School of International Service at American University were especially helpful.

I have had the good experience of presenting my research and receiving feedback from colleagues at the University of Newcastle upon Tyne, the University of Warwick, the University of Toronto, Johns Hopkins University, the Central European University, China Foreign Affairs University, l'Université du Québec à Montréal, RMIT University, Victoria University of Wellington, and annual meetings of the International Studies Association and the American Political Science Association.

Among the individuals to whom I am indebted are Jacob Stump and Priya Dixit, Ph.D. candidates at American University and coauthors of Chapters 6 and 7, respectively. I have also been immeasurably aided by capable research assistants: Priya Dixit, Daniel Dye, Carl Anders Härdig, and Timo Pankakoski. I offer my humble thanks as well to hundreds of students who have contributed in myriad ways to my education.

I owe a large debt of gratitude to Richard Falk for writing an elegant foreword to this book. Special thanks go to Robert W. Cox, Pek Koon Heng, Randolph Persaud, Manfred Steger, Linda Yarr, and John Willoughby, who painstakingly read chapters and provided penetrating criticism. Mark Beeson and Christopher Chase-Dunn offered tough and constructive comments on a subsequent draft. Pek Koon Heng and Mika Ojakangas generously shared research materials. In addition, I am grateful for the exchange of views with Barry Gills, Akihiko Kimijima, James Rosenau, Heikki Patomäki, and Raimo Väyrynen. I greatly appreciate their advice, though I have not entirely followed it, and bear sole responsibility for the results.

In addition, I have had the good fortune to work with Stanford University Press. Geoffrey Burn, director of the press and editor of Security Studies, graciously expressed confidence in my ideas and encouraged me to complete this book, several years in the making. His assistant Jessica Walsh and editors John Feneron and Jeff Wyneken helped greatly to hone the manuscript.

Above all, I acknowledge my wife, Linda Yarr, and our wonderful children, Alexandra, Jordan, and Alicia, for their forbearance, guidance, and unstinting love.

PREFACE

Matters of security and insecurity are endemic to the globalizing world that marks daily existence. Not conditions of one's own choosing, they are inseparable from personal experience. So, too, this book is about big, powerful structures. But there is also a story behind it. Not mere abstractions, the concerns in the pages ahead stem from my journey through life. Although not wanting to detain the reader with an autobiography that may be intrinsically uninteresting, I offer a brief personal history in the Preface, for I believe in the importance of self-reflectivity.

Born during World War II, I vividly recall my father and uncles recounting a history of U.S. military valor. Having served in the European and Pacific "theaters" of war, the veterans in my family returned to "the home of the brave"—in the artful language of the national anthem, which we often recited—and found it painful to relive the grit of armed conflict. Nonetheless, these former soldiers continued to fight this war as a war of words. I was tutored in passionate narratives of masculinity, heroism, patriotism, and American invincibility. As my father put it, "'We' won every war that 'we' ever fought." And some family friends, Holocaust survivors, did not have to voice their horrific stories. Tattooed in blue with numbers from concentration camps, their forearms evinced such gruesome tales. Time and again, children of my age viewed war movies that graphically portrayed threats posed by the "enemies of the free world."

At school, my teachers reinforced the narrative about U.S. military courage and love of freedom. In the wake of a shadowy war against a putative transnational enemy ("the communist threat") in Korea, distinctions between "we" and "they" were inscribed in the consciousness of American youth. During drills in the 1950s, sirens sounded an alarm, signaling that teachers and students should quickly move to the schools' interior corridors and put heads down on folded arms as a form of self-protection against impending nuclear attack. Although as a youngster, I had little knowledge of McCarthyism, I vaguely recall witnessing this scaremongering on television and radio, which alerted citizens to "enemy" agents within U.S. national borders.

Imperiled by the Soviet Union, the font of international communism, the United States no longer faced fascist dictatorships as its chief enemies. In this fearsome climate, our neighbors built "fallout shelters," as they were called, and stockpiled such home fortifications with ample supplies supposedly to help them withstand the mushroom cloud that atomic bombs would visit upon us. If one needed a reminder of the gravity of this struggle, the Soviet Union launched Sputnik, spurring the United States in the space race.

Growing up in Ohio, I resided in an area subject to restrictive covenants applied on the basis of classifications of race, class, and religion at least until the 1960s, when rioters torched inner cities. In these heady times of conflict over civil rights and black power, parts of my hometown went up in flames.

So, too, many of my memories of university life in Michigan revolve around exclusion—boundaries between friends and enemies. Of those who attended a lecture by Martin Luther King Jr., some students refused to stand and applaud; they remained seated in a show of disapproval of King's values and goals. Their behavior was a sign of resistance to restructuring in not only the United States but also the transnational realm. For me, as for many Americans of my age, the assassinations of King and John F. Kennedy, and next his brother Robert, caused a deep sense of loss and soul-searching about violence.

An intellectual awakening occurred in my courses on international relations. Political and moral awareness came in a seminar on international organization in which I was shocked to learn about the protracted conflict over South Africa's system of racial exclusion known as apartheid.

Later, less than satisfied with my first year of graduate studies in the United States, I felt a kind of intellectual itching and wanderlust. I then enrolled in an M.A. program in African studies at Makerere University in Uganda (at the time, a branch of the University of East Africa). Johan Galtung, the distinguished Norwegian peace researcher who pioneered this field, taught one of my courses.

Having arrived shortly after decolonization and a violent civil conflict in Buganda, the country's heartland area, I learned firsthand about postconflict reconstruction. I visited refugee camps for Rwandans who were fleeing a wave of genocide; met mercenaries fighting in the Congo (today the Democratic Republic of the Congo) and white fathers, Belgian priests who ran copper mines there; and traveled to or across the border (not entirely demarcated) with the southern Sudan, which was ensconced in a long, bloody conflict with the north. Some of my fellow students in Uganda had escaped violence in their own countries and were members of liberation movements. Spontaneously, I joined a demonstration at the British High Commission in Kampala to protest the decision of Ian Smith's white-settler regime to hang three blacks in Southern Rhodesia (now Zimbabwe), only to be grabbed and roughed up by a mob. Luckily, Makerere students happened by and rescued me. In a sense, I have never recovered from the good fortune of my formative experience in East Africa, a turnaround in my life.

When I returned to the United States to undertake a Ph.D. in political science, with a specialization in international organization, I was greeted by the anti–Vietnam War movement, the takeover of buildings by activists on university campuses, and fervent debates over peace and conflict. During this period, I also interned at the United Nations in New York, where I profited from a broad and practical exposure to matters of security and insecurity.

Another turning point came when I attended my first professional association meeting, held in Montreal. There, the former head of department and dean at Makerere asked what I would be doing next year. Unabashedly, I responded to the effect of "Something interesting; why do you ask?" Without hesitation, I pounced on his invitation to rejoin Makerere as a special tutor (instructor) and carry on with my doctoral research.

Not long after, on the night of January 25, 1971, gunfire disturbed my sleep. At first, I thought that it was mischief perpetrated by *kondos*, or thieves, whose gunshots sometimes troubled residents of Kampala. Living in the placid quarters of the Makerere Institute of Social Research just inside the University's secure main gate, I heard a knock at my door. I peered through the peephole and spotted a black Mercedes Benz, a government car. The man outside was a stranger, but his face looked familiar. "Sir," he said to me, "may I take refuge in your flat?" He was a minister in the government of President Milton Obote, who had just been toppled by a military coup led by Idi Amin.

After witnessing grotesque scenes in Kampala, I subsequently moved to Tanzania and then to Mozambique toward the end of its armed struggle for political independence, which was soon to erupt in civil war. There, I had an opportunity to befriend freedom fighters from neighboring South Africa, a country where, after the defeat of apartheid, I served as a visiting professor. In the interim, I lived and worked in Singapore and Malaysia, including during the 1997–98 turbulence, which provides a case study in this book. Also, on six occasions, I taught, gathered documentary material, and conducted interviews in China and Japan, similarly important to this project.

While recording my findings from these visits, I was in Washington, D.C., when the 9/11 attackers struck the Pentagon and the World Trade Center. Suddenly, political authorities defined a new "enemy"—not the same kinds of fascists or communists of earlier decades but transnational terrorists against whom a U.S.-led coalition pledged to fight a "global war."

By this point in my life, successive leaders of the United States had told me to prepare for world wars against a series of enemies: fascists, communists, terrorists. Years earlier, I had been subject to the military draft (but not called up) during the Vietnam War and, not long after, the Cuban missile crisis, when a confrontation between the United States and the Soviet Union almost triggered an outbreak of war. And overseas, on four occasions, I was on the unfortunate end of the deeds of armed combatants and thugs (no exaggeration: some of these personal stories appear in Mittelman and Pasha 1997). Yet answers to the why questions seemed to be grossly lacking.

Having carried out research on the ground on coups d'état, revolutions, liberation struggles, ethnic conflicts, civil and regional wars, and other aspects of political violence, I long puzzled about whether these pieces are part of a whole. I am convinced that a worm's-eye view of specific hotspots is invaluable, up to a point. But the big picture is perplexing. How can it be drawn? How to combine bottom-up and upstairs-downstairs perspectives from multiple research sites?

A place to begin is with the basic questions, Does globalization promote security or fuel insecurity? and, What are the implications for world order? To come to grips with these matters requires building a bridge between the geopolitics and geoeconomics of globalization, one that extends to the geostrategic sphere. Few researchers have sought to span this gulf, and these efforts have produced sharply divergent views (Chapter 2).

Some analysts maintain that globalizing processes are prone to peace because the expansion of commerce, the spread of democracy, and technological advances bring the world closer together and favor cooperation. Yet other observers argue to the contrary: the same global structures provoke conflict over trade, are used to enable criminal and terrorist networks, and lower the costs of transactions, including flows of weapons.

These debates stumble over major issues, especially on how the "fringe" zones of the world, as policy planners and strategic thinkers in Washington call them, relate to the American epicenter of power. Based in New York and Washington for most of my career, I have benefited from ample exposure to their orientations, talked to key actors in international organizations and government, collected a vast amount of data, and learned about the core processes under consideration in this book. As vital as a wealth of up-to-date information is, the standpoints adopted at these locales in the United States are wanting insofar as they focus on the here-and-now without grasping what is behind short-term events and where they are heading.

To fill the void, this book contends that beneath the exigencies of our times lie the systemic drivers of global security and insecurity. One of them may be found in the geoeconomy: a shift in the reconstitution of competition, with the development of a more belligerent form. The other driver is embedded in geopolitics, namely, the extraordinary distance between the capacities of the United States and those of other states. Furthermore, the United States is the principal node in hyperpower, which exceeds the power of a territorial state. Hyperpower includes a vast network of military bases and private security contractors, a long economic reach, dominance in the knowledge industry, technological prowess, and the wherewithal for widespread cultural diffusion, with the propagation of the American version of the English language as its most apparent sign. This argument does not however underestimate the extent to which the United States as the lead power has profound difficulty effectively using the means at its disposal.

That said, I claim that as a result of the confluence of these forces, insecurity is being globalized. And the dynamics portend *hyperconflict*. This emergent condition may be best understood as an evolving galaxy of social power relations and historical narratives. The ensuing chapters lay out the characteristics of hyperconflict, document this trend, and assess its prospects.

My main thesis does not at all cut against the findings of empirical studies of war and peace, which painstakingly show that in recent decades the frequency of armed conflict has decreased or, some say, remained level. But given structural shifts in the global political economy, why should one believe that the future will be more of the same? If the rosy view about the incidence of conflict cannot be projected in a linear manner, another perspective is worth considering.

Tilting against both classical liberal thinkers, including Adam Smith, who posited the harmony of motives, and contemporary institutionalists, who seek to trace international regimes that ensure stability, I hold that in a globalizing era, the balance is swinging in another direction. It changes course, for history is dysrhythmic and without a predefined end. If so, what are the plausible scenarios for future world order? And if the central power is imploding, how to prevent a gathering storm of hyperconflict? These themes are the landing at the close of this book.

FOREWORD

By Richard Falk

It has become increasingly difficult to frame international relations according to the realist template premised upon interaction among sovereign states.
When World War II ended, the United Nations was constructed on the basis of
such a template, conceiving of membership in organized international society
as an exclusively statist prerogative. No other political actors were considered
sufficiently significant as participants in international political life to challenge
the Westphalian paradigm that has dominated thought about world politics for
several centuries.

The UN Charter did close its eyes to the tension between its juridical affir-
mation of the equality of states and its constitutional acknowledgment of exis-
tential inequality in the form of veto rights for the five permanent members of
the Security Council. It closed them even tighter with respect to the colonized
peoples of Asia and Africa, who were (mis)represented at the United Nations
by their colonial masters. As the decolonization process rapidly unfolded in the
period between 1947 and 1980, the newly independent states were admitted to
membership in the United Nations, which meant that the Westphalian system
that had previously been mainly regional in scope and civilizational in identity
gradually evolved into a genuinely universal framework. This was the first time
that such a formally multicivilizational framework embraced all the peoples of
the world, and did seem to be a small step in the direction of what might be
called "constitutional globalization."

But it is important to appreciate that this kind of organizational framework
did little to alter the logic of security that was based, as it had been for centuries, on military capabilities, alliances, and geopolitical hierarchies. The Cold
War period, culminating this dynamic of international relations that sustained
the security of major states, made the specter of war so fearsome in what came

to be known as a system of mutual deterrence supposedly made stable by the prospect of massive devastation associated with the possession of huge arsenals of nuclear weapons by the main antagonists on the global stage. Such a bipolar world order established a condition of apocalyptic vulnerability for the entire planet that had never previously existed, and carried the amorality of political realism to the stratospheric heights of potential omnicide, or what some observers viewed as a geopolitics of extermination. This geographic extension of destruction to encompass the whole world can be best interpreted as the onset of "military globalization." An aspect of this global setting that dominated the political imagination during the Cold War was the negotiation of zones of stability (in the North), as signaled by the avoidance of intervention in Europe, and zones of interventionary rivalry (in the South), as epitomized by the wars in Korea, Vietnam, and Afghanistan.

These developments were profound but did not challenge the conceptual foundations of a Westphalian world constituted by the complex interplay between sovereign states and a supervening discipline administered by geopolitical actors exerting direct and indirect control over subordinate weaker states. A challenge did emerge in the years following the collapse of the Soviet Union due to several converging developments: the spread of what was labeled in the early 1990s as "market-oriented constitutionalism," the consequent fading away of a socialist alternative, the ascendancy of the United States as the sole surviving superpower, and a set of technological and administrative moves associated with information technology that facilitated transnational networking and socioeconomic integration. It was this series of interrelated developments unfolding in an atmosphere free from ideological rivalry that gave such salience to trade and investment trends, which were increasingly described beneath the banner of "economic globalization." The traditional preoccupations of states with security were temporarily displaced by preoccupations with economic growth as the universal engine of progress, and conflict was seen more as peripheral to world order—as disruptive encounters of mainly local, national, and humanitarian concern—and not as previously perceived, that is, as dangerously unresolved geopolitical dramas of deadly encounter.

The exception to this pattern of geopolitical calm came in the First Gulf War, when in 1990 Iraq attacked and attempted to annex Kuwait, generating a collective response organized by the United States with the backing of the United Nations. The American president at the time, George H.W. Bush, associated the military response in 1991 with a "new world order," precisely because the leading countries could agree on a common response that was given legitimacy by a decision of the UN Security Council. James Baker, the secretary of state, acknowledged a few years later that it was an unfortunate mistake for the U.S. government to have associated the new world order with collective security during the Kuwait crisis rather than to connect it with the ideological underpinning of "neoliberal globalization." More to the point, it was these emerging patterns of behavior and supportive structures, especially the combination of minimally regulated financial markets and disciplinary control of the South through the International Monetary Fund and World Bank, that cumulatively achieved the first rupture in the Westphalian framing of world politics through the prism of sovereign states delimited by territorial boundaries.

The second rupture came a decade later in the 9/11 attacks on the World Trade Center and Pentagon. These attacks were notable because they exhibited the geopolitical potency of nonstate actors and networks, demonstrating their fearful capability to disempower the traditional security mechanisms of sovereign states, which rested on their unchallengeable control of military power to deter and defend. What Al Qaeda achieved by way of inflicting harm on the dominant geopolitical actor possessing the most formidable military capabilities in the history of the world was a result that no adversary state would dare to undertake. Beyond this disclosure of a post-statist vulnerability was the awkwardness of the response, a flaying of destructive capacities without a notable impact on the terrorist threat. The response relied heavily on the military machine constructed to address hostile threats posed by adversary states but proving almost useless against this new type of threat. To the extent the threat was effectively addressed it was done through a combination of intelligence and police work that was, if anything, hampered by the clumsiness of the military undertakings. What was disclosed by 9/11 and its aftermath was a globalization of insecurity, characterized by an inability to ensure protection or to remove the threat.

But this second rupture also gave rise to a second profound shock to Westphalian verities in the form of the emergence of a "global state." The United States, with its military bases spread throughout the world, its navies on every ocean, its satellites in the skies, its special forces ignoring the constraints of foreign sovereignty, could be grasped as neither an oversized sovereign state nor as a new type of empire. It was something new and different, which corresponded to the security challenge that could not be situated territorially. Such a perception of a global state was reinforced by the reach of American diplomatic ambition and popular culture.

The third rupture took the form of the financial meltdown of 2008 and the ensuing global economic crisis, radiating its negative impacts to all corners of the planet. Whether this moment of truth for neoliberal globalization is manageable as a cyclical dislocation cannot now be discerned. If unmanageable, it would be viewed as a systemic dislocation imperiling the future of capitalism. What is already evident, and on message, is that the statist problem-solving framework relied upon to reform global economic policy is not well calibrated to the global scale of the challenge. As a result, national economic rivalry, protectionism in various forms, is likely to preclude a more benevolent pattern of response based on respecting and realizing the *global* public good.

It is with these three ruptures in mind that I find James Mittelman's book to be such an invaluable contribution to thought and action in a period characterized by confusion, turmoil, anxiety, and a pervasive sense of risk that gives rise to an enveloping atmosphere of *insecurity*. Mittelman brilliantly and presciently provides us with the first comprehensive mapping of this twenty-first century terrain of insecurity, the touchstone of his heroic effort to depict the wider implications of neoliberal globalization for the future of humanity.

What makes this undertaking truly heroic is that Mittelman accepts the daunting challenge of reconstituting a conceptual framework capable of sustaining inquiry given the obsolescence of Westphalian categories of diagnosis and prognosis. He adapts the terminology of "hyperpower," "hypercompetition," and "hyperconflict" to the originality of the global setting, whether viewed from traditional geopolitical or geoeconomic perspectives. Without questioning the continuing importance of the territorial state, the building block of Westphalian world order, Mittelman draws our attention with great erudition to how old boundaries, as between domestic and international, between self and other, between we and they, are being reconstituted to the great disadvantage of those individuals, groups, and societies that are particularly vulnerable and in various ways situated at the margins. Mittelman invokes such currently influential thinkers as Carl Schmitt, Michel Foucault, Edward Said, and Judith Butler, as well as the usual suspects found in progressive works dealing with the global setting, including Gramsci, Schumpeter, and Karl Polanyi. He also is conversant with contemporary social science approaches used to depict international trends as well as to discuss the nature and role of state and market. Overall, Mittelman builds confidence that his theory-building rests on a thorough consideration of the best thinking that has preceded his monumental undertaking. You may not agree with the assessments reached, but it is difficult to resist the conclusion that Mittelman did his very best to draw insight and support from the work of others, including those with different, even antagonistic, worldviews, such as Samuel Huntington, Thomas Barnett, and Niall Ferguson. He also does not ignore the contributions of thinkers far more congenial, including Robert Cox and Susan Strange. Such a wide net catches many ideas and approaches, making this book a pedagogical natural for university instruction.

The central argument of the book (but not its subtlety and nuanced analysis) is conveyed by the title, *Hyperconflict: Globalization and Insecurity.* Without the temerity to summarize or dissect Mittelman's worldview, I think it evident that the major conjecture underlying the text is that economic globalization is not just an extension of world trade and investment but is having revolutionary effects on the organization of political, economic, and social life of the peoples of the world; further, that the regressive ideological underpinnings of this phenomenon have been provided by neoliberalism, which privileges the market and the interests of capital and finance while neglecting the adverse consequences on people and culture. Using a series of illuminating case studies to show these forces at work in specific contexts enables Mittelman also to analyze the countermovement of resistance, both through the mobilization of civil society, as in the "battle of Seattle," and, pathologically, through the 9/11 attacks with their antihyperpower animus. Moving beyond the interactions in these examples, Mittelman provides revealing accounts of how the United States as hyperpower strives to establish a self-serving form of "security" but has unwittingly, and instead, intensified hostility and distrust to the point of generating hypercompetition, which in turn gives rise to hyperconflict. This pattern leaves in its wake a sense of heightened risk and uncertainty that is being variously experienced at different sites of struggle and vulnerability as totalizing insecurity. This experience of insecurity exhibits the novelty of this interplay of forces, making it mystifying and opaque, which in turn calls out for exposition.

Mittelman is very clear that his mission is to help us think, and not to offer simplistic solutions, much less to set forth specific policy prescriptions. He writes assuredly from a progressive perspective, movingly acknowledged in an autobiographical preface that helps establish his credential for identification and sympathy with those who find themselves victimized by forces they cannot control but strive to understand and resist. As the currently unfolding world economic crisis confirms, the tentacles of insecurity grip the hyperpower as well as the weak and vulnerable, and what is more, as clearly perceived by Mittelman, security cannot be restored by the old Westphalian reflex of militarism.

Indeed, as the neoconservative Bush presidency pathetically revealed, yielding to the militarist impulse, historically so often decisive in the high politics of global rivalry, greatly accentuated American insecurity as well as inflicted massive suffering elsewhere.

This is Mittelman's most urgent message to his readers: the old ways of power will not work, and the new ways are not yet accepted by those with the authority and capability to act. Can new leadership in this country and elsewhere, as pushed by crisis conditions and pressures from below ("globalization-from-below") and from without (climate change), restore security? Mittelman's answer, without specifying a road map, is that this hopeful possibility can only be materialized if a genuine commitment to the construction of global democracy is coupled with a drastic reorientation of globalization, basically, a shift from the priorities of capital to the imperatives of people, conceived of holistically as the human species, and not from the perspective of class, ethnicity, gender, or nation-state.

This is an inspiring book written for all those who are ready to sign up for planetary citizenship, even if this is not their current mind-set. We can keep our old identities built around loyalty to and pride in nation and state, but to move forward we will need to enlarge them as well if we are to find creative and humane responses to the multiple challenges of globalization. Mittelman not only helps us to see the world as it is but shows us how we should think about the future so as to overcome insecurity and to ground hope. This is a great achievement, warranting our attention and reflection, and eventually our gratitude.

ABBREVIATIONS

ADB	Asian Development Bank
AMF	Asian Monetary Fund
APEC	Asia-Pacific Economic Cooperation (forum)
ASEAN	Association of Southeast Asian Nations
BIT	bilateral investment treaty
CIA	Central Intelligence Agency
COW	Correlates of War (project)
DCLC	Defence of Canadian Liberty Committee
DRC	Democratic Republic of the Congo (formerly Zaire)
EU	European Union
FDI	foreign direct investment
FRELIMO	Mozambique Liberation Front (*Frente de Libertação de Moçambique*)
G-7	Group of Seven
G-8	Group of Eight
G-20	Group of Twenty
GATT	General Agreement on Tariffs and Trade
GDP	gross domestic product
IEG	Independent Evaluation Group (of the World Bank)
ILO	International Labor Organization
IMF	International Monetary Fund
IWW	Industrial Workers of the World
MAI	Multilateral Agreement on Investment
NAFTA	North American Free Trade Agreement
NGO	nongovernmental organization
NIC	newly industrializing country

OECD	Organisation for Economic Cooperation and Development
PITF	Political Instability Task Force
PRIO	International Peace Research Institute, Oslo
R&D	research and development
RAN	Rainforest Action Network
RELA	People's Volunteer Corps (*Ikatan Relawan Rakyat Malaysia*)
RENAMO	Mozambique National Resistance Movement (*Movimiento Nacional de Resistência de Moçambique*)
S&L	savings and loan (association)
SAP	structural adjustment program
SDR	Special Drawing Rights
SIPRI	Stockholm International Peace Research Institute
SSRC	Social Science Research Council
START	Study of Terrorism and Responses to Terrorism
TNC	transnational corporation
UCDP	Uppsala Conflict Data Program
UN	United Nations
WEF	World Economic Forum
WMD	weapons of mass destruction
WTO	World Trade Organization

HYPERCONFLICT

1 PRELUDE

The chief concern of this book is the relationship between globalization and security or insecurity. There are two central questions: How are they connected? And what are the implications for world order?

I want to map the debates among policymakers and scholars on these issues and develop a single concept called *hyperconflict*. It does not cut against the findings of empirical studies, which painstakingly show that in recent decades, the frequency of armed conflict has decreased or, some say, remained level. Instead, my core argument is that a novel pattern is forming. Insecurity is being globalized in an emergent configuration of hyperconflict, a galaxy of conflicts in historical motion. In other words, globalization is propelling a unique confluence of forces that portends hyperconflict. There is a reorganization of political violence, pervasive uncertainty marked by a rising climate of fear, changing structures of armed and other forms of conflict that are not necessarily in the hands of governments or their agents, and growing instability at the world level. The objective in this work is to show concretely how and why this is occurring, and what it means for future world order.

DEBATES AND VISIONS OF WAR AND PEACE

In the contemporary phase of globalization, the period from the 1970s, transnational processes rapidly slice across national territory and are also implanted inside this space. States seek to benefit from them as well as protect their citizens from threats such as global crime and pandemics brought by these transformations. The quandary is that while globalization erodes the principle of territoriality, the imperative of national security affirms the salience of homeland jurisdiction. These forces pull in opposite directions, altering the balance between security and insecurity. In this uneasy correlation of the old and the new, the national and the global blend, though not seamlessly.

In coming to grips with this shift, an oft-stated view is that globalizing processes are prone to peace because the expansion of commerce favors cooperation. It is also said that the spread of democracy fosters peace. Added to this, technological advances, particularly in communications and transportation, increase awareness and can be a spur to building commonality around the world.

Yet many of the same global structures that convey knowledge and other commodities may heighten insecurity and conflict. The Internet, the ease of travel, and financial networks enable the contagion of violence, as with cross-border criminal and terrorist organizations. Modifying the scale of action and the scope of cooperation or conflict, globalization empowers certain political actors, such as transnational advocacy networks and local civil society groups. It also reduces regulatory barriers and lowers the cost of transactions—for example, for flows of weapons and certain types of attacks. With contemporary globalization, the cost advantage now works in favor of nonstate actors. They can convert devastating strikes, such as the ones on September 11, 2001, at a price estimated at $250,000, into a multibillion dollar toll for damage and redress (Robb 2007, 31). According to Joseph Stiglitz and Linda Bilmes's calculations (2008), the overall cost of the follow-up to 9/11, the Iraq conflict, is even higher: three trillion dollars or more.

Lurking behind these factors are the deep drivers of security and insecurity, detailed in the ensuing pages. One is intensified competition that agglomerates markets. Another thrust is the amassing of power, the lead actor being the U.S. state. It, in turn, selectively induces and seeks to manage a diffusion of power that extends beyond state power. But how can the analyst bridge these geoeconomic and geopolitical realms?

To grapple with these big issues, one can trudge back over two hundred years to Immanuel Kant's philosophical writings about the quest for eternal peace. Putting forward seminal ideas about the connections between war and peace, he, like all great theorists, transcended his time and inspired thinkers to the present day. Critically, Kant's *Perpetual Peace* ([1795] 1948) offered a vision of a federation of republican states that would stave off new wars. To ensure security among themselves, states would give up lawless freedom and would agree to an expanding union based on cosmopolitan norms and world law. Renouncing a utopian perspective, Kant called for balancing morality and interests, subject to various approximations, an aspiration that was to be gradually realized by a universal order.

Striving for perpetual peace is a matter pursued by other authors mindful of the historical links between order and war. Whereas a Kantian position stresses the normative foundations of action, Marxist dialectics identify material power as the ground for protracted conflict. Both Kant and Marx knew that struggles between self-interested groups are the stuff of history—in the Marxist schema, entailing class war and ultimately the atrophy of the state. The one more ideational than the other, these sage observers were cosmopolitans who sought the means to curb the bitter antagonisms that afflict society and are used to sanctify war. These renowned thinkers understood the perils of outbreaks of war as a way to build lasting peace, later enshrined in slogans such as "the war to end all wars."

Inspired by the economic historian Charles Beard, the idea "perpetual war for perpetual peace" depicted the foreign policies of the United States in the run-up to World War II. Beard (1946, 1948) reproached Presidents Franklin D. Roosevelt and Harry Truman for steadily preparing for war while proclaiming Washington's peaceful intentions. So, too, George Orwell's antiutopian novel *Nineteen Eighty-Four* ([1949] 1950) showed how a new world order could be organized along the lines of perpetual war, represented satirically in his narrative as a quest by free peoples for perpetual peace. The notion of peace through war is thus similarly treated by Beard and Orwell: for Beard, in the sense of the "right" to conduct military operations against any power that threatens peace; and for Orwell, as an internal affair in which the state stirs up fear and uses foreign policy as a device to control its own citizens.

Fictionalizing a situation in which three major powers are constantly at war with one another, Orwell's story makes the point that "[t]he war . . . if we judge it by the standards of previous wars, is merely an imposture. . . . But though it is unreal it is not meaningless. . . . The very word 'war' . . . has become misleading. It would probably be accurate to say that by becoming continuous war has ceased to exist" (Orwell [1949] 1950, 204–5). In *Nineteen Eighty-Four*, the foremost powers do not fight one another; they live in perpetual peace; and this permanent peace is no different from permanent war. "[T]he object of the war is not to make or prevent conquests of territory, but to keep the structure of society intact" (204–5). Orwell's sinister scenario may be regarded as commentary on the historiography of his own day and more generally as a resemblance to, or an embodiment of, the meaning that Beard had conveyed.

The insight that war-makers offer urgent reasons to wage war in order to secure peace is investigated in empirical research by other revisionist historians (Barnes 1953; Divine 2000) and by various social critics. When in the throes of war, President Richard Nixon sought to convince the public that the U.S. military was extending the battlefield and bombing Cambodia so as to bring peace to Vietnam, Seymour Melman (1970, 1971, [1974] 1985), among others, showed who benefited from the war economy in the late twentieth century. A professor of industrial engineering, Melman provided meticulous empirical accounts of technological advances in the industrialization of warfare and the special interests that it serves. In this tradition, and post–9/11, dissident writers such as Gore Vidal (2002) popularized the epigram of perpetual peace through perpetual war. It may be applied to President George W. Bush's preparations for war in Iraq. In his 2002 State of the Union address, he pledged the largest hike in defense spending in twenty years and justified it on the ground that North Korea, Iran, and Iraq "constitute an axis of evil, arming to threaten the *peace of the world*" and that "the price of freedom and security . . . is never too high" (as quoted in Daniel 2006, 13; emphasis added).

Going further, the models of perpetual peace and of war for peace may be joined by a third image: perpetual peace by enduring competition. The first two are skeletal, and the third alternative adds flesh to precursor frames. It posits that the compression of time and space marking contemporary globalization brings capitalists into more direct competition with other capitalists. These head-on encounters may be deemed *hypercompetition*, a form of restructuring elaborated by Richard D'Aveni (1994), a professor of strategic management and a fellow of the World Economic Forum (WEF).[1] He documents the practices of "aggressive market disruption" and "smart bombing" to beat competitors, "counter-revolutionary strategies to buy time," and maneuvers for "building corporate spheres of influence."

The language of hypercompetition likens this combativeness to war. For example, at an AT&T plant in Denver, a poster over Northern Telecom CEO Paul Stern's photo broadcasts the statement, "Declare business war. *This* is the enemy" (D'Aveni 1994, 213, 319; emphasis in original). Researchers in strategic management (M. Porter 1990; D'Aveni 1995) interviewed many CEOs who use such war metaphors and adopt slogans like Honda's: "Annihilate, crush, and destroy Yamaha!" (D'Aveni 1994, 376). In this lexicon, strategies for escalation and conquest are expressed in increasingly aggressive terms.

Notwithstanding efforts to negotiate international competition agreements

(Chapters 4 and 6), the manner of combative maneuvering to increase market access takes on aspects of a Hobbesian "warre of all against all" on the terrain of global capitalism, with a shift in some of its bedrock. And as Michel Foucault (2003, 92–93) pointed out, Thomas Hobbes's primal state of war is not a conflagration involving actual weapons and bloodshed but a theater of presentations and representations: in Hobbes's words, "Warre consisteth not in Battel onely, or in the act of fighting; but in a tract of time, wherein the Will to contend by Battel is sufficiently known" (as quoted in Foucault 2003, 92–93).[2] When security is lacking, a "tract of time" marks the state of the field of contestation.

In our age, this field is a hypercompetitive landscape. The terrain is situated in a business environment that prizes efficiency and finds novel ways to cut costs. Speeded by new technologies, the rise of transnational capital and increasing labor mobility have had a profound impact. Yet hypercompetition is more than an acceleration of the earlier practices of capitalism. Whereas John Rockefeller and Henry Ford had sought to secure the stability of markets and their own firms, now the emphasis is on destabilizing the business environment and creating risks. Chief executives even want to knock their own organizations off balance (Sennett 2006, 41). These corporate officers are not merely competing in a benevolent manner, as imagined by conventional economists, but are carrying out a belligerent hypercompetition.

Meanwhile, national production systems are being supplanted by globalized firms that disperse activities around the world. France, for example, has long known *hypermarchés* (hypermarkets) at home. Firms based there, like Carrefour, the world's second-largest retailer, have planned a pugnacious strategy for expansion in certain overseas markets. In the words of its chief executive, "we can attack 2006 much better armed" (as quoted in Jones and Rigby 2006). Key to this agenda is transnational finance—including approximately $2 trillion per day in currency exchange—which moves rapidly across borders. Some of it locates offshore so as to avoid regulatory authority.

The growth of the Asian economies has fueled this spike in global competition. The tailwinds of rising competition from Asia brought major benefits to some sectors in the United States: an enormous volume of investments, brisk growth in overall demand for commodities, and the purchase of large dollar reserves (usually deemed an advantage though sometimes seen as a drawback). But competition over energy supply, trade, and currency-rate imbalances pose political as well as economic risks. This competition involves the explosion of highly leveraged financial instruments (unregulated hedge funds, including the use of derivatives by speculators) and the conditions for volatility of the dollar, especially as global interest rates equalize.

Intensifying competition is of course historically rooted. It became accentuated in the twentieth century with the combination of a decline in the U.S. real economy (the production of goods and services) and the ascendance of financial instruments (Arrighi 2005; Patomäki 2007). Beginning in the 1970s, there were basic shifts, notably the fall of national Keynesianism, the demise of the Bretton Woods system of fixed exchange rates, the rise of neoliberalism (a set of ideas and a policy framework for accelerating global market integration), the collapse of the Soviet Union, and the transition to a post–Cold War order.

In this restructuring, competition is not necessarily the same as conflict. Yet competition, in Adam Smith's sense of the term, involves conflicting self-interests. Or in Max Weber's usage, competition is a form of "peaceful conflict . . . in so far as it [the latter] consists in a formally peaceful attempt to attain control over opportunities and advantages which are also desired by others" (Weber [1947] 1969, 132–33). And competition can mean conflict under given conditions: sometimes from the unfinished business of the Cold War, initially in countries like Afghanistan and Angola but increasingly linked to the unevenness of globalization.

Hypercompetition is heavily but not totally American in several of its facets: the long reach of U.S. markets, the organizational technologies that originated or were adapted in the United States, U.S. predominance in spending for research and development (R&D), Anglo-American neoliberal ideas about the ordering of economy and society, the U.S. lead in information systems (as in American-fashioned software and computer operations), the spread of the American variant of the English language, and the United States' continuous capacity for cultural innovation or, one might say, the wherewithal for renewal.

These assets are associated with what Joseph Nye calls "soft power"—the means to get others to do what you want (Nye 1990). Whereas Nye posits that Washington is "bound to lead," Samuel Huntington holds that the United States is a "lonely superpower" in a transitional system in which it will become a more "ordinary" major power (Huntington 1999). Huntington is right to jettison the language in vogue during the Cold War, when "superpower" described the position of the United States and the Soviet Union relative to the standing of other countries, and to call for new analytical categories appropriate to a dynamic shift in world order.

After 1989, the United States is extraordinary in its unparalleled military capacity and its demonstrative willingness to deploy resources to get its way, unilaterally if need be (Nossal 1999, 3–4). In light of the large distance between the United States and the other major powers in a globalizing world, the apogee is not *superpower* but *hyperpower*. Having originated during a period of bipolarity to depict a split between two rivals, the category "superpower" is superseded by *hyperpuissance* ("hyperpower"), a term coined in 1998 by former French foreign minister Hubert Védrine to denote the reconstitution of the Cold War era and the astounding disparity in *capacity* between one actor and the others (Védrine 1998, as cited and elaborated in Nossal 1999, 2, 5; Védrine 2001; Duke 2003; Nederveen Pieterse 2003; Vaïsse n.d.).

Like the term "hypercompetition," the word "hyperpower" comes from both the policy community and scholarship: the WEF and university researchers in the first instance; the French Ministry of Foreign Affairs and professors such as Amy Chua (2007) of Yale Law School in the second.[3] Offering a historical analysis of the handful of societies that have reached this extraordinary level, Chua equates hyperpower with world dominance. She hypothesizes that tolerance with respect to other societies is necessary for ascendance to hyperpower. Conversely, intolerance is associated with its demise (Chua 2007, xxv).

In my usage, "hyperpower" is distinct from "superpowers," and is singular. There can be only one hyperpower, not rival or regional hyperpowers. Yet, as mentioned, hyperpower is more than state power, because it is diffuse and includes a network of overseas military bases and an assemblage of allies. In addition, hyperpower incorporates the ideological components of hegemony.

The amalgam of the world's largest national economy, unmatched technological prowess, and a defense budget greater than that of the next twenty-five states is an unparalleled form of power (Adhikari 2004). The magnitude of this range is striking. The U.S. population is 4.6 percent of the world total and generates 28 percent of the world's gross domestic product (GDP) (World Bank 2007). On the WEF's Global Competitiveness Index 2008–2009, a model with twelve categories of measures applied to 134 countries, the U.S. economy again ranks number one in the world (World Economic Forum 2008). The categories are institutions, infrastructure, macroeconomic stability, health and primary education, higher education and training, goods market efficiency, labor market efficiency, financial market sophistication, technological readiness, market size, business sophistication, and innovation. On the basis of these indicators, Table 1 presents weighted averages of competitiveness by country. It is noteworthy that just ahead of Switzerland, Denmark, and Sweden, the United States

TABLE 1

Global Competitiveness Index Rankings, 2008–2009
and 2007–2008 Comparisons

Country	GCI 2008–09 Rank	GCI 2008–09 Score	GCI 2007–08 Rank
United States	1	5.74	1
Switzerland	2	5.61	2
Denmark	3	5.58	3
Sweden	4	5.53	4
Singapore	5	5.53	7
Finland	6	5.50	6
Germany	7	5.46	5
Netherlands	8	5.41	10
Japan	9	5.38	8
Canada	10	5.37	13
Hong Kong SAR	11	5.33	12
United Kingdom	12	5.30	9
Republic of Korea	13	5.28	11
Austria	14	5.23	15
Norway	15	5.22	16
France	16	5.22	18
Taiwan (Republic of China)	17	5.22	14
Australia	18	5.20	19
Belgium	19	5.14	20
Iceland	20	5.05	23
Malaysia	21	5.04	21
Ireland	22	5.03	22
Israel	23	4.97	17
New Zealand	24	4.93	24
Luxembourg	25	4.85	25
Qatar	26	4.83	31
Saudi Arabia	27	4.72	35
Chile	28	4.72	26
Spain	29	4.72	29
China	30	4.70	34
United Arab Emirates	31	4.68	37
Estonia	32	4.67	27
Czech Republic	33	4.62	31
Thailand	34	4.60	28
Kuwait	35	4.58	30
Tunisia	36	4.58	32
Bahrain	37	4.57	43
Oman	38	4.55	42
Brunei Darussalam	39	4.54	n/a
Cyprus	40	4.53	55
Puerto Rico	41	4.51	36
Slovenia	42	4.50	39
Portugal	43	4.47	40
Lithuania	44	4.45	48
South Africa	45	4.41	44
Slovak Republic	46	4.40	41
Barbados	47	4.40	50
Jordan	48	4.37	49
Italy	49	4.35	46
India	50	4.33	48

scores well above the second and third largest national economies: Japan is in ninth place; China, thirtieth.

The United States leads in other crucial metrics as well. It is responsible for 38 percent of worldwide outlay on R&D (American Association for the Advancement of Science 2006). Fifty-seven percent of the U.S. share is military R&D (Organisation for Economic Cooperation and Development [OECD] 2006, 47).

In 2007, the United States alone accounted for 45 percent of total world military expenditure, almost as much as the rest of the global war chest. This percentage is slightly lower than in previous years due to the large rise of Eastern European spending, up 162 percent since 1998 (Stockholm International Peace Research Institute [SIPRI] 2008, 176–77). The U.S. figure takes into consideration the supplementary budget for the "war on terror," which, by itself, is almost three times more than the entire military spending of each of the next four countries with the highest defense budgets—the United Kingdom, China, France, and Japan (SIPRI 2008, 177–85). What is more, according to Department of Defense data compiled through 2005, the United States maintains 737 military bases abroad. By comparison, Britain, in 1898, at the pinnacle of its imperial era, had 36 bases (Johnson 2006, 138–39). The U.S. military's vast range is also reflected in the Defense Department's figure of 761 "sites," though this inventory includes separate installations within single large bases and not (presumably) temporary facilities in Afghanistan and Iraq (U.S. Department of Defense 2008).

Notwithstanding this scope, it is important to avoid hyperbole. Hyperpower is neither unipolarity nor omnipotence. The discourse of unipolarity centers on the nation-state without capturing globalizing processes. Gauging the number of poles in world order does not direct attention to the multidimensionality of transnational relations and the multiple scales of globalization. Unlike polarity, hyperpower signifies a relationship with distinctive mechanisms, as this book will demonstrate.

If for now, power is defined in the active, overt sense that X makes Y alter behavior, then asymmetry manifests in hyperpower. The extraordinary resources commanded by the United States and its actual exercise of power are uneven. Hyperpower is skewed in that it displays fundamental weaknesses in diplo-

---

NOTES TO TABLE 1

Source: World Economic Forum, The Global Competitiveness Report 2008–2009 (Geneva: WEF, 2008), http://www.weforum.org/pdf/gcr/2008/rankings.pdf, accessed 25 February 2009. The top fifty countries in the WEF table are listed here.

*One country that was included last year is not shown because of a lack of survey data (Uzbekistan).

matic, military, and economic performance. Suffice it to mention that hyperpower is subject to palpable constraints, as evidenced by the U.S.-led coalition's experience in the occupation of Iraq. In addition, there is distance between the United States' military might and its financial means. The United States is not only the world's largest debtor but, in the global economy, also faces an ascendant East Asian epicenter. Both Japan and China maintain persistent current account surpluses in their balance of payments—themes to which I will return. Of concern too is that although U.S. universities are highly touted, the public schools rank eighteenth and twenty-eighth in reading and mathematics, respectively, among forty-one countries participating in the Programme for International Student Assessment survey (OECD 2004).

No doubt, hyperpower encounters substantial limits to its effectiveness. Efforts to reach beyond its actual range test legitimacy and risk insecurity.

The Darwinist tendencies of hyperpower are potentially greater than those of other power centers because of both the magnitude of U.S. power and the combination of tools at its disposal. Among them are an edge in technological innovation, the scope of its knowledge industries, and a dominant role in international organizations such as the World Bank. But hyperpower may be tempered when cooperation meets political and economic self-interests. Rather than fade away, the state adapts to mutations in a globalizing world.

Increasingly, the state plays an enabling role, facilitating the competitive position of certain units of capital and seeking to thwart market failure. Yet the autonomy of the state is also constrained and disciplined by capital, as with structural adjustment programs (SAPs) in the developing world or the pressures emanating from corporations in the developed world that look to relocate certain operations outside their home countries. To varying degrees, states themselves adopt corporate logic, subjecting their own agencies to cost-cutting measures that reduce social protection. This tendency of course ranges enormously in terms of the positions of different states vis-à-vis globalization. The spectrum is from hyperpower, which is ever mutable, to the growing erosion of power in the most marginalized regions.

These trends evoke the Kantian motif of competitive attitudes among humans, inscribed in the contemporary penchant for aggressive competition among corporations and among states. Thus, at the epicenter of globalization, U.S. officials are apprehensive about fierce competition in the production of new knowledge. Although the United States is the clear leader in global R&D rankings, it trails other developed countries in R&D expenditure as a share of the national economy, basic research as a portion of R&D, and nondefense research as a percentage of the economy (Bernasek 2006; see also Epilogue). Reports that innovation in science and technology as well as research productivity are declining are regarded as danger signals. Officials worry about the drop in the American percentage of worldwide industrial patents to 52 percent, in the publication of American papers in physics from 61 percent to 29 percent in two decades, and in the American share of Nobel Prizes, an emblem of scientific leadership, to 51 percent of the awards given in the early 2000s (Broad 2004; Mandel 2004). By my calculations (based on Nobel Foundation online), U.S. laureates selected in the years 2005 to 2008 continued to constitute just over half—56 percent—of the new Nobelists.

In the face of all-time highs for federal spending on research, what explains the apprehension among Americans about a turn in scientific discoveries, which of course bear economic and military value? The perceived downward slide is variously attributed to rising foreign competition, a reverse brain drain whereby scientists and doctoral students return to their home countries, and tightening restrictions on visas brought on by the "global war on terror" (Segal 2004).

The premise underpinning statements of alarm sounded by groups such as the Council on Competitiveness in Washington and the American Association for the Advancement of Science is that the United States must be number one. The point deemed distressing is that foreign rivals are causing the pillars of national strength to crumble. In this narrative, there is an unexamined supposition about the importance of being first in a scientific domain that pits national competitors against one another. It is taken for granted that one country's gain is another's loss. There is a pronounced tendency among U.S. politicians to see Asia's efforts to attain a competitive edge as a security threat—especially initiatives in China, many of whose top political leaders are engineers by background—and to advocate forms of scientific protectionism.

But why should the primary reference point for technological innovation be defined in terms of national boundaries when, in a hypercompetitive global economy, the distinction between "national" and "foreign" is becoming opaque? The scale of many emerging problems, such as global climate change, does not correspond to territorial jurisdiction, and the search for know-how is increasingly mounted at extraterritorial levels. In the United States and some other countries, the sizable share of corporate R&D spending relative to government R&D investment means large increments in funding offshore operations. The locus of innovation is shifting from labs in a single national context to transnational networks of firms, government agencies, and universities, with emerging hubs that start up new ideas for offshore adaptation and marketing. Even with intellectual property rights, the whole world has an opportunity to benefit from global creativity, provided that technological efforts are combined to reorder the frontiers of what is possible.

Extant indices are part of the problem. They orient thinking to states. Exclusively national indices were introduced in a prior era. Although they are still important, especially owing to a proliferation of state-managed investment instruments, including sovereign wealth funds (vast pools of government-controlled money from China, Singapore, the Middle East, and elsewhere), national indices are not cut regionally and globally, as are many evolving markets and other types of human activity. Supplementing national classification are burgeoning new indices incorporating aspects of the logic of globalization itself. These gauges reflect a postmodern sensibility that offers opportunities to split statistics into different categories: global sector, dimensions of firms, industry, region, and various combinations of these. In the forefront of producing new indices are Dow Jones Wilshire (with its all-world index), Morgan Stanley International, Rimes Online, and the Eurozone Index (Authers 2006).

Still, it is not only U.S. agencies that keep score of national competitiveness, but similar patterns are apparent elsewhere. Each year, the WEF's *Global Competitiveness Report*, whose matrix of national economies was alluded to above, causes considerable pride or unease, as the case may be, in government offices and corporate boardrooms. Intellectual life is subject to the same sort of ideological effects. They are evident in ratings of universities and assessment exercises, with their productivity measures, and have direct consequences, particularly at the growing number of institutions implementing a form of restructuring known as corporatization.

This restructuring is accompanied by what Anthony Giddens (1991, 53, 65, 243) calls "ontological insecurity": a disruption in the "sense of continuity and order" within and beyond an individual's perceptual environment. Giddens's concept divulges fear of the inability to secure an order and bears an increasing global dimension in which the framework of risks is altered, its fragility becoming more pronounced. Tilting the paradigm further, Ulrich Beck (1999, 2) suggests that in a "world risk society," the very idea of security is no longer viable. According to Beck, there is an erosion of securities, hitherto considered calculable by expert knowledge but increasingly incalculable (Beck [2004] 2006).

Along with this intersubjective sense of insecurity, globalizing processes entail changing ways of contesting security in the political-military sphere. Faced with pressures from powerful substate and suprastate actors, the state's claim to control a legitimate monopoly of the use of force—in a Weberian sense—is all the more challenged, and these trends are encompassed in a changing world order.[4] In this evolving configuration, unlike the situation in Weber's day, hyperpower seeks to control the legitimate claim to violence.

THEMES

While it is useful to revive major thinkers' visions of peace and security, there are valuable ways to supplement them and further explore the themes that animated their work. Of course, it cannot be expected that the wisdom from bygone eras would provide programmatic responses to the challenges of contemporary globalization. The clues, however, offer important pointers for investigating a set of interactions, outlined below.

Marked by vast dislocation and a highly skewed distribution of benefits and losses, hypercompetition coincides with hyperpower, which seeks to secure its enabling conditions. In a globalizing era, hypercompetition and hyperpower, as it were, have grown together. They entail coercion. The application of coercive measures, in turn, precipitates a spiral of resistance to dominant structures. The result is hyperconflict, defined at the beginning of this chapter as a configuration of objective factors and a rising climate of fear.

To cut to the chase, it may be hypothesized that *hypercompetition + hyperpower → hyperconflict*.

The proposition that a convergence of conditions points toward hyperconflict is not to suggest an iron logic, an irreversible trend. Rather, the analytical formulation above may be best understood in terms of hyperconflict's seven characteristics. They are noted with discussion and examples as follows:

1. Taking shape in contemporary world order, hyperconflict is, at present, in a nascent phase.

2. With the development of globalization, hyperconflict is a displacement rather than a total break from prior patterns. The shift is not merely the well-known turn from interstate to domestic violence as the major source of conflict. Many episodes of political violence do not fall tidily into one category or another.

3. In an era of globalization, hyperconflict is a frothing up, with the poten-

tial for spillovers. The violence in the Great Lakes Region of Africa in the late twentieth and early twenty-first centuries, for example, rests on prior fighting there, transcends national borders, involves a global arms industry, and draws a mélange of local and external actors, such as private security contractors, from within and outside the area. In this instance and others, hyperconflict does not erupt automatically. One must delve into its local and transnational mechanisms to see how it happens. In all instances, hyperconflict merges with the complexity of history. Allowing for the caprice of agents and historical accidents, such as natural disasters and the unexpected appearance of deadly diseases rapidly transmitted across borders, it is impossible to foretell the tipping point or plot the time lines in advance. But we have no doubt entered an epoch in which security threats and efforts to foil them are globalized.

4. Still, the rosy view has it that the number of armed conflicts on a world basis has declined or at least remained level. Although the time lines differ among research projects, this statistical observation is consistently supported by careful calculations (thanks to Marshall and Gurr 2005; Harbom, Högbladh, and Wallensteen 2006; Mack 2006; Gleditsch 2007; compare Sarkees, Wayman, and Singer 2003; and further discussed in Chapter 8). The categories adopted by these researchers are interstate war, intrastate war, and sometimes extrastate or extrasystemic war between state and nonstate actors (in addition to the authors cited immediately above, see Holsti 1996; Strand et al. 2005; Correlates of War [project] online; SIPRI n.d). Surely, these datasets are most helpful in plotting the *incidence* of deadly conflicts among and within the categories. But the typologies themselves embrace representations of frontiers between internal and external phenomena. The empirical research is linear and needs to be supplemented by a look at foundational shifts. The analysts' classificatory lines are blurred by intersubjective frameworks and contested by the actions of local civil societies and transnational movements increasingly engaged in global governance (Wapner 1996; Keck and Sikkink 1998; Cooley and Ron 2002; Slaughter 2004; Bob 2005; Tarrow 2005). For instance, an Islamist group, Hezbollah, violates the law and wages war, deploying sophisticated missiles and guerrilla fighters. Willing to absorb heavy casualties relative to Israel's tolerance for the loss of its soldiers, Hezbollah is organized as both a militia and a Shiite political party whose members hold state office in Lebanon; does not pledge to abide by the decisions of the home state; draws support from other states; and may not represent itself in United Nations (UN) Security Council deliberations on matters of the resolution of conflict in the Middle East. Traditional lines of world

order are indistinct; borders, more porous; frontiers, altered (Sassen 1996; Rosenau 1997; Scholte 2005; Steger 2003, 2005). The transition to mixed varieties of conflict offers an opportunity to step up and rethink units of analysis. This is especially important in an era when a decrease in armed conflict does not necessarily mean less violence, as with environmentally related calamities, or more security, say, from fear of political terror. Hence, without sweeping under the rug the basic problem of how to render myriad situations intelligible, the chapters that follow adopt a holistic approach and then closely examine the pieces in diverse contexts.

5. Each signal episode of hyperconflict has a different ratio of hypercompetition and hyperpower, depending on the specific setting. Case studies in the chapters ahead show varying relative amounts. For example, in 1995, efforts to negotiate a new investment regime for hypercompetition sparked a welter of protests from transnational and local civil society groups, leading hyperpower to backpedal; however, the 1997–98 economic downturn in Asia elicited a firm assertion of hyperpower to squelch regional responses to disorder. Such variation in ratio values reflects the history and practices of distinctive places. So, too, the matrices of power competition are not at all insulated from globalizing pressures, the common underlying dynamic. In other words, hyperconflict is not a one-size-fits-all proposition but the product of a set of systemic drivers. Surely these forces are contingent: subject to proximate causes under myriad conditions. The immediate cause often becomes submerged or lost in an escalating conflict and engulfed in political violence. Collective memories are selective, constructed, and manipulated.

6. Hypercompetition in geoeconomics is in *intense interaction* with hyperpower in geopolitics. Although these realms do not cleave neatly, the correspondence between them is drawing closer during the current interregnum, a fitful passage from the old order to a new one marked by the rise of hyperconflict.

7. Although hyperconflict need not entail a sudden outburst of war, it may nonetheless spread at lightning speed. If hyperconflict is not one great blow-up, it takes shape as multiple forms expedited by new technologies that allow its elements to ricochet swiftly from one country or region to another. The cascading effects of this *contagion* may threaten mass destruction and some states' capacity to monopolize legitimate violence. The combustible parts of globalization are fueled by a combination of new systems of weaponry, a policy framework that has lowered barriers across borders, and integrated financial

markets. Transnationally, the chain reaction of hyperconflict consists of several links—channels that vary—as the ensuing chapters will indicate.

These traits are not dependent on any one administration in Washington. Rather, they form a complex that distinguishes hyperconflict from familiar forms of conflict. It bears emphasizing that hyperconflict is not a totalizing phenomenon: it pertains to only those entities, individual and corporate, that interact with global structures. There are numerous clashes, especially on a local level, that mingle indirectly with hyperconflict. They are filtered through multiple global pressures. A prime example is the community dispute that concerns schools, traffic control, or housing. At first glance, it may appear to be distantly related to hyperconflict. Yet in several school districts, there has been strife over internationalizing or incorporating global issues into the curriculum and deciding on the historical stories to tell about them. Too, the global production of automobiles makes available a cornucopia of consumer goods, further clogging the roads. And cross-border migratory flows have an impact, sometimes contentious, on the mix of peoples in formerly tightly knit neighborhoods. Many residential areas are under stress for want of rigorous banking regulations to protect borrowers from lenders, as with abuses of subprime credit, in globalized financial markets. Increasingly, evolving conflicts on the ground are the end of a global chain. The elements are interlinked.

Even so, why not conjecture a move toward more cooperation? The latter would seem to rest on a personal distaste for violence and discord, a normative preference for institutionalized cooperation, and a commitment to political and economic integration. Thus Robert Keohane reflects on the central theme throughout his writings: "If we learn more about the processes by which international commitments are taken seriously, we may understand better the conditions under which cooperation not only occurs but becomes cumulative" (Keohane 1989, 31). Noting dissatisfaction with "the realist orthodoxy," Keohane forthrightly identifies the values that animate his scholarly work: "I believe that international cooperation, though not sufficient, is a necessary condition for life, liberty, and the pursuit of happiness in the twenty-first century" (Keohane 1989, 31). But is this assertion linked to the empirical observation that cooperation is more pronounced than conflict? Does Keohane's contention open to the possibility that the actualities are the other way around? Tilting against both classical liberal thinkers such as Smith ([1776] 1904), who emphasized the harmony of motives and argued that humans are in constant need of help from their brethren, and contemporary institutionalists, who seek to trace international regimes that ensure stability (Keohane 1984, 1989), my analysis suggests that in a globalizing era, the balance is swinging in another direction.

When many authors are in a despairing mood about world order, the term "hyperconflict" provides a language that recognizes this direction and, by its very gravity, prompts questions about strategic alternatives to the present course. In this book, the prefix "hyper"—taken from Greek, in which it means over, implying excessive—is not a literary or rhetorical flourish. In my usage, "hyper" is a heuristic for opening avenues of inquiry. It is a grammar for thinking about evolving forms of world order. An approach for understanding connections, it also offers a lens on ways in which globalization brings multiple changes in scale.

I will argue that hyperconflict has the potential to constitute a historical turning point: a watershed that does not merely exacerbate transnational security threats but rather may transform world order as we know it. Of course, a future of hyperconflict is unexpected. But so was the Great Crash of 1929, which led to a restructuring of the global economy, world war, and new international institutions.

Surprisingly, there appears to be an analytical lacuna as regards this global dynamic. Observers know more about aspects of it, especially in specific hotspots, than about the general process. Because there is a wide gulf between studies of the geoeconomic and geopolitical sides of globalization, thinking on how to stanch the evolving hyperconflict remains piecemeal. For the most part, geostrategic considerations are a blind spot in globalization studies.[5] In the meantime, world order is beset by a coercive form of globalization, which differs from what other authors call military globalization (Chapter 3). Coercive globalization is lodged in not only war and militarism but also economy and society. This coercion melds diverse means of disciplinary power. The controls range from brute force to instruments of diplomacy, finance, culture, and education.

To support these claims, I will show that a series of conflicts is building momentum toward a hyperconflict encapsulating heightened coercion and weakening consensus. This trajectory signals that different world orders are possible, and I will examine their peril and opportunities.

To assess the likelihood of these outcomes, one must identify the agents and ground them in their context. Inasmuch as generalization is fraught with the risk of contingency, my contentions will be anchored in empirical evidence—in the main, a large corpus of historical detail. It is worth repeating that my claims are not meant to take the form of universal laws.

The method adopted here is to inspect a chain of conflict points that gathers force, shifting the framework of risks and possibilities of world order. In view of the French economic historian Fernand Braudel's entreaty about different speeds of time (1980), this analysis probes "the history of events"—the short run, the recent past—but as rooted in deep structures. Attention thus turns to continuities and discontinuities with the *longue durée*, that is, origins and gradual, slow-moving transformations: a churning of globalizing processes that are fluid and disorderly, in some respects less visible and perhaps more profound and wrenching than surface phenomena.

To delimit these processes, four case studies are offered as a detailed account of the mechanisms of hyperconflict. In an effort to increase variation and the explanatory payoff, my research strategy deliberately rests on heterogeneous instances:

- the 1995 Multilateral Agreement on Investment (MAI), a treaty introduced by the United States in the OECD in order to remove barriers to market competition, but blocked by a coalition of citizen groups that adroitly used the Internet and formed a transnational network of activists
- the 1997–98 debacle that burst the Asian bubble, immediately rippled to other regions, and caused discontent with international financial institutions in which Washington is the most powerful actor
- the 1999 Battle of Seattle, the scene of street violence surrounding a meeting of the World Trade Organization (WTO), followed by the eruption of similar battles in other cities on five continents
- the 2001 attacks on the Pentagon and the World Trade Center, icons of U.S. military power and a globalizing economy, followed by the "global war on terror."

In addition to the case chapters, the Epilogue traces this trajectory through the U.S. wars and market turmoil of the early twenty-first century.

The rationale for selecting dissimilar cases is to allow for the possibility that evidence does not fit my central thesis. Anomalous findings that do not support the argument will be grounds for repudiating, sustaining, or qualifying it.

That said, the four case studies examine the texture of different contexts, social power relations, and micro-macro links. By paying close attention to intricate ways in which globalization touches down at specific sites of contestation, the cases help dispense with unduly universalist accounts of this process. Moreover, all four cases hover around historical moments that signify potentially transformative politics. Although each conflict was not altogether crippling in its own right, together they are storm signals that may portend upheaval in world order. In ways that will be shown, all the cases involve geostrategic dimensions of globalization, although to varying degrees.

In tracking the accumulated evidence, it is important to recall the antecedents of my cases, including protests by students and black power advocates in the 1960s, the peace movement, feminism, environmentalism, riots over the policies of the International Monetary Fund (IMF), and the Zapatista uprising.

As one could also identify other cases and add them to the list, why select these four for anchoring my study? Although their forms and the degree of structural violence differ, each case crosses borders, draws in local and global actors, involves both bottom-up and top-down processes, and calls on the state to maintain security in the face of threats to its claim to a legitimate monopoly on the use of force. The four cases entail both challenges to the legitimacy of the state and political unrest. In each instance, the outbreak of conflict is not merely a matter of mistaken policies but is tied to globalizing forces. The connective tissue among the cases is conflict over the governance of globalization.

The four cases stand astride two centuries, the last century being a prelude to the hyperconflict looming over ours. Blending hypercompetition and hyperpower, the cases are signs of hyperconflict. In Churchillian terms, if the twentieth century was the calm before a gathering storm in globalization, the twenty-first may prove to be the gale that threatens to foil the pursuit of security in a globalizing world. Although Winston Churchill's prognostication about an impending war was greeted with skepticism, if not derision, his early warning proved to be prescient.

On the basis of evidence adduced through a combination of methods appropriate to each specific case study (textual analysis, documentary research, and patterns of discursive practices), Chapter 8 will provide scenarios for future world order. These are not conjecture or make-believe in the sense of utopias or dystopias that never happened. Rather, each scenario is grounded in real historical tendencies, and embodies lived practices. Insofar as scenarios offer insights about trends, they can help to find ways to prevent or mitigate hyperconflict—an outcome that does not have to be.

PRISMS

The themes foregrounded here may be viewed through the prism of insecurity. The politics of fear is of course not new. It was characteristic of the last century, with its world wars and the Cold War. Today, however, a narrative of safety and protection—"homeland security"—is employed by political authorities who disseminate stories about immigrants, environmental dangers, weapons of mass destruction (WMD), and health pandemics that transcend borders. Many aspects of these representations are of course warranted. Yet scaremongering in the name of national security carries a price in terms of civic activism, a pillar of democracy. The message that destructive forces are transforming the world may be used to promote a sense of anxiety and powerlessness as well as to limit agency (Furedi 2002). More than elsewhere, many developing countries experience this sense of vulnerability as diminishing control over events and processes, a hallmark of globalization.

Insofar as what follows in this book hinges on clarification of meaning, it is worth lingering over basic concepts, ideas that I will develop in subsequent chapters. Not only a matter of control, globalization is a set of transformative processes. It is a transformation of human interactions across several domains—politics, economics, ideology, culture, society, and environment—as I have sought to delineate in my previous research on globalization (Mittelman 1996, 2000, 2004b; Mittelman and Norani Othman 2001). While accelerating prior trends, globalization is not merely interdependence, or a surge in global flows such as trade, investment, migration, and information. A transformational concept includes, but cannot be reduced to, increasing interconnections. This construct also delves into social relations and human organization, and holds that structures are relatively enduring yet subject to shifts. In other words, globalization, at least in its contemporary form, is encountering resistance, an issue that chapters of this book detail. However, it is not sufficient to leave the discussion there. To delimit a historical transformation does not in itself indicate the form that change could take.

As part of this transformation, the concept of security has evolved since the notion of national security emerged in the 1930s with the ascendance of the realist approach to international relations and at the first signs of the Cold War in the 1940s. New fears related to threats subsequently posed by nuclear war and ideological foes coincided with the rise of the United States to a preeminent position. In this milieu, policymakers and public intellectuals securitized military issues entailing international violence.

To be sure, there are different kinds of security. Although security has traditionally meant to be free from danger and threats, one person or group's security may be perceived as another's insecurity. Seen through a second lens, then, security and insecurity are states of mind. They are bound up with fear, paranoia, and prejudice that divide people into alignments of friends and enemies. Designating an issue as a matter of security is subjective also because it treats certain threats as more important than others.

Whereas national security as a construct gives priority to military-strategic matters, the 1990s discourses on security expanded to human security, which includes nontraditional threats to people's rights in the interrelated spheres of gender, race, poverty, development, food, water, health, employment, and the environment. In the twenty-first century, the debates about what to specify as security and who may decide on these matters are more comprehensive and involve global security. Absent a consensus on the meaning of this concept, especially in the aftermath of 9/11, there is at least agreement that global security is an evolving, not an absolute, idea, and that the old answer for what to do when security breaks down—namely, to balance power—is inadequate in light of dire nonterritorial threats.

Although narrow and wide interpretations remain, with differences over what counts as a threat, the trend is to render the notion of security more inclusive than in its earlier formulations. The extended conceptualization of security shows multiple levels and different standpoints without ranking the relative priority of types (military, ontological, energy, food, environment, credit and finance, and so on). Establishing a hierarchical order among them would be a dubious if not misguided undertaking, for they cannot be clearly separated and because their salience differs according to time and place. It is right to think of security and insecurity as encapsulating potential physical danger, fear, and other threats in a single yet multifaceted construct. Nonetheless, the exercise of throwing more and more adjectives at security to expand conceptual boundaries invites immersion in bottomless controversies. If entirely stripped of national jurisdiction, the notion of security could become hollow, lack decision-making capacity, and fail to identify who achieves security. Threats to national security, such as the one carried out on September 11, 2001, are real enough. While perils are partly wordplay and social constructions, understanding security involves more than examining how images of enemies are produced.

That said, the security dilemma extends beyond the realist conundrum that when, out of necessity, each state pursues its own security, the general condition among states is, ironically, insecurity. The national state must protect its citizens also from threats emanating from nonstate and transnational actors, which are elements in a globalizing system. Globalization both sows destruction and bears the potential for a genuine worldwide order. But the earlier forms of national security have been partial in their reach. And attempts to extend security through multinational alliances are still subject to decisions by national states.

Now, hyperpower is mostly concentrated in a single state that remains the nucleus of military coercion, albeit with considerable difficulty, as demonstrated in the manifold problems surrounding its occupation of two countries, Afghanistan and Iraq, each with fewer than thirty million inhabitants. The United States relies on direct and indirect methods of coercive power—brute force and influence. But owing to ill-judged policies that turned public opinion against its occupation of Iraq, Washington has failed to optimize the means at its disposal and take full advantage of hyperpower.

At its epicenter, coercive power is seen through an ideological filter of safeguarding national interest (even when in concert with collective legitimacy) in which states face relentless competition. For some analysts, globalization is represented as serial wars over drugs, illegal aliens and alien smuggling, arms trafficking, and organized crime (Naylor 2002; Naim 2003). For others, this warfare is famously imagined as a conflict of civilizations, the West against the rest (Huntington 1996). For still others, global conflict is a matter of imperialism and empire, the focus of a vast literature (for different perspectives, see Ferguson 2003; Hardt and Negri 2004).

Distinct from these accounts, I plot globalizing processes as the driving forces of hyperconflict, which in turn points to a convulsion in world order. It is the changing dynamics of control and transformative action that propel conflict. They are rooted in material power and values and are embedded in social structures. In some cases, violence becomes the instrument of agents who incite conflict, which in a globalizing epoch is not a momentary or purely local problem. Certain thinkers, including ones named in this chapter, regard conflict as perpetual, and today its dimensions are more far-reaching and systemic in that it represents an adaptive response to structural forces. More specifically, hyperconflict, which entails insecurity, is spurred by the polarities and vulnerabilities that come along with globalization. Hyperconflict also arises out of the tension between the logics of statecentric and polycentric worlds (Rosenau 2003, 62, 271). They often collide and, in some cases, are at war with one another, as on 9/11 when state and nonstate actors joined battle.

In light of the conditions that drive discrete instances of conflict, hyperconflict must be regarded as more than an inventory of events or a matter of scale beyond the local and regional levels. The latter are tied to the global, albeit in diverse ways. As noted, while allowance must be made for contextual nuances, local and regional conflicts are chapters of the whole.

Additionally, there is a distinction between hyperconflict and crisis, a woolly term if it is thought to be the great *déluge*—a cataclysmic or ultimate episode. Sometimes used in a primarily economic manner, as in accumulation, underconsumption, or overproduction, a logic of crisis gives the impression that this state of affairs is unremitting until its terminal stage. Far from automatically imploding, hyperconflict remains open to adaptive and transformative outcomes. In the meantime, its instances differ in intensity, their range is from manifest to latent, and there are several types of catalyzing moments.

Notwithstanding this diversity, hyperconflict springs from a decline in legitimacy and a restructuring of hegemony. Legitimacy is key because power can rarely be exercised without it. To get people to obey, power holders must strive for legitimacy. People willingly comply with decisions if they believe that authorities and norms are justified. Thus, as Weber taught us, power seeks to justify itself, and the power of an order is deemed legitimate if it is grounded in rational rules and norms; but legitimate domination may also rest on personal authority rooted in tradition or a belief in charisma endowed in "a saviour, a prophet or a hero" (Weber 1978, 954).

Regarding legitimacy as more of an ideal of an agreement between free and equal citizens, Jürgen Habermas (1973) addressed the condition of a legitimation deficit. For him, a lack of legitimacy stems from unequal distribution of surplus and the chances to meet needs, or from the absence of widely shared norms and institutions for public decision-making. Habermas held that a variety of legitimating tools, such as the ideology of formal democracy, may be used to address the challenges set in train by advanced capitalism. In some cases, coercive measures are a response to this deficiency, but they risk provoking more conflict and a further reduction in legitimation.

In this connection, Antonio Gramsci (1971) maintained that the supremacy of a social group manifests as domination, which rests on coercion, and as intellectual and moral leadership, whose power generates consent. If consent rather than coercion is the chief element in the mix, a hegemonic order prevails. Yet with increasing coercion relative to consent, hegemony falters. Within this Gramscian realm are not only state power but also the vitality and maturity of the institutions of civil society, including the family, schools, and religious organizations. Although Gramsci wrote mainly about domestic society, his major insights, generated from a fascist prison in Italy when the great powers prepared for war, still appear fresh. They may be profitably melded with contemporary peace and conflict research. One may extrapolate from Gramsci's ideas and extend them to the historical transformation known as globalization as it realigns world order.

Popularized by President George H.W. Bush, the term "world order" is used in various ways by scholars (Hoffman 1978; R. Cox 1996; Falk 2004). The classic definition is provided by Hedley Bull: "those patterns or dispositions of human activity that sustain the elementary or primary goals of social life among mankind as a whole" (1977, 20). Understood in this sense, world order is "wider than order among states" and "is morally prior to international order" (Bull 1977, 22). Although Bull's concept is foundational, some scholars, such as John Ikenberry (2001), reject a broad definition and give primary emphasis to state security. However, critics of this adherence to a realist paradigm believe that it is wrong to privilege the role of the state to the extent of underestimating that of other crucial actors and processes.

Barring a restrictive interpretation, world order may be construed as a constellation of norms, rules, ideas, and institutions entwined with power relations. This configuration is not static but contingent on myriad attempts to maintain and undermine it. In other words, a world order is an entrenched though not perpetual structure whose security and insecurity are subject to transformative processes.

INTERREGNUM

A great deal of thinking about contemporary world order is rooted in old realities from a state-centered world. Ideas that pertain to a passing order weigh heavily on the minds of analysts and policymakers grappling with the reorganization of conflict in our times. Apparently on the cusp of a transformed order, we might well recall Gramsci's observation: "the old is dying and the new cannot be born; in this interregnum a great variety of morbid symptoms appear" (1971, 276).

Similarly, the analysis undertaken here is an attempt to comprehend the dynamics of an interregnum. As emphasized, underpinning hyperconflict is a confluence of shifts in security, legitimation, and hegemony. To capture this incipient condition, I have dwelled on the United States, because it is the night watchman of globalization. Its material power is at the global epicenter. Given its vast resources, hyperpower is by definition asymmetric and sets terms for all, though not without constraints. Other actors accommodate the structural forces that hyperpower fuels, resist them, or combine options for engagement. The strategies and struggles that ensue vary greatly from one region to another. Some of these stories, contexts, and standpoints will be presented in this book. But the justification for the focus here on the United States is that if globalization retreats, the main impetus, I believe, will come from its core.

The next chapter searches for answers in the literature to the central questions posed in this book. Chapter 2 thus highlights major hypotheses and debates, gleans insights from diverse authors on the nexus of globalization and conflict, and offers critical reflections on these discourses. Chapter 3 goes beyond critique to suggest an alternative conceptualization. Then, Chapters 4 through 7 (plus the Epilogue) dig into specific conflicts. In Chapter 8, the impact of these narratives will be gauged as a sum total. The balance includes not only factors that incline toward hyperconflict but also countervailing tendencies. The task is to pull together the several themes in this research and project scenarios for future world order. If I am right in my overall assessment, this analysis will invite creative thinking about ways to avert hyperconflict. Other outcomes are possible, for history is an open-ended encounter without final resolution. This final chapter, on postnational security, is thus about avoiding hyperconflict and initiating enduring peace.

2 PRELIMINARY ANSWERS

To what extent are answers already available for the research questions that guide this book? To recapitulate: what is the nexus of globalization and security? Buried in this issue is a double query: What are the interactions among globalization, conflict, and world order? In a globalizing era, what is the evolving structure of power relations?

My contention is that the stored knowledge on these themes, drawn especially from the fields of peace and security studies, resembles a cat-o'-nine-tails: a whip used in the British navy during the eighteenth and nineteenth centuries.[1] During the Napoleonic wars, the cat was composed of a baton or handle made of rope or wood, and attached to nine knotted thongs. Likewise, the accumulated knowledge takes the form of nine braids. It separates conflict by identifying different strands, select aspects of outbreaks that are often refracted into regional variants (Väyrynen 1984; Wallensteen and Sollenberg 1998; Hettne, Inotai, and Sunkel 1999; Buzan and Waever 2004). Indeed, given myriad types of contemporary conflicts, there is reason to disaggregate global conflict. The sharp distinctions in the literature and empirical research have added to understanding and produced many insights, particularly important because the bulk of globalization studies has sidestepped the issue of military-strategic security, the salience of which was punctuated on 9/11.

Now let us examine each of global conflict's nine tails: national security, democratic peace, peace through trade, ethnopolitical fragmentation, the weak state, warlordism, resource wars, greed and grievance, and new wars. I shall trace their main features, taking care to do justice to them without touching on all the variations of each one. My treatment of this vast and rich literature must be telescopic—an overview, not a lengthy exegesis of the core ideas. The divisions among the branches of knowledge are not watertight compartments but pointers that help focus my contrasting approach. The aim here is to delve into intellectual history and offer critical reflections. In addition, the goal is to draw insights from a large corpus of research in order to establish a springboard for the rest of this book, which will attempt to pull together the several braids of peace and security research as well as thread these themes through the concept of hyperconflict. At the end of this chapter, I will suggest how to do so.

NATIONAL SECURITY

Invoking the root concept of national security, analysts like Victor Cha (2000) have sought to come to grips with "the 'new' security environment" at the outset of the twenty-first century and have proposed how to address threats posed by transnational groups such as drug smugglers, terrorists, criminal organizations, and ethnic insurgents. Cha charts trends, largely innovation in bureaucracy and other forms of policy adjustment engendered by the security challenges of globalization. It would seem that post–9/11, certain countries have enacted some of these recommendations—for example, the United States, in the USA Patriot Acts and the Homeland Security Act.

Such modifications in policy nevertheless pertain to the infrastructure of national security but not its bedrock problem, namely, parametric shifts that constrain the state.

To reiterate, policymakers must safeguard citizens who stand in harm's way. But to what extent can a powerful structural force, globalization, be converted into a management problem? More basically, can national security, reflecting the logic of the Westphalian system, respond adequately to problems of global security? Or is national security structurally handicapped? National security, even when pooled in interstate regional organizations and alliances, is imbued with a pregiven logic. Yet matters of global security transcend territorial borders and operate according to a more fluid framework in which transnational flows, facilitated by policies of deregulation and liberalization that lower barriers, and speeded by new technologies, increasingly penetrate the jurisdiction of "sovereign" states. In this sense, the language of "*homeland* security" itself conveys nostalgic significance, harking back to the stanchions of a Westphalian order, albeit in a more complex globalizing era. Is there a way to escape this dilemma?

Recognizing the conundrum, Thomas Barnett, a national-security planner and an insider in the Washington strategic community, notes the pointlessness of the Pentagon's dominant scenarios of the 1990s: the military mind-set focused on would-be competitors like China with the potential to deliver a big blow and, periodically, authoritarian rulers such as Slobodan Milosevic and Saddam Hussein, but not holocausts in far-off places, as in central Africa. After the Cold War, experts on defense thus misconstrued the "defining historical process of our age" (Barnett 2004, 147).

Adopting a systemic view of this era, Barnett holds that the common enemy is disconnectedness from globalization. The major world conflict on the horizon is between the "Functioning Core" connected to the global economy and the "Non-Integrating Gap," which is not integrated into the sets of rules of the broader economic community. To resolve the problem, military security must be targeted against those who exploit the disenfranchised and losers in the states that constitute the Gap. Nonstate actors, such as terrorist networks, maintain and promote disconnectedness from globalization and fight the rules for keeping it stable. The larger security challenge is to expand connectivity, which is the way to advance peace and prosperity. Key to reducing violence is endorsement of the system of security rules for allowing globalization to flourish.

But which rules, and whose rules? Barnett makes no bones about it: "security must flow from the Core to the Gap, but most specifically from the United States" (Barnett 2004, 241). The reason why the United States must play this role is not merely its enormous capacity for warfare but because it "come[s] closest to perfecting [globalization's] historical equation: the individual pursuit of happiness within free markets protected from destabilizing strife by the rule of law" (296). Moreover, "we seek not to extend our rule but merely our *rules*" (296; emphasis in original). In that "we are globalization's wellspring, its inspiration" and its "godfather," "America's task . . . is to serve as globalization's *bodyguard* wherever and whenever needed throughout the Gap" (301, 298; emphasis added).

His zeal for globalization aside, Barnett identifies the new security dilemma: states must prepare for myriad threats not only in the context of war but also "within the context of everything else" (Barnett 2004, 95). However, to plan a system-level response to globalizing processes, one must have a sound understanding of them. Whereas Barnett knows the culture of the Pentagon, offers trenchant criticism of military doctrine, and rightly draws attention to the importance of global governance, his historical analysis is lacking.

A phase of capitalism that originated in Europe, contemporary globalization may be heavily American, as with the long reach of CNN, McDonald's, and Coca-Cola. But the sources of globalization range widely, as evident in the 1980s when U.S. industries borrowed post-Fordist organizational technologies from Japan. Similarly, just as evolving global structures disrupt ways of life outside the United States, so mid-America too faces similar pressures, as with migration and outsourcing. In addition, global cultural products come in many forms, including the croissant, reggae music, and Japanese animation (Mittelman 2000, 18).

In integrating market competition into planning how to secure U.S.-led global hegemony and share some of its benefits, Barnett fails to recognize that hypercompetition is linked to neoliberalism, which is entirely absent from his account. Surely an accurate depiction of globalization turns on an appreciation of the set of ideas and policy framework to which it is joined. Another problem is Barnett's lack of systematic evidence. Empirically, Barnett's thesis that war-prone states are less connected to globalization than are peaceful ones is a dubious proposition. According to measures of connectivity in the fifth annual A. T. Kearney/*Foreign Policy* Globalization Index (A. T. Kearney, Inc. 2007), Croatia and Israel, both in recent times involved in armed conflicts, are ranked 21 and 26, respectively, out of seventy-two countries. No higher on measures of global integration, however, are countries not lately enmeshed in interstate violence: Germany ranks 22; Japan, 28; and Spain, 29.

In view of statistical indicators of ties to globalization, how would Barnett explain that certain highly globalized *and* conflict-ridden states in bad neighborhoods come in ahead of or close to democracies that have known international peace since the end of World War II? Or that Malaysia and Singapore, whose leaders have expressed sharp criticism of Western values inscribed in globalizing processes, are nonetheless among the top twenty-five in the globalization index and have often been at loggerheads with one another? Or that irrespective of conflict measures, small states which produce less for the home market than do large ones generally have a higher globalization valence?[2]

Finally, as with other notions about the West against the rest (Huntington 1996), Barnett's twofold distinction between a Core and a Gap is more constraining than revealing in terms of making clear the dynamics of conflict. Not only do multiple divisions and redivisions of global labor and power belie an image of a bifurcated world, but his contention that the United States has earned the right for unilateralism (Barnett 2004, 176) begs questions about Washington's relations with other democracies and their role in world order.

DEMOCRATIC PEACE

It is often argued that in an interdependent world, the route to national security is through building democracy. This position often rests on the "democratic peace" hypothesis that democratic states do not wage war against one another and, by extension, that the spread of democracy promotes peace throughout the world (Russett and Oneal 2001, 116).[3] In light of ample statistical support for this Kantian proposition—Kantian in that peace is not only the absence of hostilities but a positive and enduring condition—refinements on the basic claim have developed.

But why would two democracies not go to war with each other? What inhibits violence? In Russett and Oneal's formulation, democracy fosters international peace through a combination of measures: domestic legitimacy, checks and balances, transparency that comes from open communication and political competition, the credibility of international agreements, and a sensitivity to the costs of violent conflict (2001, 79). The Kantian elements that underpin peace are said to be triangular: republican constitutions, the expansion of trade beyond national boundaries, and participation in international institutions. This proposition is upheld by rigorous empirical investigation and interrogation of historical data (E. Robinson 2001; Oneal, Russett, and Berbaum 2003).

There are variants of the democratic peace thesis. One of the most important debates concerns the vexing question, Are liberal states prone to peace only in relations with other liberal states (Doyle 1983a, 1983b), or are they also peace-prone in relations with illiberal states? If the former proposition is valid, what inhibits a more general peace (Rummel 1983; MacMillan 2003)? For Max Singer and Aaron Wildavsky (1993), the answer is the twofold division of the world into "zones of peace" and "zones of turmoil." The former is characterized by wealth and democracy; the latter, war and development (1993, 3). Although "zones of peace" maintain internal peace, they engage in economic conflict with "zones of turmoil." The latter will eventually become democratic and wealthy, the avoidance of war being a matter of continuing democracy in the principal powers, especially the United States (1993, 31). Yet democratization itself, particularly when incomplete and without requisite institutions, is frequently tinged with bellicose nationalism that increases the likelihood of war (Mansfield and Snyder 2005).

Also emphasizing national identities but complicating the dichotomous distinction between two zones, Robert Cooper (2003) first posits a "zone of safety" in democratic Europe that faces zones of "danger and chaos." Although European democracies form a postmodern community and relax their sovereignty, they coexist with both modern states, driven by nationalism given to aggressive behavior, and premodern, often "failed states," bedeviled by civil war and endemic criminal activity. The democratic, postmodern zone can be threatened by the modern zone, especially by states equipped with WMD, and by the premodern zone, whose chaos "preys upon" and can "suck" in "the civilized world," thus disrupting peace (R. Cooper 2003, 77). But some observers might ask, Who is doing what to whom, and why? Suffice it to say that there are disagreements among researchers over both the causal mechanisms of democratic peace and the ways in which it relates to the fringes of world order. A consensus cannot be found.

To grapple with causality, it is most useful to adopt a historical perspective. The image of a democratic peace fogs the quandary of the relationship between liberal democracy and the growth of capitalist market relations, which, as Karl Polanyi ([1944] 1957) showed, were aided by the coercive power of the state. Indeed, from a critical standpoint, it may be argued that the peaceful orientation of Western democracies arose out of the violent history of capitalism. As Karl Marx put it, "unheroic though bourgeois society is, it nevertheless needed heroism, sacrifice, terror, civil war, and national wars to bring it into being" (Marx 1852, 116, as quoted in Jung 2003, 10). Democratic rule in the West was based on not only class conflict within national societies but also wars among European powers and violence inflicted in the form of colonialism in other parts of the world. A zone, or zones, of capitalist peace among liberal democracies could be juxtaposed to a zone of conflict elsewhere, but this formulation leaves open questions about worldwide interactions at various levels. For example, is liberal peace, linked as it is to hypercompetition, prone to generate liberal war (Duffield 2001, 15)?

Whereas Kant and his followers have argued that free peoples are peaceful, what about other polities? Just as democracies rarely become embroiled in war with one another, so too well-established oligarchies infrequently make war among themselves; but they have often warred with other forms of state. Peace is maintained by the same forms of state among themselves (Weart 1998, 14, 36). But then what about relations between liberal democracies and illiberal states? Clearly, well-established democracies are inclined to fight autocracies and engage in wars outside the West, as during World War II and the aftermath of colonial and postcolonial conflicts. Launched by the United States in 2003, the preemptive, "democratic war" in Iraq is but one example. Mindful of such cases, social constructivists have drawn attention to the ways in which "warlike democracies" undercut the democratic peace by identifying the Other. "[D]emocracies to a large degree create their enemies and their friends—'them' and 'us'—by inferring either aggressive or defensive motives from the domestic structures of their counterparts" (Risse 1999, 19–20, as quoted in Hough 2004, 44).

All things considered, the democratic peace hypothesis has not really come to grips with asymmetric power relations. Even if many of its purveyors claim to be able to separate facts and values, their research is about how to maintain and harmonize contemporary world order. But some postpositivist critics would say that the task is to transform a world order that rests on the principle of state sovereignty and that is shot through with inequalities. One need not entirely endorse this critique to note that a major difficulty with the democratic peace hypothesis is that it sidelines the large-scale transformation known as globalization.

PEACE BY TRADE

Another strand in the liberal argument is that trade advances peace—a proposition that we have seen is connected to democracy in Kantian ethics. The claim that international commerce supports peace may also be found in the writings of John Stuart Mill, Montesquieu, and other philosophers. Basically, the liberal conviction is that trading states increase the general welfare. Not only are there mutually beneficial economic gains from commercial intercourse, but also social interaction resulting from trading relations helps build a peaceful world. However, this position should take into account that long before mainstream economics embraced the liberal stance about the pacific benefits of trade, philosophers in antiquity and early Christian theologians such as Augustine registered skepticism about long-distance commerce. Later, mercantilists—among them, Jean Baptiste Colbert—worried about security, specifically that trade would precipitate war in Europe. Seeking to propel economic nationalism, mercantilists like Alexander Hamilton and Friedrich List argued for government intervention in the economy so as to avert rash liberalization and upheaval among states (Schneider, Barbieri, and Gleditsch 2003, 6–7).

While liberal writers deemed trading relationships to be harmonious, development economists carried out research that cast doubt on the putative nexus of trade and peace. Albert Hirschman, who investigated Nazi Germany's trade relations with Eastern Europe, and others underlined abusive power anchored in trade ties and asymmetrical relations among actors (Hirschman [1945] 1980, as cited in Schneider, Barbieri, and Gleditsch 2003, 7). Adding to this critical stance, dependency theorists detailed the ways in which unequal exchange benefits interests at the center and harms the periphery. Inequality is of course at issue in conflict between the global North and the global South and, by extension, supposedly detrimental to world peace. Some Marxists and neorealists (Waltz 1979, 138, as noted in Schneider, Barbieri, and Gleditsch 2003, 7) also reasoned that close economic links do not reduce conflict in the long run.

In the wake of decolonization and the collapse of the Soviet Union, scholars have looked anew at the trade-conflict relationship. Liberal theorists of international relations still adhere to the proposition that economic openness lessens the prospect of hostilities among states; mercantilists are not alone in insisting that increased trade can be a source of political friction; and still others hold that trade is not directly related to outbreaks of conflict, given the anarchic nature of the international system (Mansfield and Pevehouse 2003, 234, picking up on Waltz 1970, Gilpin 1981, Keohane 1990, Mearsheimer 1990, and Doyle 1997). Lately, there has been a proliferation of rigorous empirical studies on how economic openness affects militarized conflict (Barbieri and Schneider 1999; Oneal 2003; McDonald 2004). In this vein, Stephen Brooks (2005, 266) finds that there is no evidence to sustain the claim that international commerce advances peace among the great powers.

All told, this literature largely argues about both measurement procedures and contextual factors. The results are a plethora of qualified hypotheses concerning relative gains and intervening variables. The amount of quantitative evidence for different positions in this debate is impressive, or, one might say, daunting.

In switching from the classical debates over the ethics of commercial intercourse and its impact to contemporary investigations, formal theory and statistical research have abandoned a more holistic approach in favor of a separation of economics and politics. The presupposition is that these spheres can be divided. So, too, it is thought that independent and dependent variables may be unbundled. Meanwhile, the external arena of interstate behavior is scrutinized, while the domestic realm is set aside. As postmodernists would charge, the difficulty is with the use of binaries, dichotomies that betray positivist underpinnings. If anything, globalization obfuscates either/or splits. The analytic task is to bridge these divides.

Apart from the epistemological assumptions ingrained in positivism, the peace-by-trade approach suffers from a triple conflation: trade is often equated with economics, while finance and investment are assigned little or no weight; trade is used as a proxy for global economic integration; and interdependence is construed as globalization. For example, extremely useful at one level is the chapter cited above, "Does Globalization Contribute to Peace? A Critical Survey of the Literature," which appears in *Globalization and Armed Conflict* (Schneider, Barbieri, and Gleditsch 2003). The problem with this analysis, though, is the authors' failure to grasp the core concept that they purport to interrogate. As they candidly acknowledge,

> The catchword globalization has been applied to a host of activities in the economic, social, political, and ecological realm. Researchers investigating globalization have yet to resolve the basic issue of what we mean by globalization and whether or not globalization has changed over time. . . . Establishing a consensus about what we mean by globalization is the first, but also the most important, step to pursuing a research program. [Schneider, Barbieri, and Gleditsch 2003, 26]

By all indications, this research program is not sufficiently familiar with the globalization literature. In these authors' opus, the concept of globalization is undertheorized. The empirical instruments are sharper than the theoretical tools. Surely much is to be gained by carefully examining pieces of a puzzle, but especially if they are reassembled into a whole.

ETHNICITY AND POSTETHNICITY

Another strand of global conflict is ethnicity, or ethnonationalism, as it is sometimes called. Social theorists have focused on ethnic politics as a double-edged sword. It is both a source of solidarity and a deep-seated tension: communities come together around and fight about shared meanings. The concept of ethnicity also has various permutations: among others, communalism and tribalism. Such terms have many connotations, and it must be emphasized that these loyalties are not primordial.

For example, in postcolonial Uganda, a locus of civil war and coups d'état, members of different solidaristic groups have killed one another. But at root, is the bloodshed really about tribalism, as some accounts have maintained? Yes, tribe A comes into conflict with tribe B; however, it is a tautology to say that A fights B because of tribalism. And how was tribalism produced in the first place?

Take Ankole in southern Uganda as an illustration. Before the colonizers arrived there, the people of Ankole, the Banyankole, were what Americans would call rugged individualists. They farmed the ranks of steep slopes in a mountainous area. These farmers and their families shared only an oracle for worship; they did not identify as a single group. However, the British strategy of divide and rule provided incentives for indigenous peoples to band together and establish a hierarchical system with a chief in return for material rewards such as weapons to use against would-be enemies. Later in the colonial period, the British favored certain groups and groomed them for roles in the civil service and local government; others were channeled into the military and were supposed to be warrior-like "natives"; and still others were left on the margins. Then, in the nationalist interlude leading to decolonization, political parties formed in good part around these differences, and conflicts became more entrenched. In some cases, such as Nigeria, the Democratic Republic of the Congo (DRC, formerly Zaire), Rwanda, and Burundi, these cleavages became inflamed and ignited political violence (Mittelman 1975; Mittelman and Pasha 1997).

In a compelling account of ethnic conflict, Chua (2004) focuses on the hostility, sometimes deadly, visited on "market-dominant minorities," such as the Chinese in Southeast Asia, Asians in East Africa, Lebanese in parts of West Africa, and Jews in Russia. Her thesis is that free markets have concentrated large amounts of wealth in the hands of nonindigenous ethnic groups. At the same time, democracy augments the political power of the destitute majority, who use it to ravage an "outsider" minority. With globalization, the "spread of free market democracy has thus been a principal, aggravating cause of ethnic instability and violence throughout the non-Western world" (2004, 187). This explosive combination plays out not only in developing countries but also at regional and global levels, with the United States assuming the worldwide position of an advantaged minority group.

However, a difficulty with this way of thinking is that nondemocracies also encounter the same dynamic of blaming well-to-do minorities for their problems (as with Idi Amin's brutal regime and the Asians whom he expelled from Uganda). Another is the unquestioning acceptance of narratives of "us" and "them." Seemingly in an unreflexive manner, Chua grants—nay, sanctions—the construct of insider and outsider groups as a presupposition without at all analyzing how or why social differences become ethnicized in the first place (Dixit 2005).

Social constructivists, among others, examine the ways in which ethnic identities are created or, as Benedict Anderson famously argued, "imagined" (Anderson 1991). From this vantage point, emphasis is given to ideational factors, the subjective components of social relations. The focus is on identity politics. Attention turns to Othering—the mechanisms of constituting "we" and "they," especially important in genocide and "ethnic cleansing" (Chapter 3). This approach helps to make sense of the enigma of violence-ridden, homogeneous societies. An arch case is Somalia, a country with one language (Somali) and a single religion (Sunni Islam) ensconced in persistent conflict. Historically, the main axis of this strife has been warring clans. In conditions of intense competition for scarce resources, feuding there takes place among oppositional groups whose identities are created and maintained at an intraethnic level. Clannism is based on olden genealogies, in turn linked to family networks, bands of pastoralists that fought over water holes. Paradoxically, now this process of constructing identities is sometimes accentuated and politicized by peacemakers seeking to foster cross-clan dialogue.

Closely related, sophisticated research on ethnopolitics offers warnings about minority ethnic groups at risk. Ted Gurr (2000) has gathered a vast amount of data in order to pinpoint the incidence and specific types of conflicts. With Monty G. Marshall and Keith Jaggers, Gurr provides coded information on "regime and authority characteristics for all independent states . . . in the global state system" from 1800 to 2002. The objectives in this project are to establish a basis for analysis of the impact of democracy and autocracy on civil and international conflict and to contribute to the peaceful settlement of disputes (Marshall, Jaggers, and Gurr n.d.).

That said, it is important to comprehend the blending of ideational, material, and political factors in people's lived experience. In other words, beyond the question of how conflicts originated is the vexing issue of how to cope with them. After all, in places like Sri Lanka, many people have endured war for their entire lives. Levels of military spending have escalated and offer sizable economic opportunities. War can provide a cover for crime. It begets economic gain for certain international actors, insurgency leaders, as well as the holders of state power and their key supporters. Spending by the state is also supplemented by remittances from diasporic networks seeking to support those perceived as brethren. Then, too, there is humanitarian assistance from international organizations, nongovernmental organizations (NGOs), and bilateral agencies. With these infusions of funds, members of rival ethnic groups not only survive but also use the war economy as a way to build their livelihoods.

In this situation, war is represented in light of ethnopolitics and bound up with making a living. The expansion of violence can enlarge the basis for incomes. This expansion is in turn even greater with neoliberal policies that open economies. Hence, a rise in ethnic identity and neoliberal globalization can fuel one another. And postethnic wars, which have a basis in nonethnic spheres of life and are profitable endeavors, reproduce themselves (Nafziger and Auvinen 2003; Winslow and Woost 2004). Although it is usually thought that wars are irrational, given the interests of the combatants and their accomplices, there is, within severe limits, a rational choice to be made, as evident in the planning of armed conflicts in locales such as Rwanda, the site of premeditated genocide in 1994 (Murshed 2002, 388). In executing political violence, some combatants do not seek to win a war but to perpetuate it.

WEAK STATES

Quite clearly, the state is implicated in this perpetuation of conflict. Particularly susceptible are the postcolonial state and states in the former Soviet sphere trying to navigate transitions to democratic rule and market economies. Some of them are regarded as "weak" states and, in the worst cases, "failed" or "failing" states that hardly satisfy the Weberian criteria of statehood. These "frail" entities are seen as catalysts for, or cauldrons of, domestic and transnational violence. Normally, weak states are defined as lacking capacity (Migdal 1988; Jackson 1990). Capacity, in turn, is gauged in terms of efficacy and legitimacy. States that are not capable of providing basic services, protecting their citizenry from harm, and monopolizing the legitimate means of coercion within their borders are deemed a threat to a peaceful order.

However, many states, including ones in the West, fail to protect citizens from basic insecurities. The developed as well as the developing states not only put their nationals in harm's way on the battlefield but also founder in major ventures. An egregious instance is Washington's failings in 2005, when Hurricane Katrina took 1,800 lives and caused $81 billion in damage, and the government's emergency relief was notably lacking.

In addition, if the adjectives "failed" and "weak" are relative terms, it seems fair to ask, Compared to what? Are states weak compared only to other states? Or also to their domestic civil societies, to the putative strength that they had some years ago, or to market forces? Unfortunately, from one author's account to another, the meanings of failure and weakness vary enormously. They remain an approximation employed to highlight an aspect of local and global conflicts.[4]

States are weakened when they become mere managers or facilitators for market forces and other actors, such as powerful international economic institutions. Courtesan states lose autonomy and relinquish functions of governance. All states, even the strongest ones, are facing increasing pressure from above in the form of markets and international organizations such as the WTO and the European Union (EU), and from below in pressure exerted by civil societies. And all states are experiencing difficulties in harnessing global flows of capital, information, knowledge, technology, migration, and weapons. If so, it is misleading to suppose that there is a neat distinction between weak and strong states. The issue may be transposed to the amount of reduction in autonomy and loss of control vis-à-vis globalizing processes, but of course the magnitude of state power still differs from one case to another.

Indeed, hyperpower may use the nomenclature of "failed state" as a technique to justify intervention and occupation, as it did in Afghanistan and Iraq (Duffield 2007). Naming the cause of ills in certain countries as state failure, weakening, or fragility can serve as a route to state destruction under the banner of state-building, which is precisely what happened in post-2003 Iraq (Mittelman 2009).

Actually, failing, or fragility, is a catchall for many kinds of vulnerability to diverse risks. This grouping obscures numerous basic differences among actors placed in the same schemata. Countries' capacities to cope with extreme shocks range widely according to the case and specific localities. The historical paths and hinges to globalization are so dissimilar that it is not helpful to force these highly disparate situations into a single residual category.

WARLORDS

Sometimes, warlords such as Aideed in Somalia and Charles Taylor in Liberia step into the breach of state power. Especially when national institutions lack capacity and legitimacy, these contenders can be somewhat effective. They pursue private gain and build networks as bases of support.

In an impressive study of African politics, William Reno (1998) skillfully goes beyond the earlier tendency of specialists on the armed forces who focused on the idiosyncratic variable—the traits of autocrats like Idi Amin (Decalo 1976). Reno explores the structure of power relations that constitutes warlordism. He indicates that in weak states, leaders may aim to serve the public interest, but warlords are bent on capturing rents for their own benefit. Grounding his research in case studies of Liberia, the DRC, and Sierra Leone, with attention also to Nigeria as a potential example of warlord politics, Reno examines the interplay between the fluidity of power and conflicts over economic means. In his case studies, warlords have little or no concern for public welfare. They amass gains by working with international institutions, bilateral agencies, and NGOs, siphoning aid and circumventing, penetrating, or seizing the state. They benefit as well from foreign trade, especially exports of primary commodities and imports of arms. Consequently, this kind of war economy fuels patronage, which in turn feeds warlord politics.[5]

This line of inquiry shows that for large numbers of people, political life is being transformed. Different spaces are established. The rules are shifting. Symbols, such as emblems of sovereignty, are appropriated by combatants. Icons are important because they can lend legitimacy. Symbolic representations count heavily in contesting power.

Warlord politics fuses the local and the global. In a post–Cold War order, there is no more largesse from two superpowers at loggerheads with each other. Rather, a neoliberal framework of deregulation, liberalization, and privatization eases borders and pressures the state, as with SAPs that mandate reducing public enterprises and budgets. These policies also call for enhancing market access, which as noted, means fierce competition among capitalists in both the national and global realms. When economies are pried open, national capital must go up against foreign firms. In developing countries, conditions set by the World Bank and the IMF are accompanied by WTO decisions on facilitating free trade.

In this conjunction of globalization and local conditions, permutations of warlord politics may be found in venues from Somalia to Afghanistan to Colombia. The instances abound. But if leaders can forge ties to external interests, what about transnational social movements as actual or potential partners for other strata? And at the local level, more attention needs to be given to cases in which power seekers do not become warlords even though conditions are opportune for them (Dixit 2004a). How do analysts account for the lack of warlordism in an environment that in certain respects is less favorable for development than in another context? Is there a crucial distinction between, say, Ghana on the one hand, and Sierra Leone on the other, given their dissimilar resource endowments? The former, where warlords have not dominated politics, lacks the latter's diamonds, used by combatants in lucrative trade (Väyrynen 2000, 444–63, cited in Nafziger and Auvinen 2003, 148). Are valuable primary commodities a prerequisite for, or an enabling factor in, the rise of predators that thrive on the spoils of war?

RESOURCE WARS

No doubt, local and regional warlords and corrupt officials—in some cases joined by unprincipled businesspeople and arms smugglers—benefit from the exploitation of natural resources. For example, at the time of writing, the killing in the Darfur region of the Sudan is described (along with that in the DRC) as the worst case of genocide in the world. Known as *janjaweed*, brigades of mujahedeen on horseback are drawn from the ranks of nomadic Arab herders and have committed grotesque crimes against African farmers. The *janjaweed* are loyal to Musa Hilal, whom human rights groups and foreign officials cite as leading the carnage carried out by his gunmen. Observers are quick to point out that the conflict is between different Muslim groups, and race appears to be a prime axis in it; however, an underlying issue is the dispute over land and water rights (Sengupta 2004). This conflict has spilled into Chad, where Sudanese refugees are camped, the Central African Republic, and adjoining areas in other neighboring countries. Additionally, the protracted, apparently settled conflict elsewhere in the southern Sudan between the Arab and Muslim north versus rebels who practice Christianity and indigenous religions has been caught up with oil deposits.

At various times, Sudanese rebels found refuge in northern Uganda. This border is not clearly demarcated, and from early in the postcolonial period to the clash with the Lord's Resistance Army in this century, the Ugandan government has sought funds for military activities in the north. It gained revenue by looting the DRC, where Uganda's army fought alongside rebels and troops from other countries.

Conflict diamonds have contributed to the bloodshed in the DRC, Angola, and Sierra Leone. The extraction of oil has been a factor in the continuance of conflicts in Angola and Nigeria. The exploitation of timber, much of it illegally exported to the EU, Japan, and the United States, prolongs conflicts in various countries in Africa, Asia, and Latin America.

Nature's bounty is tapped to fill the void in sponsorship left from the era of competing superpowers. The revenue is often used to buy small arms from regional or global suppliers. A brisk weapons trade exacerbates violations of human rights. Unlike struggles in which ideology is a central factor, resource wars are more likely to involve the recruitment of young boys who serve as child soldiers, and girls as sex slaves. Typically, they are forced to engage in atrocities against family members, traumatized, and made to feel complicit in these actions (Renner 2002, 14).

Importantly, the availability and pillaging of lucrative resources are rarely or ever the sole or root causes of wars. By itself, the abundance of resources does not explain why some countries and regions bleed.

Rather, resource pressures may aggravate local conflicts that have regional and global channels through culture, markets, and arms. Resources have fueled struggles for power in Angola and the DRC. But not all countries endowed with ample resources are part of this conundrum. Diamond-rich Botswana, for example, has not been embroiled in violent conflicts in southern Africa. This country is attempting to use its resource riches to jumpstart other sectors of the economy and create linkages among them. The point is that lavish natural resources themselves are neither a curse nor a blessing. Resources are subject to agents with political will and interests. Policy frameworks and the ideologies that guide them are major factors in exploiting nature's bounty.

That said, the ramifications of conflicts with major resource components extend to environmental devastation of land, water, and forests (Homer-Dixon 1999; Klare 2001). Although some countries and regions possess generous resources, many of them are a nonrenewable form of wealth. Environmental conflicts spring from intense competition over this munificence and also scarcity, particularly where there is strong demographic pressure, as in Nigeria, whose wealth in oil is contested in terms of just distribution among different regional, ethnic, class, and religious groups (Renner 2002, 6–17). Indeed, there are also various water war scenarios.

Yet again, it must be emphasized that conflicts should not be reduced to strife over natural resources. Even when resource endowments are assigned exchange value and treated as commodities, it would be a mistake to read conflicts in a manner that stresses economics to the neglect of other dynamics, as for example do observers who claim that the 2003 invasion of Iraq was primarily about securing oil resources. Of course, the long-term commitment by the British and Americans to protect what they defined as their vital interests in the flow of oil from the Persian Gulf region should not be underestimated. Hence, when the United States alleged that Saddam Hussein threatened to send troops into Saudi Arabia, following Iraq's invasion of Kuwait in 1990, the U.S. defense secretary, Dick Cheney, expressed Washington's concerns:

> We're there because the fact of the matter is that part of the world controls the world supply of oil, and whoever controls the supply of oil, especially if it were a man like Saddam Hussein, with a large army and sophisticated weapons, would have a stranglehold on the American economy and on—indeed on the world economy. [as quoted in Koppel 2006]

A major change since 1990 is not only the accentuation of competition in the global economy but also the spike in demand for the eighty million barrels a day pumped by the world's oil producers. The chief oil consumers now include India and China. Noting that the United States wants to avert political instability in the gulf region, columnist and television editor Ted Koppel nonetheless underscores what, in his view, drives American foreign policy there: "For now, the reason for America's rapt attention to the security of the Persian Gulf is what it has always been. It's about the oil" (Koppel 2006). Also recalling the United States' long-standing geopolitical interests in the Persian Gulf, and adding nuance to the argument, David Harvey (2005, 20–24, 220) holds that the U.S. invasion of Iraq has everything to do with access to oil reserves: this spigot is crucial to security in the sense of maintaining effective control of the global economy.

Lending credence to this line of reasoning, Alan Greenspan, chairman of the Federal Reserve Board from 1987 to 2006 and often regarded as the "maestro" of the U.S. economy, acknowledged "what everyone knows": "the Iraq war is largely about oil" (Greenspan 2007, 463). For him, the geopolitical stakes center on energy resources.

Still, it is claimed, other factors are also at work. The fundamental issue remains, Why do people engage in battles over resource wealth and scarcity? Some analysts frame this question as a matter of greed and grievance.

GREED AND GRIEVANCE

In the context of natural resource endowments, many instances of deadly conflict over capturing rents, such as diamonds and copper, are traced to greed. This is a motive for the accumulation of wealth that may merge with criminality. Unquestionably, too, an accumulation of grievances reflects economic agendas. Some scholars thus ask whether greed or grievance drives contemporary civil conflicts (Berdal and Malone 2000). The issue may be formulated in terms of which element is primary in causing war. Or is there a balance between them, and how then do greed and grievance interact in propelling armed conflicts?

In an influential study, economists Paul Collier, while director of the Development Research Group at the World Bank, and Anke Hoeffler (2001) draw on a dataset of wars from 1960 to 1999. They note that the overwhelming majority of the outbreaks were cases of internal strife, and seek to predict the occurrences of civil war. The authors weigh political scientists' conception of conflict, defined in terms of motive, and economists' notion of opportunities as the basis of rebellion. Resting on these two approaches, a model is constructed that pits greed against grievance as rival explanations. Introducing refinements in the "motive-opportunity dichotomy," Collier and Hoeffler (2001) identify types of each category and the importance of perceptions and misperceptions.

Collier and Hoeffler's empirical investigation employs proxy variables, quantitative indicators, and measurable allowances for scale, especially the size of countries. Regression analysis is used to predict the risk of the eruption of civil wars over a five-year period. Controls for random effects and cases of outliers are introduced.

A major finding is that a model that centers on the opportunities for rebellion is robust to the authors' statistical tests. The main factors that influence the opportunities for rebellion are the availability of finance, the cost of rebellion in earnings, and military advantage attributable to the dispersal of population and terrain. Diversity makes rebellion more difficult because cohesion among rebels is costly, and grievances mount with increased population owing to greater heterogeneity. Finally, this research shows that the amount of time that has elapsed since a prior conflict is significant: "time heals."

The conclusion is that opportunity provides the best explanation for rebellion. Economic viability is deemed the key to results robust to the methodology. Opportunity explains the risk of conflict and is consistent with greed-motivated accounts if the latter are given an economic reading. What motivates rebels is not social concerns of inequality, rights, and identity. Economic opportunities are decisive in explaining civil conflicts. Over time, "[g]rievance has evolved into greed" (Collier 2007, 31).

At bottom, the debate of greed and grievance falls into rational-choice analysis and cost-benefit calculations. But a large part of civil conflicts does not involve voluntary calculations. Many child soldiers and sex slaves do not have a choice. Few of them voluntarily engage in coercive activities. It is the lack of alternatives that impels them to violent behavior.

Yet there is no mistake about the impact of this debate among analysts. The categories of greed and grievance affect where resources flow in postconflict situations. Multilateral financial institutions and bilateral agencies employ this knowledge set to help decide about the allocation of funds.

There are other important contributions to the debate about greed and grievance as drivers of war that go beyond descriptive statistics and correlation analysis (Addison and Murshed 2003; Ballentine and Sherman 2003). Some of this research first looks at the overlap and intersections between greed and grievance. The next step is to investigate exactly how greed often escalates into grievance, as in Sierra Leone. There follows the matter of specific ways in which resource depletion and unsustainable consumption (as during Nigeria's oil boom) can spur grievances over corruption.

Or one might define grievance in a manner that does not treat economics as decisive and rather offer a multilevel conception that incorporates collective memories, including myths, such as the strong narratives that emerged during the 2002–3 violent conflict between Hindus and Muslims in Gujarat, India, ostensibly over which group could legitimately claim the original site of a mosque or a temple. Also, what needs to be added to the research that focuses on the internal aspects of war is the bleeding of resources from certain parts of the developing world. Privatization of the extractive sector entails incentives and tax breaks for transnational corporations (TNCs), which are taking, for example, substantial rents from Ghana's and Tanzania's mineral exports and Chad's oil revenues. This outflow heightens competition for scarce resources among the local population and compounds the problem of good governance. The political conflict then is over access to the share of resources that remains in the home economy. In this vein, there are efforts to reframe the debate over greed and grievance in a manner that surmounts the separation of internal and external issues, a suspect dichotomy in a globalizing era.

NEW WARS

As we have seen, globalization has altered the conditions for conflict, leading from old wars to new forms of organized violence; and contemporary wars are not predominantly between states. Prefigured during the Cold War, and particularly apparent in Africa and postcommunist states, new wars grow out of guerrilla and counterinsurgency campaigns as well as from a decline in state authority (Kaldor 1999; 2003, 119). Mary Kaldor emphasizes that this transformation is linked to a reduction in the autonomy of the state and, in many cases, its claim to legitimately monopolize coercion. Though implemented by the state, neoliberalism diminishes the scope of its activities and lowers tax revenue.

To add to Kaldor's point, debt structures require a sizable outflow of capital from developing countries so that they can pay their interest on principal—a transfer from the world's poor zones to the rich zones—and international financial institutions insist on austerity measures. As a result, the state encounters great difficulty carrying out its part of the social contract and maintaining support from the general public, especially the strata experiencing the most pain from budget cuts and a lack of protection against the jagged edges of opening the market.

Another factor propelling new wars is innovation in technology, particularly in communications and transportation. Technological development facilitates the rapid transfer of money used for the purchase and shipment of small arms and light weapons. With deregulation and the liberalization of trade, borders are increasingly porous and rebels gain easy access to a flourishing global arms industry. Nonstate actors thus have greater capacity to use violence and try to turn asymmetric power to advantage (Brzoska 2004).

Hence, a major feature of new wars is a localized conflict that involves extensive connections to NGOs and international organizations. United Nations peacekeepers, forces deployed by the North Atlantic Treaty Organization and the African Union, Oxfam, and Save the Children are among the actors in these wars. Second, as mentioned, an aspect of the dialectic of integration and fragmentation that comprises globalization is the rise of identity politics. A surge in conflicts over identity, frequently represented in religious and ethnonationalist narratives, supplements traditional aims in geopolitical and geostrategic rivalries. A third characteristic of new wars is that the combatants are not primarily states but also networks. The agents in this warfare are an assortment of politicians, traditional security forces, warlords, mercenaries and paramilitary units, traders, refugees, diasporic groups, and terrorists. War is increasingly fought by competitive networks of state and nonstate forms of authority hooked to the global political economy (Duffield 2001, 190).

Fourth, as suggested, the conflicts are not contained within the juridical borders of sovereign units but splice them. Fifth, globalization complicates the binary distinction between legal and illegal activities. The so-called illicit elements may be found within the state itself, as in Russia, or tacit deals are made between state agencies and criminal networks. Covert actors sometimes operate as overt actors, say, within intelligence agencies, some of which now recruit members of the underworld. Criminality is a major characteristic of new wars. In this respect and others, globalization clouds the lines between state and nonstate actors. Finally, new wars involve large-scale violence against civilians. Notwithstanding the elaboration of international law since the Nuremberg trials, ethnic cleansing in the former Yugoslavia and the Great Lakes region of Africa in the 1990s and the early twenty-first century are but two examples of flagrant abuses of human rights in which perpetrators employed violence as an instrument to sow fear and insecurity. In these cases, organized rape has been used to dehumanize victims.

The effort to distinguish old wars and new wars advances understanding of the problematic nexus of globalization and conflict. A major strength is that this approach calls attention to the interactions of conflict, race, and gender.[6] Kaldor's work, in particular, contributes powerfully to explaining globalized wars: globalized not as a matter of universal scope but in underlying dynamics. The twofold distinction between the old and the new warfare is especially useful if it is regarded as a heuristic and an ideal type, not as hard-and-fast categories.

Yet when it comes to the state, it is important to be precise about the concept. If one employs a Weberian concept of the state, as does Kaldor, then the fine point is that the state lays *claim* to a monopoly over organized violence (Dixit 2004b). For Weber, "a state is a human community that (successfully) claims the monopoly of the legitimate use of physical force within a given territory" ([1946] 1973, 78). By implication, there can be competing claims and multiple actors. The state is not the sole agent to attempt to wield the legitimate use of force.

Moreover, the new-wars approach to global conflict invokes Kantian ethics by which cosmopolitan rights override sovereignty as a condition for peace. These norms are likened to a "global 'civilising process,'" which entails a global social contract and a global civil society as the long-term remedy for new wars (Kaldor 2000, 7). But does this Promethean image of *la mission civilisatrice* suggest that enlightened cosmopolitans imbued with Kantian ethics are the agents for preventing new wars (Dixit 2004a)? Is this civilizing mission projected from the West elitist? Is cosmopolitanism a discourse from above that fails to resonate with those of social forces at the base, especially on the margins of globalization? Is the cosmopolitan approach too top-down? Surely for the multitude in Africa, the contemporary discourses are mainly about food, water, work, health, education, and physical security—not cosmopolitan ethics. At best, there is potential for cosmopolitanism from below, though its realization does not appear imminent.

Mozambique

Consider a case in southeast Africa: Mozambique, still one of the world's poorest countries despite an increased rate of economic growth in the twenty-first century (Mittelman 1981, 2000). There, peasant resistance to foreign control dates from the advent of colonialism in the fifteenth century. The best-known peasant rebellion in Mozambique is the war launched by the Ngoni people in Gaza province in the nineteenth century. Mozambicans of diverse ethnic backgrounds joined together in attacking colonial rule in 1917, formed a mass movement to oppose the occupation by Portugal, and continued during the *Estado Novo*, the corporate state that held the reins of power throughout the longest period of fascism in world history, the regimes of António de Oliveira Salazar and Marcello Caetano.

The modern phase of the armed struggle began with the founding of the Mozambique Liberation Front (FRELIMO) in Dar es Salaam, Tanzania, in 1962. Initially, FRELIMO represented a merger of three separate movements based in different neighboring countries and encompassing myriad language clusters, ethnic units, races, and religions. In addition to nationalist groups that operated legally, semilegal organizations, such as the Núcleo dos Estudantes Secundários Africanos do Moçambique, provided a framework for the covert activities of militants, who promoted strikes, labor unrest, and other forms of popular protest in ports and on plantations. Eduardo Mondlane, FRELIMO's first president, returned from exile with Marcelino dos Santos and others to help concert the struggle for national liberation. After Mondlane's assassination in 1969, the war continued with Samora Machel as FRELIMO's top leader. Supported by the Organization of African Unity Liberation Committee, the United Nations Committee of Twenty-Four (on decolonization), bilateral agencies, and NGOs, FRELIMO fought until the fall of Portuguese fascism in 1974.

Following political independence in 1975, FRELIMO encountered the Mozambique National Resistance Movement (RENAMO), a contra force initially organized in Southern Rhodesia (today Zimbabwe) and later sponsored by a combination of white settlers, Portuguese fascists who maintained major business interests in southern Africa, and apartheid South Africa. Backed by the U.S. policy of "constructive engagement" during the presidency of Ronald Reagan, the South African Defense Forces supported RENAMO, insurgents responsible for grotesque human rights abuses. RENAMO lacked programmatic goals other than wanton destruction and made no effort to construct meanings about the Mozambican landscape and people. During this sixteen-year civil war, which concluded in 1992 (with RENAMO becoming part of the government), international organizations, NGOs, and states such as in the Nordic region sought to bring humanitarian assistance and an end to the conflict.

In postwar Mozambique, the discourses among impoverished peasants and unemployed workers center on survival; and among employed city dwellers, including the educated and political leaders, on national unity and development as well. Cosmopolitan ethics resonant with Kant do not enter these discourses. Or it could be argued that an indigenous cosmopolitanism, Pan-Africanism and the spirit of *ubuntu* (an epistemology that originated in southern Africa, with emphasis on community and solidarity), may be detected and could become more pronounced. However, the main point is that beginning early in the colonial period, a medley of bandits, resistance fighters, mercenaries, a private militia, states in the region and beyond it, transnational business, and international and nongovernmental organizations have sought to bring their power to bear in Mozambique. In this country's colonial and postcolonial history, there is at most a difference in emphasis but by no means a well-marked threshold between old and new wars.

Finland

Another illustration of the blending of old and new wars may be found in Finland.[7] The mixed nature of its civil war in 1918 is reflected in the ongoing debate about what to name it in Finnish: *kansalaissota* (literally, war of citizens), *sisällissota* (internal war), *vapaussota* (war of liberation, or war for freedom), *kapina* (revolt), *luokkasota* (class war), or *vallankumous* (revolution) (Pankakoski 2004). The various constructions reflect the partisan nature of the war and the fact that different wars were fought in Finland at the same time.

Ostensibly, after the 1917 revolution in neighboring Russia, the warring parties were Reds and Whites. (A grand duchy of Russia since the end of Swedish rule in 1809, Finland became an independent country for the first time in 1917.) The Bolsheviks channeled arms across the border and trained the Reds, but the troops of the old imperial Russia remained in Finland. Also present was the German military, which since 1915, instructed Finnish volunteers for the army. They formed the *Jäger* battalion to fight alongside the Whites. Germany supplied weaponry paid for by the Finnish government, an arrangement that not only was financially beneficial to German arms producers but also provided a military bridgehead against Russia. Sweden, too, had interests in Finland, especially in occupying the Ahvenanmaa (Åland) Islands, and Swedish volunteers fought for the Whites.

Not yet having a permanent army of its own, Finland's government thus brought together a group of White officers mostly trained in Russia, Germany, and Sweden. They helped fill a vacuum arising from the dissolution of tsarist power, which left the municipalities in Finland without control of the means of coercion. Several organizations sprang up, initially with a mutual aim—to maintain order and to stop the retreating Russian troops from pillaging. There emerged working-class militias, bourgeois countermilitias or paramilitary police, and security corps composed of farmers, all with different interests and objectives.

Out of a population of just over 3,100,000 people in 1918, more than 36,000 people died in the Finnish civil war, but only 9,400 in direct action (*The War Victims of Finland 1914–1922 Project*, as cited in Pankakoski 2004). Direct violence against civilians was common on both sides and often justified as "cleansing." In fact, as many as 13,000 prisoners perished in camps during the war. When it ended, the government was not prepared to feed the more than 80,000 prisoners or treat epidemic diseases (Mäkelä, Saukkonen, and Westerlund 2004 and Manninen 1993, as noted in Pankakoski 2004).

In sum, this case exemplifies a combination of myriad interests, multiple groups of combatants, and varied aims. Clear-cut distinctions between internal and external actors, public and private spheres, and the military and civilians cannot be drawn. The Finnish civil war of 1918, like the violence associated with the centuries-old peasant rebellions culminating in the decolonization of Mozambique and the ensuing civil war there, indicates that the old wars are postmodern in that they contain elements of the new.[8] The two cases betray messy conflicts that complicate well-hewn categories.

NINE TAILS

Where does this stocktaking leave us? It shows many important contributions by scholars and an extraordinary fragmentation of knowledge. In the main, the nine analytical frames are partial and detached from one another. There is little coherence among them. With exceptions (inter alia, Sandbrook and Romano 2004, apropos "poor countries," and the citations in my Chapter 1, note 5), this literature does not focus on the big picture of globalization, security, and world order.

The discussion in this chapter layers critiques of strands of security, peace, and conflict analysis, and indicates that in comparison to Kant's vision of worldwide "perpetual peace" or Beard's inspiration for the idea of "perpetual war for perpetual peace," contemporary state-of-the-art research lacks globality. A large part of it stumbles on the nexus of liberal democracies and the fringes of this zone, and loiters outside the conditions of people's daily practices without getting inside their intersubjective frameworks. Although substantial reframing is warranted, the conceptualization heretofore on offer takes the form of nine tails, with the braids disconnected from a baton, the handle for attaching them together.

Why is the big picture decidedly lacking? One reason is the sheer messiness of the complex problems with which analysts are grappling. Different forms of conflict, sundry types of regionalism, and diverse local conditions are in play. Indeed, more research is done on local and regional conflicts than on global conflict. An enormous amount of quantitative and qualitative data are adduced. Econometric and case-study evidence is assembled in order to examine internal and international factors, and economic and political variables. The dominant tendency in this domain of knowledge is to separate variables, inventory them, test hypotheses, and identify correlations.

In this regard, Raimo Väyrynen makes a telling point: "the bulk of Nordic peace research was structured as an epistemic community around the Galtungian core" (2004, 32). The reference here is to the enormous influence of the Norwegian scholar Johan Galtung. A founder of peace studies, he is a sociologist with training in mathematics. The positivism ingrained in Galtung's scholarship is manifested in his book *Theory and Methods of Social Research* (1967). This empiricism is now patent in the orientation of major scholarly journals, such as the *Journal of Conflict Resolution* and the *Journal of Peace Research*. One could also trace this imprint in the development of knowledge structures such as the Peace Research Institute, Oslo (PRIO) and SIPRI, which as Väyrynen (2004, 37) observes, married with realism. It must be said that these knowledge sets extend beyond Europe to universities, research centers, and think tanks staffed by intellectuals who buttress and are at times supported by hyperpower or conjoined funding agencies.

True, the world is complicated, and each local conflict is distinctive in certain respects. But the connections between them are understudied. Although a lot of conflict is no doubt local, it is conditioned by global forces. When all is said and done, the links between conflicts and transformations in world order have not been adequately comprehended. It is time to reaggregate the separate pieces of knowledge without pinning diverse phenomena on a single cause. The concept of globalization, which interrelates myriad processes, is the handle on the nine tails of conflict. Surely this concept can be enriched by the literature on peace and security, which helps to explain the intricacy and variability of its components and battlegrounds.

No doubt, there is a risk, I want to say emphatically, in shoehorning multiple subject matters that are difficult to encapsulate intellectually into a single body of knowledge. Can a sprawl of issues that seemingly run apart from one another really be joined? Also, there is a danger of turning structures into structuralism by banishing or diminishing agency.

Yet, while remaining sensitive to these analytical traps, it is worth underscoring my points about macrostructures: the geostrategic side of globalization and its impact on world order have not been properly understood. There is insufficient attention to the ways in which the social relations of power and violence are being reconstituted. One can gain an appreciation of these linkages without pretending that globalization is a juggernaut. Multidimensional and not a singular or totalizing process, the globalization syndrome includes emblematic events and actors. But of what are they emblematic?

A way to answer these questions is to build a new concept of *coercive globalization* by drawing on philosophical insights in the run-up to a major conflagration, World War II. This era was the fulcrum of a "gathering storm," just as storm signals, albeit with distinctive features, have emerged in our troubled times.

3 COERCIVE GLOBALIZATION

"The hidden hand of the market," notes journalist Thomas Friedman, "will never work without a hidden fist. McDonald's cannot flourish without McDonnell Douglas, the designer of the U.S. Air Force F-15" (1999, 373). A champion of globalization, he contends: "And the hidden fist that keeps the world safe for Silicon Valley's technologies to flourish is called the U.S. Army, Air Force, Navy and Marine Corps" (373).

But with the incipient conditions of hyperconflict, the fist is anything but hidden. After pledging a peace dividend when the Soviet Union collapsed in 1991, Washington redirected the available resources to secure the structures of neoliberal globalization. The United States has increasingly relied on the military component of hyperpower to protect territory and promote its interests in a hypercompetitive world, as with bolstering the oil-service giant Halliburton in the Middle East. At the same time, the cumulative effects of market-driven globalization in the former Soviet Union and Eastern Europe, Asia in 1997–98, and Argentina when it closely adhered to the neoliberal prescriptions of the Bretton Woods institutions discredit the Washington Consensus of the 1990s and prompt policymakers to search for an enhanced consensus.

In a climate of growing uncertainty about emergencies and new risks, these tendencies flag ways in which globalization is being renovated and fortified. To elucidate these dynamics, the burden of this chapter is to suggest that militarizing globalization should be understood in tandem with the changing balance of social forces. The discussion that follows will develop a framework for analyzing hyperconflict by interrogating political discourse and scholarly literature—power and knowledge.

Distinct from many approaches, the discussion will argue that military power and social relations are co-constituted. Explanation must go beyond state-centered framings of security and account for exclusionary practices that attend to hyperconflict.

MILITARY GLOBALIZATION

Military globalization consists of an extensive network of bases, combatants, weaponry, and related technologies. Several elements support this web. One is a global arms market in which sourcing takes place at numerous sites around the world, reflecting the logic of a highly specialized division of labor and power. In other words, the production of weapons systems is primarily transnational rather than national. The emergence of this market includes the proliferation of large and small munitions. Second, innovations blur the distinction between civil and military technologies. Enabling one to feed the other, new developments in electronics span these spheres. Computer-based systems, for example, are used for long-distance detection and lethal damage. Such means are advanced to counter chemical, biological, and other instruments of destruction that fall into the hands of insurgents. And by cheapening weapons systems and the delivery of them, technologies alter cost-benefit analysis.

Third, detection is not merely an activity that takes place in distant locales but also involves broadened police and surveillance functions at home; it becomes a cross-border strategy with varied modalities. Finally, reliance on private security contractors is a major feature of this pattern. In Iraq, these private services are hired by most American news agencies and even protect the U.S. ambassador. But states are not the only clients. International organizations, NGOs, and TNCs widely use private security firms (Singer 2003; Avant 2005).

Observers of different persuasions subscribe to the notion of military globalization but offer different formulations. For Ellen Frost, a former U.S. deputy assistant secretary of defense, this problematic is about a new aggregation of force reflecting the overall characteristics of globalization and "prompted in part by global competition" (2001, 55–56); for Joseph Nye, it is the slow evolution of "a geogovernance of military globalization" (2001, 83); for David Held, the need to reform "the world military order" (2004, 85); and for Richard Falk, a shift from "modern geopolitics" built on conflict and relations among sovereign states to the construction of "postmodern geopolitics," that is, the subversion of a Westphalian world order and the resort to wars without territorial enemies and against nonstate combatants (2004, 93–94).

The concept of military globalization provides insight into aspects of the reorganization of political violence when the truncheons are increasingly privatized and to the extent that the meaning of security expands broadly beyond actual fighting, especially in comparison to prior eras. Businesses conduct the business of war. Private contractors, along with military consulting firms, are indeed key actors that offer a range of services, including equipping the troops, gathering intelligence, training a national guard, as well as protecting key corporate and political personnel. Former military officers and scientists sell their knowledge and weapons. Paramilitary forces are deployed in battle. There is little regulation of firms that fill in where a stretched-out U.S. military or demobilized armies are unable to deliver security. By all accounts, the private military industry is booming, generating $100 billion in annual revenue and operating in more than fifty countries ("The Jobs of War . . ." 2003).

Yet questions about the correlation of morality and force abound. Private firms know no loyalty to the political authorities who hire them; their allegiance is to the captains of the market. What are the implications for security if a concern quits the job, switches clients, or trades secrets? Similarly, if weapons production is based on a geographically dispersed form of economic globalization, and if an overseas contractor proves unreliable, could security be easily breached? Taking into account issues such as production, technology, finance, and morality elicits varied responses and requires revising the notion of military globalization.

NEOCONSERVATIVES AND MILITARY GLOBALIZATION

Neoconservative policy intellectuals have played a major role in constructing the discourses on globalization. A source of neoconservatism is a group of students, many of them Marxists, mostly Trotskyites, who attended the City College of New York in the 1930s and 1940s, and later moved to the right. They include Irving Kristol, Daniel Bell, Seymour Martin Lipset, Nathan Glazer, and Daniel Patrick Moynihan. Another root of neoconservatism is the teachings of Leo Strauss, a political philosopher at the University of Chicago who believed in eternal verities that could be traced to classical Western texts. His writings primarily examined the great books from earlier centuries. Strauss was not one to offer counsel on policy matters. But from his own childhood in Europe, he knew the perils of the Russian pogroms and the Nazi Holocaust, and reflected on the West's uncertainty about its purpose in his time. Strauss maintained that unlike the foundation laid by classical political philosophy, the modern project, which he did not advocate, could no longer be understood as "contemplative and proud" but rather for "the sake of human power" and to master nature.

He averred, "[T]o make the world safe for the Western democracies, one must make the whole globe democratic, each country in itself as well as the society of nations" (Strauss 1964, 3–4).

Strauss and his disciples, such as Allan Bloom, author of the influential book *The Closing of the American Mind* (1987), and Albert Wohlstetter, a mathematician and military strategist, shaped the ideas and values of their heirs.[1] Among them are William Kristol, founding editor of the *Weekly Standard*; Paul Wolfowitz, deputy secretary of defense in the George W. Bush administration and subsequently president of the World Bank; and Richard Perle, chairman of the Defense Policy Board and managing partner in Trireme Partners, a venture-capital firm heavily involved in homeland security. Bloom taught Francis Fukuyama, a former State Department official and now a professor at the Johns Hopkins School of Advanced International Studies in Washington, D.C.; and Straussian Harvey Mansfield at Harvard mentored several leading power holders (Atlas 2003). Linking knowledge and power, these policy intellectuals claim the mantle of Ronald Reagan's beliefs and designed their hawkish policies in the 1990s. Documents such as the 1992 "Defense Policy Planning Guideline" drafted by Wolfowitz and the 1997 Project for a New American Century cosigned by Wolfowitz, Dick Cheney, and Donald Rumsfeld propounded a militaristic view of U.S. power.

Embracing many aspects of neoliberalism, neoconservatives uphold the principles of free markets and free trade. Whereas neoconservatives abide by the ideal of unrestrained enterprise, this "neo" is also wedded to patriotism, American exceptionalism, and masculine images of authority. Neoconservatives and neoliberals alike have global aims. Compared to neoliberals, however, neoconservatives are more favorably inclined to state intervention in the economy, public provision for security, and assertions of economic and military force (Steger 2005, 16). Whereas neoliberals look to soft power but are not averse to hard power, neoconservatives turn readily to the use of brute force, albeit tinged with the values of freedom and democracy.

From a neoconservative perspective, the outliers are a medley of enemies. One is a transnational network of terrorists led or inspired by Osama bin Laden. It includes cells embedded in the homeland that need to be rooted out. Their religious idiom of political violence is deemed an expression of globalized Islam largely detached from ethnic cultures. A globalizing *ummah* (the Muslim community of believers or nation) is represented as a new Caliphate tied to radical identity politics. Part of this web is deemed to be rogue or weak states, such as Afghanistan under the Taliban, which harbor and assist these extremists. There are also other nondemocratic regimes, among them North Korea and Iran, which possess actual or potential nuclear capability.

Although neoconservatives are not univocal, they agree that future world order is about securing freedom. They believe that democracy can be exported—if need be, with the collaboration of allies—and advocate a muscular strategy. In principle, when other means of security fail, the unilateral impulses of the modern state, at least at the hub of hyperpower, must prevail. And with the ascendance of neoconservatism, Washington sought to reassert state power by waging a "global war on terror."[2]

In the United States, "neo-liberal conservatism"—to use Anthony Giddens's felicitous term (Giddens and Pierson 1998, 152)—means opening markets and maintaining traditional cultural values. Added to this, it signifies hunting enemies, sometimes preemptively, as well as going it alone or engaging in multilateral pacts when convenient. Ideologically, the hybrid neoliberal conservatism is dynamic, adjusting to rapidly changing conditions and allowing for new elements. This mixing of frameworks along with policy setbacks eventually prompted an uprising among some neoconservatives, as evinced by Fukuyama's critique of this movement, including the ways in which it became associated with American hegemony (Fukuyama 2006).

There has been an apparent swing toward a *security-state* that braces market power. In contradiction to the view of analysts who hold that the state is in retreat, declining, or redefining itself from a nation-state to a *market-state* (Strange 1996; Bobbitt 2002, 228–38), the United States, whose dominant strata are chief beneficiaries of economic globalization, demonstrated its resolve to militarily preempt any power that allegedly abets an enemy. But in making this move, Washington also felt obliged to try to gain legitimacy and multilateral assistance from the United Nations and through a "coalition of the willing."

After 9/11, policymakers and defense planners in Washington know that globalization is a significant security issue and are struggling to come to grips with it. The response is not only unilateral action when need be, while pursuing multilateral options, but also to focus on process—reform and reorganization in government. Accompanying organizational changes for adjusting to globalization is a renewed interest in the concept of "Revolution in Military Affairs," which entails proposed technological transformations pertaining to weapons, information, and doctrine. Such recommendations include network-centric warfare and the use of increasingly sophisticated technologies (nanotechnology, robotics, and biotechnology).

Cognizant of this thinking, President Bush's 2002 National Security Strategy states, "the distinction between domestic and foreign affairs is diminishing. In a globalized world, events beyond America's borders have a greater impact inside them.... This is where our national security begins" (U.S. President 2002). His 2002 document, largely unchanged except perhaps in tone in 2006 (U.S. President 2006), also holds that the simultaneous rise in competition in the marketplace and the military arena is producing threats of global reach.

Indeed, conservatives—whose ranks include neoconservatives, realists such as Brent Scowcroft, and nationalists like Pat Buchanan—acknowledge the conjunction of military power and market power, and have called on the government to provide the security that a global economy requires. In the minds of conservatives, military power makes market power credible, as Henry Nau, an official in the Ford and Reagan administrations, explains:

> Market power is an illusion if there is no military power to safeguard the marketplace.... Military power not only defends national security and freedom, it underwrites the stability that a prosperous global economy requires. ... [C]onservatism is more comfortable with competition both in the economic arena and, as a basis for balance and safety, in the military realm. [Nau 2004/2005, 20]

From these principles, several studies flow and support President George W. Bush's position on the changing nature of global security. An exemplar is *The Global Century: Globalization and National Security* (Kugler and Frost 2001), a research project carried out at the National Defense University. According to the coeditors of this collection of essays by leading strategists, their study is a departure from past thinking in that the Department of Defense had not previously considered globalization as a major factor in defense planning (2001, 5). Now, for these planners, it is up to the United States to safeguard order:

> The United States will need to remain the world's strongest military power. Working in concert with allies and partners, it also will need to use its military forces to shape the strategic terrain in peacetime, to respond to crises and other situations, and to win the wars of the future. [2001, 5]

Understood as increasing interconnections "in which networks and flows surmount traditional boundaries or make them irrelevant," globalization is said to place new stresses on the international system and cause strategic chaos (Frost 2001, 37). The coeditors of *The Global Century* maintain that the task is to strengthen the policymaking process and military capacity in order to meet global challenges. Globalization presents new risks, especially the proliferation of WMD and missile technologies, as well as escalating ethnic and religious violence. Transnational security threats are exacerbated by rebel armies, drug traffickers, and extremist religious groups that span borders. Emblematic too of this genre of strategic analysis, the U.S. National Intelligence Council's 2020 Project views globalization as a "mega-trend . . . that . . . will substantially shape all of the other major trends in the world of 2020" (2004). The authors of this study conclude that globalization places enormous strains on government and that a pervasive sense of insecurity results from threats such as terrorism, transnational organized crime, cyberwarfare, and pandemics.

This way of thinking portrays globalization as posing a vast and orderless assortment of cross-border challenges to peace. Security analysts generally construct long lists of sundry threats brought or accentuated by globalization. A catalog, of course, cannot substitute for a well-rounded understanding of interactions or of globalization as a propellant. Strategic planners not only lack a holistic approach to how the items in their inventory are interwoven but also give the impression that globalizing threats will last indefinitely. The implication is that military preparation must be undertaken forever. In short, the mission is to wage perpetual war for perpetual peace.

BEYOND MILITARY GLOBALIZATION

Another approach to explaining security challenges is to develop a concept that is more probing than military globalization. A way to do so is to give greater scope to the role of ideas in the globalization syndrome and to revisit the work of classical authors, including master strategists. In rendering their contributions, Martin Shaw provocatively argues that military-strategic theory, beginning with the foremost classical theorist of war, Carl von Clausewitz, lacked social theory, and that the pioneers of sociology, from its founder Auguste Comte on, failed to make war central to their understanding (Shaw 2000, 58–62).[3]

To assess Shaw's thesis, and to grasp the relationship between war and society, one must judge how much autonomy to grant war. Akin to premising the primacy of production, as in Marx's schema, is warfare the primary human condition? Or is firepower just one more element in the mix?[4]

First, it is worth complicating Shaw's contention, even in its refined formulation: Clausewitz provided "a primitive sociology that began to examine *warfare* as a social institution" (Shaw 2005, 40–41; emphasis in original). True, long before the discipline of international relations was established, military theorists, preeminently Clausewitz, focused on armed conflict; and sociologists, following Comte, on social relations. As is well known, the main thesis in Clausewitz's magnum opus, *On War* ([1832] 1968), is that politics and war are inextricably interrelated. In advancing this proposition, Clausewitz offered a global vision of a cataclysmic breakdown in world order caused by historical forces engaged in war, pushing the system beyond its limit. In the maelstrom, it is not only sovereign states that clash with one another, but also "People's War" erupts. For example, patriots formed the backbone of the revolutionary French army and believed that they were fighting for rights throughout Europe. Mindful of this rebellious ardor, Clausewitz showed great respect for the power of ideas.

Although the Clausewitzian philosophy of international relations postulates the centrality of sovereign states, which strive to increase their power relative to that of their rivals, and normalizes war among them, it does not one-sidedly emphasize military might. Rather, Clausewitz points to openings to other factors, subsequently explored by thinkers such as Raymond Aron, whose *Peace and War* (1966) purports to present a "world sociology" built on Clausewitzian underpinnings (Rapoport 1968, 65–66; also Van Creveld 1991).

Within social theory, there are, of course, different traditions. For some thinkers, war is *conditioned* on industrialism and capitalism.[5] In this mode, Polanyi's account ([1944] 1957) is certainly one of the most compelling explanations of the dynamics of industrial capitalism. He provides an institutional analysis of the international order in which the Industrial Revolution occurred. According to him, the pillars of this order were the balance-of-power system, the international gold standard, the self-regulating market, and the liberal state ([1944] 1957, 3).

In the nineteenth century, the market became disembedded from social and political control. There developed the utopia of the self-running market, a utopian idea in the sense that it was anything but self-adjusting. Its rise was abetted by coercion: the enclosures in England, sanctified by acts of parliament; the use of the royal navy to enforce England's role as the principal balancer of power in Europe; and the spread of the capitalist market to other parts of the world. The state most often favored the interests of the budding industrial class. Political authorities passed legislation and collected taxes that aided them. But the rulers also maintained public order and sought to regulate aspects of capitalism so as to gain legitimacy, not least so that citizens would back war-making.

Nevertheless, the extension of the market had deleterious effects on large numbers of people, some of whom were pauperized in the shift from their peasant lifeways to proletarianized, urban conditions. Stripped of their cultural moorings in this transformation, victims of the thrust of capitalist industrialization fomented a countermovement as a manner of redress. In Polanyi's analysis, this configuration became a propellant of large-scale conflict in Europe, culminating in World War II.

Another landmark effort to meld war-making and social theory is the oeuvre of historical sociologist Charles Tilly, who famously argued, "War made the state and the state made war" (1975, 42). For him, only the strongest states in Europe survived the "giant competition" of warfare (1975, 42). With the demobilization of lords' private domestic armies, absolute monarchs assembled centralized militaries for external defense and police forces to maintain law and order at home. There emerged a panoply of institutions to fund, supply, and conscript personnel for armies and navies. To centralize rule and pay for war, the crown coopted, neutralized, and suppressed opposition (Tilly 1986, 136).

Tilly thus tells a story of capital and coercion. The former is the sphere of exploitation; the latter, the realm of armed force, which extends to other means created by soldiers and large landlords in Europe and sanctified by states (Tilly 1990, 16–19). And as war became more expansive and expensive, the state helped sustain collaboration between merchants and landlords and increasingly relied on a growing bureaucracy (Tilly 1993, 107, 145).

Deepening his social theory of war, Tilly analyzed the application of cultural control, especially with regard to the development of national languages and national education systems, including museums and expositions. This transformation in state-building occurred when war became increasingly deadly (Tilly 2002, 165, 179). Overall, Tilly assembled a sizable corpus of evidence to show the four ways in which state agents carry out organized violence: state-making, war-making, protection, and extraction. Aspects of this process, he claimed, are on the same spectrum as that of organized crime (Tilly 1985, 171, 182).

Another way to meld social theory and war is to invert Clausewitz's dictum that war is policy by other means. Taking a broad view of power as a relationship of force—a mode of repression—Foucault contends that "politics is the continuation of war by other means" (Foucault 2003, 15). Not only does political power rest on force, but also it relies on a "silent war ... to reinscribe it in institutions, economic inequalities, language, and even the bodies of individuals" (2003, 16). In this sense, power is a warlike operation.[6]

In light of these interpretations, it is possible to add nuance to Shaw's claim that the theory of war is deficient in social theory and that social theory lacks military theory. Moreover, the historical explanations advanced by Polanyi and Tilly, as well as Foucault's reformulation of Clausewitz, help to think about the interactions among globalization, hyperconflict, and world order. Different but complementary analyses show ways in which *military power and social relations are co-constituted.* There is no primacy of one over the other. Primacy arguments assume a separation that does not exist in practice. These are analytically futile moves.

It is organized violence that is being reconstituted through various processes, implied in notions of structural and soft power. There are myriad mechanisms of coercion. Not only do production, technology, finance, and morality need to be enveloped in a robust concept of coercive globalization, but also culture is a central element—and, as indicated, an important theme in branches of social theory.

To illustrate, with the crescendo of fears about a Muslim presence on European soil, debates about migration and multiculturalism are stirred by political violence: in Madrid, the 2004 train bombings linked to resident terrorists and aimed at changing the Spanish government's policy of supporting the U.S. occupation of Iraq; in reputedly peaceful, open, and tolerant Amsterdam, the 2004 murder of Dutch filmmaker Theo van Gogh, who portrayed abusive treatment of Muslim women; in several cities in France in 2005, clashes with authorities over the policy of banning head scarves and other signs of religious affiliation in the schools and, more generally, myriad barriers to advancement by immigrant communities; and in cosmopolitan London, the 2005 coordinated bombings in three underground trains and a double-decker bus, all by British Muslims raised in northern England, again prompting questions about cultural politics.

Meanwhile, discourses about multiculturalism in Germany are largely directed at guest workers and their descendants, many of whose families came from Turkey. As Angela Merkel, a conservative German politician, declared in the run-up to her 2005 election as chancellor, "Multiculturalism has failed, big time." "Those who refuse to embrace German values as their own," Edmund Ströber, Bavaria's premier, affirmed, "picked the wrong country." Jörg Schönbohm, the interior minister of Brandenburg, warned immigrants that they must adopt the *leitkultur,* Germany's national culture. Referring to German Basic Law, he implored, "We cannot allow foreigners to destroy this common basis" (Bernstein 2004).

Sectarian violence, notably arson attacks on mosques and schools in the Netherlands, as well as on synagogues in France, stirs controversies about its spread in the German "homeland." Apparently, German popular vocabulary first included the term *leitkultur* in 2000, when then-parliamentarian Friedrich Merz urged non-Germans residing in Germany to fully become part of the country's "mature, liberal Leitkultur." Merz's statement gained currency with other officials, national language becoming a leitmotif in the debate. The widespread use of Turkish and Arabic on the streets, as well as by imams in mosques, worries many Germans. But there is also outrage that *leitkultur* includes racism and serves as a way to further marginalize immigrants (Kumanoff 2004).

Indeed, when globalization becomes more fearsome and coercion-intensive, the case of the absorption of immigrants in Europe points to crucial issues. One is that migration is palpably a transnational process, with not only objective flows of population and remitted capital but also intersubjective frameworks easily crossing borders. Second, cultural channels of coercion can be potent mechanisms in the reorganization of political violence. And third, as Clausewitz ([1832] 1968) contended, violence is instrumental. It is not for its own sake but a way to compel others, advance interests, and achieve goals.

Taking this point from Clausewitz, at present, when large numbers of Germans and Europeans generally, as well as many people elsewhere, have renounced national wars, what does political violence instrumentalize? Who is coerced? How is the enemy identified?

CONCEPTUALIZING COERCION

For help in answering these questions, it is worth probing the work of Carl Schmitt, a German philosopher and legal scholar who joined the Nazi Party in 1933.[7] He adopted an expansive and systemic view of power, in some respects similar to that later advanced by Michel Foucault. Schmitt offered many insights into security and insecurity, some of which are remarkably prescient for the twenty-first century, and sought to link them to world order. Extrapolating from Schmitt's formulations helps bring to light coercive globalization. Four byways in his writings are most pertinent here: the concept of *nomos*, the transformation of political life, the distinction between friends and enemies, and the role of war in society.

For Schmitt, *nomos* depicts the constitutive processes of order and orientation. Orders are world historical events that may be distinguished from one another, and suggest a political and juridical rule. They also instill orientation, which springs from the local, the earth in a spatial sense (as in an attachment to the land), and thus below the heights of the economy and the state. Historically, the old orientation and European order of independent economies and liberal markets, balanced by self-centered states, were eventually supplanted by a move toward spaceless universalism (Schmitt [1950] 2003, 192–98).

So, too, the rule of *nomos* involves a measure of legitimacy, as with the laws that sanctified land appropriation, originally by violence. Enclosure entailed erecting fences, drawing border lines, and forming identities, all of which in time became the stuff of rituals and territorial zones that required protection. In other words, *nomos* expresses orders that unite as well as divide.

To the extent that history remains open and fluid, a new *nomos* may emerge. With the continuing reapportionment of space, the nexus of order and orientation shifts. Hence, after 1492, with land appropriations and changing forms of spatial consciousness, global lines were redrawn. The global template demarcating hemispheres originated in the eighteenth century, and the United States later proclaimed its right to control the Western one. In other words, this line enabled the United States to introduce the concept of a New World and challenge the European spatial world. Although international law pronounced territorial sovereignty to be inviolate, many states—the ones controlled and dominated from without—found this space to be an external shell marked by linear borders yet without the social and economic content to maintain territorial integrity (Schmitt [1950] 2003, 150, 252). Meanwhile, the United States established a "sphere of *spatial sovereignty*" in the Western Hemisphere (Schmitt [1950] 2003, 253; emphasis in original).

Nomos is thus a totality of conditions replete with unresolved tensions that emanate from inside and outside. A main tension is the dualistic construction in liberalism between the economic and political, the fiction that an apolitical economy exists apart from the state. Schmitt also noted the liberal proclivity for engaging in perpetual discussion of the political, a substitution for firm decisions by the sovereign. Furthermore, the conjunction of liberalism and democracy weakens the political, setting in train a system of depoliticization and giving scope to illiberal elements. These tendencies can provide an opening for the "total state."

Yet politics remains the brain, even if the state wages war, which is expressed in its "own grammar" (Schmitt [1932] 1996, 34)—an allusion to Clausewitz's maxim that war is an extension of politics. It is only political authorities who can definitively prohibit their citizens from fighting a war and thus remove an adversary from conflict. In doing so, power holders invoke concepts such as justice and freedom to legitimize their own political ambitions and discredit the enemy (Schmitt [1932] 1996, 66). While propounding ideological humanitarian values, the state helps spawn "an economic-technical system of production" (Schmitt [1932] 1996, 72). In short, liberalism seeks to protect individual freedom and, ultimately, transforms the state into a weak institution, rendering a bundle of compromises and an arena for endless discussion.

Distinctive to political life are groupings of friends and enemies.[8] Today, this sort of line-drawing is taken for granted—as in "foreign" policy and "foreign" students.[9] Schmitt's reflections on such tacit categories give pause. For him, an enemy is the Other, the alien. Not a private opponent, the enemy is public because of strife between collectivities. Whereas Schmitt's attention turned to armed conflict between organized political entities, including religious communities, he was also concerned about the enemy within. In Nazi Germany, Schmitt found this enemy among people who live together. The enemy is a friend of Christians who, in fact, are threatened by Jews, because the identity of the superordinate group is held together by this form of exclusion. Therefore, the assimilated Jew becomes anyone, an element to destroy (Ojakangas 2003, 417, 420).

An ardent anti-Semite himself, Schmitt advocated that Jews are the absolute enemy, not because of racial inferiority but because they constitute a political enemy. The exclusion of the enemy binds the dominant community, that is, a political identity of friends, which sees itself as the enemy of the enemy. Jews are the absolute enemy because in diasporic Judaism, they evade identification as the Other, and this ordinary existence as assimilated people is a genuine threat to the sense of belonging among friends. Thus, according to Schmitt, the exclusion of the enemy, within and without, is a vital function for the unity and spiritual well-being of political life (Ojakangas 2004, 78–79).

Deemed an exception to the normal juridical order, the absolute enemy is outlawed, and the sovereign may legitimately decide when to suspend normal constitutional protections. As the contemporary Italian philosopher Giorgio Agamben puts it, the paradox in Schmitt's theory of exception is that the sovereign is thus both inside and outside the law (Agamben 1999, 161–62; 2005). There is an exclusion. The individual case is not governed by the general rule. Yet the rule applies to what is excluded as a suspension. The exception is on the outside of the community, outlawed by the power of excluding, or in Schmitt's words, "The exception is more interesting than the regular case. The latter proves nothing; the exception proves everything. The exception does not only confirm the rule; the rule as such lives off the exception alone" (Schmitt 1985, 15, as quoted in Agamben 1999, 162).

Agamben's writings build on Schmitt's theory of exclusion and Foucault's notion of biopower wherein the political melds public and private space, especially bodily sites. Resting on this foundation, Agamben's claim is that the concentration camp represents a state of exception par excellence. I hasten to add that it brings to mind the post–9/11 exception invoked by U.S. leaders—whose predecessors had adopted the 1798 Alien and Sedition Acts, including the Alien Enemies Act, to jail and deport opponents, and had interned Japanese-Americans during World War II—for detaining suspected Muslim terrorists at Guantánamo Bay. During the "war on terror," the United States has employed a doctrine known as extraordinary rendition (outsourcing intelligence) and sends suspects to secret prisons in other countries for torture. The justification for these actions is that they are deemed necessary for securing freedom. This containment and dehumanization of peoples—the building of walls—reduce foes in these camps and torture chambers to sameness, a homogeneity that stokes fear (Butler 2004, 119–21). For Agamben, the lockups may be understood as a space of exception, for they are outside the usual juridical order. This exception, initially a temporary provision, becomes a regular procedure (Agamben 1998, 169–75; 2005).

The state of exception is part of outlawing and coercing the enemy. The ultimate form of coercion is war among sovereign units. In international law, "the bracketing of war"—a contest of forces with regulations to guard against "nihilistic hatreds" and "meaningless destruction"—is a cardinal aspect of order (Schmitt [1950] 2003, 187). Indeed, long ago, abstract rules came to encode perpetual war for perpetual peace—far different from the achievement of perpetual peace in Kantian terms. Schmitt, in fact, decried the limitations of abstract principles that entail coercive enforcement, as after World War I when the victors criminalized Germany as an aggressor for exercising its right as a sovereign to wage war. For Schmitt, war is the hallmark and proving ground of political life. Conversely, according to Schmitt, perpetual peace—Kant's vision of a world government—is tantamount to the demise of politics.

Setting aside Schmitt's own political commitments, his framework may be gainfully employed and adapted in two ways. First, Schmitt's writings may be read as cautioning against the use of Self/Other as a universal. It is not a nominal construct. In a Schmittian sense, Self/Other is anything but a static category, a dehistoricized template.[10] Second, if *nomos* is a concrete order and orientation to the local, then in the current epoch, these processes are being constituted as disorder and reorientation. And just as the principle of territoriality and the contradictory pressures for deterritorialization operate simultaneously, so the dialectic of inclusion and exclusion is unfolding. In our times, the enemy appears in different guises: the "failed state," rogues encamped in sleeper cells in the West, or as the threat of extreme poverty that feeds these impulses. The political violence, uncertainty, and instability characteristic of hyperconflict evoke an emergency.

While the old *nomos* disintegrates, a new *nomos* begins to form.

The task in the ensuing chapters is to trace the displacement of the old and show the extent of a budding hyperconflict over its successor, as well as the forms that it could take.

4 CONFLICT 1: THE MULTILATERAL AGREEMENT ON INVESTMENT

In an oft-cited statement, Renato Ruggiero, the first director-general of the WTO, underlined the importance of instituting an enhanced investment system, the proposed MAI: "We are writing the constitution of a single global economy" (as quoted in Kobrin 1998, 105; Melloan 1998; Tabb 2001, 196; Faux 2006, 18). This vision of global governance began with specific competitiveness policies, broadened to a new regime for global trade, and ultimately extended to the basic rules of world order.

The struggle over the competitive environment in the 1990s quickly turned into a conflict over ideas, the lines between friends and enemies, and the question of exceptions that would secure order. In addition, the MAI became a lightning rod for attachments to localities and a battle fought by states and certain globalizing forces—the basic themes of order and orientation characteristic of a Schmittian *nomos*.

Reading the MAI as an instance of globalization together with security thus permits working with concepts vetted in the preceding chapters. Attention now turns to the formation of hyperconflict as it is embodied in contestation over a new *nomos*. But what are the actual mechanisms? How do they operate in the interplay of order and orientation, disorder and reorientation? And in what respects, if at all, does hyperpower enter on the terrain of efforts to lock in a regime of hypercompetition?

The objective in this chapter is to gain insight into these issues, using the MAI as a case study of a concrete institutional initiative to normalize the practices of power. It will be shown how the efforts of a range of actors to promote the MAI roused stiff resistance to the deepening of globalization. The drive to secure investment conditions in fact produced greater insecurity.

CONTEXT

The MAI was launched in Paris at the OECD, an intergovernmental poli-cymaking body and venue for then twenty-nine (today thirty) countries, in-cluding the wealthiest ones. The 1995–98 negotiations there came on the heels of the North American Free Trade Agreement (NAFTA), signed in 1992 and made operational in 1994, as well as the amplification of the General Agree-ment on Tariffs and Trade (GATT) in the form of the WTO beginning January 1, 1995. Policymakers justified choosing the OECD as a forum for talks on a legal framework for foreign direct investment (FDI) on the ground that the bulk of these flows is among its members: at the time, 85 percent of outflows and 65 percent of inflows (Picciotto 1998, 744).

But if one adopts a long perspective, the inspiration for the MAI may be traced to the origins of economic liberalism itself more than two hundred years before. Resting on this foundation, the global market expanded; it grew espe-cially rapidly in the 1970s and 1980s and even more greatly after the fall of the Soviet Union in 1991. From 1980, the volume of world merchandise trade rela-tive to global production, and the ratio of the stock of FDI to world output, surged. (Investment and trade flows are complementary in that the former cat-alyze the latter.[1]) Although flows of FDI slowed in the early 1990s, they picked up again in 1995.

Against this backdrop, there were sustained efforts in the 1990s to protect and promote trade and investment. Rapid increases in the number of bilat-eral investment treaties (BITs), for example, were part of the move to secure the rights of foreign investors. BITs have helped to establish the principle of nondiscrimination for investors, safeguards against expropriation and strife, the freedom to freely transfer capital, and dispute settlement procedures. The spread of BITs resulted in a plethora of more than 1,300 agreements by the mid-1990s, leading to a search for a coherent multilateral framework to super-sede a patchwork of bilateral and regional agreements (Vandevelde 1998).[2] The idea was to arrive at a more comprehensive compact delimiting the rules of the game. This would require building confidence and ultimately consensus on not only easing regulatory policies but also normative features of globalization.

In proliferating multilateral trade agreements, states have sought to use in-ternational institutions such as the OECD as means for lowering barriers to movements of capital and setting up conventions for doing so. Elements of this process are two codes adopted in the OECD in the 1960s: the Code of Liberali-sation of Capital Movements and the Code of Liberalisation of Invisible Transactions (Henderson 2000, 3, 6–7). Technically, they became legally binding instruments, but in the absence of a juridical instrument within the OECD that could ensure compliance, enforcement was problematic and reliant on pressure from members. In fact, the scope of the MAI greatly exceeded these precursor codes.

The aims of the MAI were to extend liberalization and spread privatization. The new rules would, for all practical purposes, reduce a state's regulatory authority over both foreign and domestic companies that do business within its national boundaries. In comparison to other treaties, the MAI adopted an unusually expansive view of foreign investment so as to encompass portfolio investment and any asset, including real estate and intellectual property, belonging to noncitizen owners. Indeed, the actual terms of the MAI were far more comprehensive than the stipulations of its forerunners. The MAI not only augmented the investment section of the NAFTA but also was to be employed worldwide. After adoption by the OECD states, accession was to be offered to other countries. Thus, the MAI would be a stepping-stone on the path to broader membership organizations, presumably the WTO and perhaps the United Nations Conference on Trade and Development.

HYPERCOMPETITION

Throughout the MAI deliberations in Paris from 1995 to 1998 on key features of hypercompetition, the discursive power of language—the ways in which the platform was framed—took on special importance. Following are the specific issues negotiated there:

First, a key provision of the proposed MAI was national treatment: signatories were required to grant at least the same rights to foreign investors as to their own investors. Under the MAI, preferences such as tax concessions or economic assistance programs could not be granted to domestic firms. Known as indigenization decrees in some countries, laws that require hiring a certain percentage of managers locally would be barred. Other performance requirements for foreign corporations—technology transfer, domestic equity participation, and mandatory allocation of a percentage of profits in local development—were disallowed. Additionally, foreign investors would be assured equal access to natural resources in a host country. But there would be no prohibition against offering special incentives to foreign investors.

Second and closely related is most favored nation status, wherein foreign investors and foreign countries would be received without discrimination. Regulatory laws, albeit eased, would apply equally to domestic and foreign firms. Under the MAI text, the most favored nation specifications permitted challenges to acts such as economic sanctions against countries violating human rights.

Third, investor guarantees required states to compensate foreign investors at market value if their investments were at all jeopardized by governmental actions. Expropriation was broadly construed as not only direct seizure of property but also state policies equivalent to expropriation. Under the MAI, countries could not interfere with the free repatriation of profit or the movement of capital. Nor could host countries stop or stall the transfer of assets such as stocks or currency. The MAI text specified that these capital transactions could be entirely made in convertible currency and at the current market rate of exchange.

Fourth, in a radical shift in the legal framework of international economic pacts like the GATT, wherein only governments could bring complaints against governments, private investors would now be able to sue national governments as well as press for monetary compensation if the government were to renege on investor rights delimited in the MAI. Transnational investors would have standing to take their cases before domestic courts in the host country or to go to an international tribunal.

Finally, "rollback" and "standstill" clauses ensured access for outside investors to newly emerging markets. Countries would be obliged to dispense with laws that contravened MAI provisions and not pass these laws in the future. State and local laws came under this rule. Any other provisions that pertained to fair competition, labor standards, and environmental protection—for example, in a code of corporate conduct—would be nonbinding (Sforza-Roderick, Nova, and Weisbrot 1997).

Clearly, these tenets are about transforming the conditions of competition, a bedrock feature of capitalism. At root, the MAI negotiations concerned the rules that structure market-polity-society relations and the rights of local communities in determining their own fate. And as one would expect, sharp disagreement emerged over the proposals among states, varied interested groups, and ultimately the public at large.

Before the release of the draft treaty, the delegations of OECD states could easily anticipate the basic interests of diverse stakeholders: for environmentalists, protection of policies already in place, ones that could be deemed obstructions to investment. For instance, some local laws prohibit the sale of unprocessed timber to foreign countries or the sale of land to foreign residents on the ground that local residents have a larger stake in the community. Typically, environmental standards that are most stringent at the subnational level regulate surface mining, fishing techniques, and oil shipment so as to prevent leakage, pollution, and so on. From the outset, it was evident that foreign investors would regard tax incentives granted by states for environmentally friendly practices and technologies as discriminatory (Tuomi n.d.; Singer and Stumberg 1999).

Fundamentally, these issues of local initiative and homegrown development pose the question long ago raised by Aristotle: What is the proper scale of the polis? At what point is political community too large or too confined to allow for both self-determination and, as social contract theorists as well as philosophers such as John Rawls (1993) added, sufficient autonomy for political life?

More concretely, if small employers at home were to be rendered less competitive relative to global capital, then certain jobs would be curtailed, potentially contributing to income inequalities. Yet the countervailing factor would be job gains as a result of the inflow of investments. But the risk is that corporations could use this lever to restrain labor standards, fight unionization, and depress wages in a global race to the bottom: a downward ratchet making it easier for investors to shift production facilities from one country to another, thus increasing the pressure on all locales to compete more vigorously for investment capital. In some developing countries, states facilitate this process by establishing "special economic zones" or "export processing zones."

With this intensified competitive landscape, developed countries have experienced not only the outsourcing of jobs but in certain cases an alteration in the corporate-supported social contract established after World War II, a pillar of labor-industrial relations: the pension and health benefits of union and nonunion retirees. To compete against overseas rivals with limited costs for benefits or younger workforces, many large private corporations no longer offer a secure retirement plan and have reduced the package for current employees and retirees, adding to uncertainty about the rules and the future.

These considerations were real concerns before the start of the negotiations in the OECD. But not surprisingly, advocates of the MAI pointed out substantial gains from unfettered capital flows. The contention was that heightened competition and more efficient allocation of resources outweigh any losses caused by rising flows of capital across borders. Just as more goods and lower prices advantage consumers, the new job opportunities that come with FDI can improve workers' lives. It is exposure to strong competition and increasing trade that brings technological advancement and the stimulus deriving from the growth of capital. Proponents of the MAI also contended that the conditions for the injection of transnational capital include reducing regulatory practices, thereby gradually eliminating "distortions" in the host economy. After all, a multitude of distortions are the result of political pressures wrought by special interests and create putatively adverse forms of protectionism.

In contrast, critics maintained that the MAI represented an undemocratic structure, part of the tendency to vest power in unelected officials in international economic institutions that lack accountability. Opponents of the MAI feared a growing democratic deficit when globalizing processes scale up political power to organizations such as the EU (which variously acts as both a component of and a response to globalization), the Group of Seven (G-7), the IMF, NAFTA, the World Bank, and the WTO. To be sure, according to the principle of national treatment, foreign corporations would have no obligation to abide by local laws. Where such laws gave preferential treatment to minorities or helped promote small businesses, they could be challenged on the ground of discrimination against foreign capital. With the dispute settlement mechanism, the MAI explicitly empowered foreign corporations to sue governments without granting the same rights to civil society groups that would want to challenge these firms.

Thus, under the NAFTA investor-state procedures, Ethyl Corporation, a U.S.-owned firm, sued the Canadian government in 1997 for banning an Ethyl product, the petrol additive MMT. Parliament in Canada prohibited the import and transport of MMT, deeming it a dangerous toxin, as did the U.S. Environmental Protection Agency in proscribing this item. Arguing that the Canadian decision violated the provisions of NAFTA (subsequently toughened in the MAI) concerning expropriation and compensation, performance requirements, and national treatment, Ethyl claimed damages. Ultimately settled by the parties, this case was not only about indemnity but also the prerogative to safeguard public health against harmful products.

In this light, its opponents came to view the MAI as a potent weapon for large industries ascendant in the globalization process. According to critics, some of them cited later in this chapter, political authorities sought to endow corporations with greater power. In a hypercompetitive world, states adopted measures to ensure investors' security, even though some parties regarded the actions as tantamount to threats of coercive globalization.

HYPERPOWER

Seemingly about economic globalization, the MAI also raised basic issues about power relations and military-strategic security. These dimensions of globalization coalesced around the proposed MAI.

In the run-up to the talks, the representatives of European states, facing political parties on the left in both national parliaments and the EU, wanted the venue to be the WTO, which has a much larger membership than does the OECD. However, U.S. strategists pushed for holding the negotiations in the OECD (Egan 2001, 87). Like all participants in the negotiations, the U.S. delegation aimed to parley the terms that it wanted into a treaty. From 1996, Charlene Barshefsky, who also led the American negotiators at the 1999 WTO gathering in Seattle (Chapter 6), headed the team of officials from the State Department and the Office of the U.S. Trade Representative, and was required to seek congressional ratification for the adoption of an accord.

Throughout the proceedings, the United States, of course, continued to pursue its own agenda, as did other states. Mindful that the OECD countries received 81 percent of the stock of U.S. firms' direct investment and provided the greater part of the inflows of FDI (Witherell 1997, 39), U.S. official discourses centered on the ways in which the MAI could spread ideas propagated by the Americans: to wit, "a well designed MAI has the potential to advance American values in such areas as environmental protection and internationally recognized core labor standards. .... Certainly, American companies generally take their high standards with them when they operate abroad" (Larson 1998, 32–33). In the same statement by the U.S. assistant secretary of economic, business and agricultural affairs, emphasis is given to securing the "freedom" of investors and the "legitimacy" of the U.S. proposals (Larson 1998).

Redolent of debates about hegemony, U.S. negotiators sought to legitimize the right of sovereign states to maintain their national security. This effort was to assure that hard power, the coercive component of globalization, could be bolstered.

In so doing, the MAI language that provided for security exemption fused the objectives of neoliberals and those of rising neoconservatives in the United States. Coupling their interests, the MAI would protect the arms industry against interference in production and sales. Governments would be free to subsidize national weapons manufacturers. There would also be a free flow of trade in arms, both in imports and in exports. Transactions pertaining to defense industries and national armies were to be shielded from restrictive measures in the MAI.

Typically, treaties forged in international organizations are widely subject to bureaucratic politics, rival policy preferences, and national security exemptions. The MAI would appreciably extend the latter. The MAI security exemption would apply to R&D expenditure on military innovation—for example, in regard to warships—though not public transportation supported by civilian R&D. This distinction relates generally to spending on military and nonmilitary science and technology. It also has major implications for public health and education, including universities and research institutes that are part of the vast network of Pentagon and related defense funding.

In this vein, it is important to bear in mind the manner of representation. Not only was the Paris conclave conducted by political authorities from the wealthy states, home to the world's largest military industries, but these countries included all sixteen members of the North Atlantic Treaty Organization, a security alliance. For them, surely peace was an ideal shared in the negotiations. In the MAI forum, the route seemed to be peace by trade, with special rights for those in the arms business, whose freedom was to be securitized: prerogatives almost immediately contested by different actors with varying strategies.

HYPERCONFLICT

An initial sign of conflict appeared within the high-level Negotiating Group itself. The issues proved troublesome; the scope of the treaty, vast; and the conception, complex. Trying to find common ground was an arduous task.

Tension emerged over access to the negotiations. Early on, the WTO secretariat was invited to attend the proceedings. One year into the talks, South Korea joined Mexico and Turkey, the only developing countries at the table in 1995. To address concerns that the MAI would be exclusionary and undermine development, some meetings of the negotiators were eventually held outside Europe. In principle, the MAI would subsequently be open to participation by non-OECD countries able and willing to meet its conditions. Notwithstanding this tenet, the 1995–98 negotiations were really among three parties: the United States (hence NAFTA) paramount among them, the EU, and Japan.

All the seats at the table whose occupants were entitled to vote belonged to representatives of states. Formal consultation with NGOs began only in October 1997, when thirty organizations representing every region of the world sent delegates (Mabey 1999, 60). It was late in the process. Negative publicity about a potential deep restructuring by elites conferring in Paris had begun to circulate. There were concerns from below about a top-down process, an inter-elite framework hammered out in secret or with negligible consultation. In other words, the lines were drawn between friends free to participate in the proceedings and outliers who would be deemed eligible at some undisclosed time when ready to assume the characteristics of their forbears, the countries considered advanced. The MAI explicitly posed the issue of political identity—the differences between insiders (OECD members) and outsiders (nonmembers)—in terms of legal and market security. The treaty contained techniques of inclusion and exclusion, and the us-and-them outlook provoked hostility.

Conflict surfaced when civil society organizations obtained the script, a restricted internal document, and posted the leaked version on the Internet in the spring of 1997, before the official release of the text on October 1, 1997 (Organisation for Economic Cooperation and Development 1998a, 1998b). In various countries, groups such as Public Citizen, Amnesty International, Oxfam, the Sierra Club, and Third World Network used their Web sites to alert the public to the MAI proceedings. An "International Week of Action" in several locales in February 1998 drew attention to the MAI and decried its provisions.

Troubled by the ways in which flows of trade and investment would bring down barriers to the protection of national culture, French artists designed placards and performers sported puppets and other symbols of resistance. (In all likelihood, some of these dissenters directly or indirectly benefited from state subsidies for cultural industries.) Environmental, labor, women's, and church groups wrote letters to the OECD, demanding a halt to the negotiations. The campaigns included demonstrations in Washington, D.C., and protesters occupied the entrance to the office of the chairman of the Dutch MAI negotiators in The Hague. Rallies were also staged in front of the Department of Trade and Industry in London and were followed by actions in Oxford, Brighton, and Essex. The London *Guardian* published a critical analysis of the MAI, a defense of the treaty by the U.K. minister of trade and industry Lord Clinton-Davis, and a response from leaders of NGOs. Actions took place in Australia, Finland, and Sweden as well, and a coalition of 565 groups made demands on OECD member states, including a call for transparency and a halt to the negotiations (Khor 1998).

Diverse constituencies brought increasing pressure to bear on their governments. The Vancouver-based Defence of Canadian Liberty Committee (DCLC) initiated legal action against the federal government in the Federal Court of Canada. Arguing that the MAI is unconstitutional under Canadian law, the DCLC held that the draft accord "gives entrenched rights to international banks and foreign corporations guaranteed by international law which Canadian citizens do not have." The DCLC also contended that "[t]his is contrary to the principle of equality before the law which is part of the Canadian Constitution enshrined in the Charter of Rights and Freedom" (as cited in Chossudovsky 1999, 449). The lawsuit challenged the secrecy of the measures and the undemocratic character of the process, thereby raising questions about the legitimacy of this kind of constitution-writing.

In Canada, a grassroots movement fought the proposed treaty. The members consisted of national culture associations, such as the Canadian Conference of the Arts and the Council of Canadians; ecumenical church groups; the Canadian Labour Congress; environmental organizations; the Canadian Center for Policy Alternatives; the federal New Democratic Party; the provinces of British Columbia and Prince Edward Island; the territory of Yukon; and numerous community movements. At the local level, officials on four continents passed resolutions to establish "MAI-free zones." Enacted in several cities, this legislation was adopted in places such as Wollongong, Singleton, and Hastings, Australia; Montreal, Toronto, and Vancouver, Canada; Edogawa Ward in Tokyo, Japan; Geneva, Switzerland; and Boulder and San Francisco, U.S.A. This broad network quickly thrust out to become increasingly transnational in scope and resisted the efforts of corporate coalitions: among them, the U.S. Council of International Business, a cluster of more than three hundred TNCs, including American Express, Intel, and Philip Morris.

Tactical weapons in this battle were the Internet and symbols, the MAI itself becoming emblematic of the promise and problems of globalization. The advantages of the Internet were its speed, low cost compared to other methods of disseminating messages, and the ease of transmitting information. It offered a means to counter the vast amount of data in the hands of business, government, and the OECD. It also provided a way to coordinate local, national, international, and transnational strategies—an extensive sharing of know-how. The drawbacks included unreliable reports, the sheer quantity of flows, uneven access to this technology (skewed in favor of white males), and the sometimes imprudent language. Nonetheless, this tool helped to open political space for different discourses and to refocus the agenda for debate (Smith and Smythe 2000).

As the resistance gained momentum, the MAI widely signified a changing balance between market forces and the sovereign state. While pursuing investment security in the form of a multilateral treaty, corporations continued the proliferation of BITs as a course toward a more comprehensive regime. But under mounting pressure, Lionel Jospin's government, which provided the venue for the OECD in France, withdrew from the negotiations in 1998, as did Canada. Meanwhile, the U.S. delegation was constrained because in 1997, President Bill Clinton had failed to gain congressional approval of fast-track negotiating authority for trade agreements. Bureaucratic politics, too, became a more limiting condition. The State Department's enthusiasm for the agreement was not matched by support from the Office of the U.S. Trade Representative. And the Department of the Treasury was at best lukewarm until it cooled when the Asian debacle began in July 1997 (Dougherty 1998, as cited in Egan 2001, 94; and see Chapter 5).

By late 1998, the MAI was blocked in the OECD, though it later resurfaced in other international institutions, especially the WTO. The contagion was striking. As if by wildfire, the issues swept from one venue to another. The range of factors that came into play in this conflict included ideologies (economic liberalism, nationalism, internationalism, cosmopolitanism, and other identities), culture, paradigms, and several types of crossborder transactions. The agents were states, localities, international bodies, corporations, and civil societies. This contestation over "which rules and whose rules" is at the heart of constituting global governance, betrayed in the MAI strife as highly fragmented and loosely cast in an organizational maze.

NOMOS

These themes may be elucidated by means of the Schmittian concept of *nomos*, which focuses on world historical events. As elaborated in Chapter 3, this way of exploring order and orientation trains attention on a political and juridical regime in relation to the base of society as well as the environment. The ensemble is multidimensional. Embedded in the MAI governance structures, *nomos* consists of local agency, a transformation of political life, lines drawn between the Self and the Other, and the state of exception as a coercive measure.

Viewed through Schmitt's prism, the idea of the MAI was to secure a neoliberal order for promoting global market integration. To give teeth to this accord, the negotiators sought to ensure legal security for the interests for which they stood, legitimized by a formal agreement in a club of mostly rich states, the OECD. They wanted an augmented orientation to a free market extended all the way to the local level, ultimately raising knotty questions about power relations and global governance.

The MAI provisions on national treatment, most favored nation status, and compensation guarantees against expropriation would vie with community development and environmental goals as well as with the scope of sovereignty. To underscore a point made earlier in this chapter, the MAI proposals did not confer upon local governments the standing to defend their laws in disputes with overseas firms or to bring actions against foreign investors. Rather, localities were obliged to rely on national governments to enforce their laws in court cases involving a foreign company or government.

A potential conflict immediately arose in that local requirements—for example, on environmental standards—were often, as noted, more stringent than national ones, partly due to local stakeholders' concern for the long-term development of their community, and not only short-term interests. Yet under the MAI, overseas investors and governments could declare such legislation to be discriminatory. Local governments would not have the right of reciprocal challenge in the judicial system and would be represented by officials responsible to larger constituencies, perhaps with somewhat different interests or persuasions.

In this manner, the locality became a site of globalizing processes. Not only was the reach of hypercompetition extended, but also the extant structure of competition at the local level shifted. The scale expanded. As shown, this structure also had legal and political components, altering the balance of forces. Specifically, the points of conflict were local laws formulated by democratic means, and the right of representation. The proposed agreement would strengthen investors while weakening local governments. It would secure the freedom of movement for capital, extending protections to various types of capital, including trading in speculative instruments. The MAI thus throws into sharp relief the contradiction between economic globalization and the democratic right and legitimacy of elected officials to make decisions on behalf of the electorate.

A leitmotif throughout the 1995–98 deliberations in Paris was rights, underpinned by notions of "us" and "them." Lines drawn between the prerogatives of corporations and core states on the one hand, and additional levels of community on the other, served to distinguish between the Self and the Other. With the backing of states belonging to the OECD, the treaty would establish a political and juridical border between the rights of TNCs and unprotected citizens concerned about respect for human rights.

In addition to limiting national and subnational regulation of economies, the MAI commitments would retract norms elaborated by the International Labor Organization (ILO) and at the Rio Earth Summit as well as the 1974

United Nations Charter of Economic Rights and Duties of States affirming that all states have the right to regulate foreign investment within their national borders (Tabb 2004, 404). If an investor's human rights record could not be used as a standard of treatment, international human rights action would be restricted.

At the national level, the MAI's most favored nation clause would bar boycotts or other sanctions, viewed as forms of "discrimination," against countries that violate human rights and degrade the environment. Thus, the MAI's detractors pointed out that foreign policy instruments for influencing countries that abuse human rights would be diminished.

Also problematic, affirmative action and related practices of hiring ethnic minorities would not be permitted. Inasmuch as subnational levels of authority would be subject to the treaty, indigenous peoples, among others, could be challenged if they interfered with transnational investment, say, on land claim settlements or the use of natural resources on their land (Barlow and Clarke 1998, 77–78; Goodman and Ranald 2000, 107–66).

Another concern was the impact of the MAI on human rights outside the MAI perimeter. If the MAI membership were to be enlarged, and if its growth entailed the spread of TNCs around the world, new jobs would be created in developing countries. At first, such opportunities are usually concentrated in labor-intensive factories and often export-processing zones that employ mostly young female workers. Trade unions are circumscribed, sometimes by violent means. Protected by private security forces, these free-trade areas are typically fenced off and exempt from national and local laws.

Hence, in redefining market boundaries and accommodating different actors, the MAI text explicitly laid bare the issue of foreignness. It implicitly trod on political identities behind the categories of "inside" and "outside," effectively the Self and the Other. In such instances, power holders seek to maintain identity in relation to difference, demarcated in terms of domestic and foreign. Yet identities are increasingly fluid, subjectively mobile, and shaped by the dynamics of globalization. In a contradictory manner, globalization both helps enforce border lines and undermines them.

To deepen and channel globalization, a primary technique is the exception, which in a Schmittian sense, perpetuates the rule. It shores up order. The MAI performed this crucial task in multiple ways. This chapter, thus far, has touched on three such issue areas: national security, civil society, and development. Three others are also noteworthy: national financial instability, taxation, and cultural protection. Taken together, these six elements illustrate a principal aspect of global governance: consensus-building on general rules and the power of exclusion from them.

In the arena of MAI talks, Washington sought to protect its "essential security interests." For the United States, this meant fighting for the extraterritorial application of U.S. law. While other powerful actors also wanted to look after their privileged positions, Canadians and Europeans viewed facets of the general exemption for national security as infringing sovereignty. They objected to the U.S. attempt to impose its laws and policies on other countries. For example, the United States wanted to safeguard the Helms-Burton legislation penalizing countries and companies for investing in and trading with Cuba. This law would enable the United States to apply sanctions on investors from other MAI countries. Remaining steadfast, the United States insisted on a general exemption for securing interests during war or other emergencies relating to the proliferation of WMD and for arms production. This exception could be decided by a state itself, for the dispute-settlement procedures grant other parties only the right to consultation (Picciotto 1998, 762).

For hyperpower, exclusion takes on a special meaning: a belief in the uniqueness of American history and the benign role of U.S. hegemony. The MAI exemptions thus buttress American exceptionalism, the long-standing belief that the United States could deploy its power where other actors could not because it has greater moral standing than do others.

Surely the text as well as the subtext in the Paris negotiations pertained to defining the Other, that is, the border between "us" and "them." Meant to enhance security in the context of globalization, the MAI was supposed to redraw the lines of market and legal security but actually sharpened differences and heightened insecurity. Whereas Washington identified Havana as an "enemy," its model and potential spread as a threat to free-market democracy, some U.S. allies wanted to maintain their thriving relations in trade and tourism with Cuba. Countries with a social democratic tradition, among other states, were prone to engage, not boycott, Cuba's socialist regime. This difference applied not only to the identity of the MAI as a spatial zone but as an intersubjective region. Hence, underpinning the MAI debates was the move to define "us" in terms of "our" values? And what are the threats from "our" enemies from "inside" and "outside" the MAI sphere? Resolving these questions would help to buoy legitimacy.

Within the MAI area, excluding civil society groups from this forum on state-to-state and investor-to-investor mechanisms became a contentious matter. According to the Negotiating Group, consultation with NGOs began at the end of 1996. The OECD channeled discussion through its Business Industry Advisory Committee and Trade Union Advisory Committee. Labor and environmental groups wanted specific clauses for protection. Major corporate lobbying groups, such as the U.S. Council for International Business and the International Chamber of Commerce, not only advocated for their interests but also began to express disquiet at the prospect of special language on labor and environmental issues, the large number of exemptions, and what increasingly appeared to be a diluted form of neoliberalism (Egan 2001, 90). By the time the formal dialogue with NGOs started in October 1997 (Organisation for Economic Cooperation and Development Negotiating Group ... 1998, 3), resistance had stiffened. In the guise of an investment treaty, disembedding the market from social and political life brought counterthrusts from multiple actors.

Notably excluded from the table in Paris were almost all developing countries, some of them loci for value systems that differ from dominant cultural norms in the West. To bring these sensitivities into negotiations, ostensibly over competition and regulatory policies, the MAI Negotiating Group invited Argentina, Brazil, Chile, and Hong Kong (as well as the Slovak Republic and, later, the Baltic countries) to participate as observers beginning in September 1997 (Organisation for Economic Cooperation and Development Negotiating Group ... 1998, 3).

For developing countries, increased net flows in external finance during the 1990s came from the rapid growth of private foreign capital. The share of official development finance in aggregate flows to developing countries declined between 1991 and 1994 (Dhar and Chaturvedi 1998, 845). The intraregional differences were patent, with Asia, especially China, drawing almost 21 percent of overall FDI inflows to developing countries in 1995. Together, the developed countries and Asia received more than 84 percent of inflows in 1995, leaving the combined total for Africa, Latin America, and the Caribbean at less than 10 percent (Dhar and Chaturvedi 1998, 445). Thus, for non-OECD members, the MAI offered a means wherein the power of the owners and managers of capital had the potential to advance free capital movements. Yet, unlike elites in the developing world who wanted to become part of this consensus-making, critics saw the MAI as an effort to perpetuate or even increase world inequality.

In terms of development, major balance-of-payments difficulties and national financial instability would be treated as a special category. For example, a balance-of-payments emergency such as occurred in Mexico in 1994, in which the United States and the IMF provided a bailout, would be freestanding. It would be a specific exception falling under "reservations" in early MAI drafts, which allowed a safeguard clause. The safeguard provision could be applied, with surveillance by the MAI Parties Group and the IMF.

Complex problems, too, surrounded taxation, which it was decided would be carved out, unless assets were expropriated and the MAI compensation provisions for investment would then secure fair treatment. To garner support from OECD member states, the treaty excluded taxation from the nondiscrimination clause. The taxation issue was linked to cultural carve-outs, opposed most forcefully by the Business and Advisory Committee to the OECD, the U.S. entertainment industry, and giant media companies like Time Warner.

Meanwhile, Canada and France wanted to protect linguistic diversity. Canada also sought exclusions for cultural subsidies for artists, musicians, writers, and publishers. Notably, its magazines benefited from tax measures that favor domestic content. Of concern as well were films produced at home, parliamentary subventions for the Canadian Broadcasting Corporation, and government policies facilitating distribution rights for movies by producers, as well as the development of its national book publishing industry, which was faced with U.S. competition and massive bookstore chains. Thus, some Canadians regarded the MAI as a threat to national culture and the industries that offer a local perspective on the arts, news, and history (Clarke and Barlow 1997). But the key point about the exception is that the rule feeds on what is excluded. And which rules, whose rules, and how are they defined?

THE RULE

Plainly, the MAI was a site of contesting rules. More than a document or a discrete event, the proposed agreement decidedly began as a top-down process. The discourse about "negotiations" was in fact a way to try to produce consensus about competition policies. Consensus, however, can be a means to exclude the less privileged and least powerful actors. If anything, the MAI process fueled public distrust and suspicion, thereby diminishing state-led efforts to promote globalization.

An attempt by state managers to expand the space for neoliberal globalization, the MAI was to be part of the infrastructure of global governance. Nonetheless, it actually opened space for countermovements, inchoate and heterogeneous groupings whose participants decried the democratic deficit in powerful institutions and the spirit of the neoliberal ethic. Even so, state officials and corporate executives emerged from the MAI anything but dispirited, and determined to fight for other free trade agreements, such as the Free Trade Area of the Americas. These actors continued to press for the MAI framework and took the battle to another site, the WTO, where under the rubric of "Trade and Investment" and "Competition Policy," the MAI provisions still exist, and not only nominally—even after they were apparently dropped in 2004 and not ostensibly on the agenda during the ongoing Doha round of world trade talks.

Meanwhile, BITs have proliferated, now buttressed by a network of private arbitration and third country enforcement (Van Harten 2007). Additionally, the Multilateral Investment Guarantee Agency, set up as part of the World Bank Group in 1988, has maintained its efforts to promote FDI into developing countries. It specializes in facilitating investment in conflict-ridden areas and, more broadly, investment among developing countries themselves. Of course, this effort is not without its critics, who take issue with the risks posed by projects such as mining ventures, the threats to the security of local communities and the human rights of their citizens, and the alleged linkages between this finance and violent conflict, as in the DRC.

A more basic source of conflict is the paradigm that informed the MAI negotiations and the overall investment regime. Like the peace-through-trade thesis (Chapter 2), the investment-dominated perspective adopted in Paris emphasized a single issue. The FDI orientation gave priority to one channel of globalization and limited perceptions of the interplay with related aspects of globalization, especially impacts on the environment and implicit notions of economic citizenship; hence, the enormous range of exceptions—in the language of MAI drafts, "general exceptions," "country-specific exceptions," "temporary exceptions," and "carve-outs." As the negotiations evolved, the canvas expanded and became cluttered. Featured on it were investment flows as they related to regional agreements (namely, the EU and NAFTA), ideologies, and resistance politics. Major components of global governance appeared in this collage. The challenge was to blend them.

But the result was a large panoply of conflicts: between states, between the OECD and social movements, between the OECD and some representatives of capital, and between the global North and the global South. Not at all envisaged when the state-to-state negotiations began under the auspices of an international organization, the terrain of battle expanded with multiple contestants entering the fray. The contention over the MAI ranged from debate to political maneuver, to friction spilling out into the streets, to government pullouts from the proceedings. While muted in comparison to what followed, these transnational expressions of discontent with globalization were emblematic of hyperconflict. The MAI stirred disputes that carried over to the WTO meeting in Seattle. The route was via problems in the political economies of Asia and their openings to global market integration. Let us now turn from this foreshadowing by the MAI to the next case.

5 CONFLICT 2: ASIAN DEBACLE

The crash of Asian economies in 1997 appeared as an exception to the pattern of fast market growth in the newly industrializing countries (NICs). Policymakers in Asia framed it as an emergency linked to globalizing pressures, necessitating interventions that impinged directly on the everyday lives of people. But this state of exception showed the general rule or, more precisely, the manner for there being rules of globalization and conflicts over them. In this sense, the exception was not uniquely Asian or primarily lodged in the geoeconomic realm. Rather, its scale was global; the scope extended to geopolitics.

At its most basic, the Asian debacle shows the downside risks in hypercompetition in the absence of an effective regulatory framework. The uncertain situation, which carried risks for the global economy, drew measures of hyperpower along the lines to be traced in this chapter. To salve from loss, the United States used unilateral and multilateral instruments at its command in efforts to realign economies, societies, and polities in Asia. Evident in this case are bedrock traits of hyperconflict: manifold forms of political violence, coercion wielded by state and nonstate actors, a growing climate of fear, and contagion.

To explain the sudden breakdown of a group of Asian economies, one must identify the conditions that precipitated their rise in the first place and the specific factors that led to their descent. The discussion also turns to the spillover within and beyond Asia. The tremor immediately spread to Africa, Latin America, and Russia. Finally, it is important to delineate the new risks associated with globalization.

BEFORE THE STORM

Analysts have long debated whether the high growth rates of the Asian NICs as early as the 1960s resulted from domestic conditions or propitious global circumstances, such as strategic ties to the United States and a favorable international economic environment. [1] The most frequently encountered account has it that at bottom, an outward-looking, export-oriented strategy, augmented by generous inflows of foreign capital and technology, is the basis of the Asian "miracle" economies. This position points to a high rate of crude factor accumulation (inputs of land, labor, and capital into the production process). The market is said to have played a central role in catapulting the Asian economies up several notches in the world hierarchy in a mere thirty-year period.

Notwithstanding efforts to define an Asian model, the experience in this region among the so-called super-NICs (Hong Kong before it returned to Chinese rule in 1997, Singapore, South Korea, and Taiwan) and the second-tier NICs (Indonesia, Malaysia, and Thailand, with the Philippines somewhat lagging) is heterogeneous. In light of this variation, myriad elements are woven into the explanation for the ascendance of the Asian NICs: the right macroeconomic policies of trade and investment; human capital endowments, especially an educated and disciplined workforce embracing a quasi-Confucian ethic; and the role of a strong state. Picking up on Kaname Akamatsu's writings in Japanese in the 1930s, later popularized in English (1962), economists have often referred to a "flying geese" formation of growth: starting with one country, followed by others, a pattern of harmonious transition from labor-intensive, export orientation to more sophisticated industrial production. Although this configuration has sometimes been uneven, Japan is clearly identified as the initial leader guiding the Asian way.

To grasp these disparate factors, observers advance three theses, primarily neoclassical, cultural, and statist arguments. Neoclassical authors focus on an outward bearing as the key to the NIC phenomenon. Embodying the law of comparative advantage (lower relative production costs for particular goods than is the case elsewhere), the NICs developed the capability to turn out cheap manufactured commodities, thereby facilitating an optimal response to opportunities presented by the global economy. Especially in Hong Kong and Singapore, trade and exchange-rate policies, despite state intervention, were largely left to the market. According to neoclassical economists, the Asian economies are, above all, market-based and subject to less regulation than are their counterparts. Private initiative is encouraged, and the state is generally predisposed toward market solutions. An outbound industrialization strategy allowed NICs to successfully exploit the world market, carve out greater shares of manufactured exports, and move up the ladder of world production.

For other analysts, it is culture that distinguishes the NICs in Eastern (East and Southeast) Asia. Confucian values of temperance, collective purpose, and sacrifice are delimited as distinctive features underpinning NIC development in this region. A work ethic and obedience to authority are regarded as hallmarks of societies infused with Confucian ethics. Filial piety, a collectivist order, and respect for hierarchy provided the footing for entrepreneurship and gave the Asian NICs a competitive edge. By mobilizing cultural resources, a strong state could reap advantages from the moral economy so as to enforce discipline.

Departing from neoclassical and culturalist explanations, the third position highlights the contributions of a Japanese-style developmental state, imbued with purpose and capacity to turn adversity into advantage. Scholars point to strong bureaucratic agencies like Japan's Ministry of International Trade and Industry and the Ministry of Finance, as well as their counterparts in other Eastern Asian countries. These bureaus had the capacity to form and implement a vision for long-term economic growth and industrial upgrading (Johnson 1982; Deyo 1987; Amsden 1989). Crucial to the NICs' effort were the policy instruments for vaulting forward in development and ensuring coordination with indigenous business groups. Institutional arrangements—namely, the existence of a centralized, meritocratic system and a certain autonomy from special interests—facilitated sustained cooperation in pursuit of a vision and with little interruption. A talented managerial class gave direction to society and advanced mutually reinforcing interests of both capital and the state. The political leadership in the Asian NICs drove these economies to expand. Providing stability, administrative guidance for infrastructural investment, and the upgrading of strategic sectors, the developmental state is thus deemed to be the author of miraculous economic growth.

The state was particularly effective in integrating the agricultural sector into the national economy. Weak forward and backward linkages between the agricultural and industrial sectors are the proverbial thorn in the side of developing economies, often impairing the rate of overall economic growth. But by incorporating the rural economy, the NICs increased efficiency, especially in the distribution of resources between the rural and urban sectors. An expanding global political economy may have provided a conducive environment, but from this third perspective, the key to success was the role of the developmental state—a form of state that the MAI, with its provisions for guaranteed national treatment for foreign investors (that is, a prohibition on host-state restrictions on FDI), would have circumscribed.

In addition, the political climate for these start-up economies featured U.S. assistance to countries that occupied a key geostrategic position during the Cold War. After the 1949 Chinese revolution, Washington coordinated a trade embargo in an attempt to prevent the Beijing model from becoming a form of competitive security in Southeast Asia. Having fought two major wars in this zone after 1945, one to a draw on the Korean peninsula, and the other to a defeat in Indochina, the United States sought to apply its power to shore up market-based, export-oriented economies friendly to its own interests. The measures included introducing supply-chain technologies like containers and satellite communication and creating the conditions for buyers to purchase consumer goods and absorb U.S. dollars in Southeast Asia. It must be stressed that these hot wars and the Cold War catalyzed inflows of capital and kindled economic growth in this part of Asia (Stubbs 2005; Hearden 2008).

The backdrop to the Asian debacle also included relentless competition among investors in financial markets. The magnitude of the spike in the rate of cross-border financial flows and currency transactions is noteworthy. The ratio of daily foreign exchange trading to world trade was 2:1 in 1973, and reached 70:1 by 1995 (Dicken 2003, 438). A regulated system under the Bretton Woods agreement of pegged exchange-rate regimes shifted to competitive deregulation. The United States abandoned the gold exchange index partly owing to the impracticalities of a policy of guns and butter (war in Vietnam and provisioning at home). That is, persistent war is a major factor that produced a more competitive financial system. In addition, information technology and computerization facilitated the advent of new financial products and services. With the acceleration in speed came changes in scale, spurring the transformation of markets across the globe. Securitization meant that new kinds of loans and borrowings could be bought, repackaged, and sold (Dicken 2003, 444; also see note 6 in Chapter 8, and the Epilogue). But hypercompetition in financial markets increased risk. With fewer restraints against economic volatility, shocks could now easily spread from one geographical market to another, as came to be the case in Eastern Asia following several decades of outstanding performance.

There should be no mistake, however, about the extent of real achievements in this region: annual GDP growth in the Association of Southeast Asian Nations (ASEAN)-5 (Indonesia, Malaysia, the Philippines, Singapore, and Thailand) averaged almost 8 percent in the decade up to the late 1980s. Over a thirty-year period, per capita income levels mounted by multiples of ten in South Korea, five in Thailand, and four in Malaysia. Per capita income levels in Hong Kong and Singapore actually exceeded those in some Western countries. By 1996, Asia drew nearly half of total capital inflows to developing countries (Fischer 1998b, 9). This immense influx of foreign capital, short-term loans, and equities fueled soaring economic growth rates, stoking the boom economies and pumping up asset bubbles as well.

IN THE EYE OF THE STORM

Yet the boom contained the seeds of a bust, the reverses moving rapidly from one national economy to another. Some of the conditions that had propelled fast growth in Asian economies also triggered or added to the downward spiral. The capital inflow quickly swung to massive capital outflow.

With Japan, the dominant economy in Asia, mired in a deep recession in the 1990s, exports to Tokyo from countries such as Thailand plunged and trade deficits mounted. Essentially, the chief engine of economic growth, the Japanese locomotive, stalled. Added to this, China devalued the yuan by 50 percent in 1994, thereby cheapening its products and furthering the decline in Southeast Asia's exports. Then, growing anxious about Thailand's overvalued currency, Bangkok entrepreneurs purchased dollars, a decision that signaled foreign speculators. Firms like the New York-based Tiger Management bet against the Thai bank, and other large funds followed suit.

The downturn began in earnest on July 2, 1997, when the Thai central bank allowed the baht to float. The bank had already tried to maintain this currency's value by large-scale spending amid capital outflows and conjecture about devaluation. In order to avoid a parallel drop, other central banks in the region sought to purchase their own currencies in foreign exchange markets and sold reserves. Nonetheless, the Philippines permitted the peso to float freely on July 11. Malaysia allowed the ringgit to float on July 14; Indonesia, the rupiah, on August 14. Next, after months of unsuccessful market intervention, was the depreciation of the Republic of Korea's won in November 1997. All five currency values declined precipitously by December 1997: the baht, almost 80 percent compared to its value at the end of May; the peso, 50 percent; the ringgit, 52 percent; the rupiah, 110 percent; and the won, 74 percent (Rivera-Batiz 2001, 48–49).

According to Robert Wade (1998, 362), the "whipsaw movement" of net private flows into and from the most heavily affected countries (Thailand, South Korea, Malaysia, Indonesia, and the Philippines) ranged from plus $93 billion in 1996 to negative $12 billion in 1997: a shift in one year of 11 percent of the combined GDP of the five countries. The slump in Asia led to the loss of 6 percent of world GDP (United Nations Development Program 1999, 2). There is no doubt about the severity of this ordeal. Senior political economists of different persuasions, such as Robert Gilpin and Susan Strange, concurred about its impact: "The world was plunged into the worst economic crisis since the Great Depression" (Gilpin 2002, 162). Gilpin and Strange alike noted that the basic weakness of the international financial system showed the vulnerability of certain countries and regions, imposing an unacceptably enormous toll on them and many bystanders (Strange 1998, 106–18; Gilpin 2002, 161–62).

Yet up to 1997, many macroeconomic fundamentals in the most affected countries had seemed secure. Apart from the Philippines, the economies maintained manageable inflation rates. Exchange rates remained steady; debt service ratios were fairly sound; and savings rates continued to climb. However, with the exception of Indonesia, the current account of balance of payments (goods and services) plummeted. In addition, the savings-investment gap grew. Notable deficits in human resource development (such as R&D scientists and engineers) and overall shortages in skilled labor constrained higher technology manufacturing in Indonesia, Malaysia, and Thailand. Weak internal linkages among certain sectors in the national economies reduced the domestic spinoffs from value-added chains (Rasiah 1998).

Facing the pressures of hypercompetition, especially with short-term debt, currency traders bet that some regional currencies could not maintain their value. Trying to manage uncertainty and reduce risk, speculators put their money into forward contracts on foreign exchange rates, a market without effective control. Some countries in Eastern Asia were less tied to this volatile market of external capital flows than were others: China, without a convertible currency and with capital controls; Vietnam, also with a nonconvertible currency and fixed exchange rates; Burma/Myanmar, whose military regime and weak infrastructure rendered it unattractive to foreign investors; and the Philippines, only beginning to recover from the devastations of the Ferdinand Marcos dictatorship.

By comparison, Indonesia, Malaysia, Thailand, and South Korea had high convertibility of currency, borrowed substantially from foreign creditors, and eased barriers to foreign participation and ownership on the local exchanges, thus heightening vulnerability to speculative attacks. In this context, speculators were positioned to challenge fragile domestic institutions, whose supposed role was to mediate the impact of global financial flows (Winters 1999, 83–84).

Without heavy regulation, hedge funds (Chapter 1) aggregate money from firms and wealthy individuals, are highly leveraged, and mobilize sums far in excess of the GDPs of small, open economies. In Eastern Asia, managers of these funds and currency traders borrowed on local markets and bought foreign exchange from reserves. When the currencies fell, the debts could be repaid at a large discount, enabling the speculators to realize enormous profits (Winters 1999, 84–85). In other words, the speculators could enter the markets of the most affected countries, quickly raise prices by virtue of the massive size of their firms' holdings, suddenly exit, reenter when prices sank, and then repeat the whole cycle (Rasiah 1998, 23).

At issue is market power in transactions that link firms and individuals at the center of globalization and on the margins. In a globalizing environment in which hypercompetition ratchets up and capital flows instantaneously, speculators pulled funds from Asian economies, sparking the problems in one country that swiftly touched off troubles in competitor countries. Not only are the most affected countries located in the same neighborhood, but also they had adopted many of the same policies. All the worst affected countries experienced large current account deficits and deteriorating prudential regulation of their banking and financial systems. Globalization joined the economies so that the impact of speculation was quickly transmitted to the currency markets in nearby countries, adding to the free-fall drop in value (J. Lim 1998, 215–16).

Noteworthy then are the links in the contagion that engulfed a constellation of countries in 1997–98. It started with weakening currencies. Foreign exchange problems emerged as well. Failures in domestic banking systems, particularly with nonperforming loans and bankruptcies in certain enterprises, recurred. The decline in the financial system brought a broader economic malaise: a meltdown of stock markets in the most-affected countries, a dip in real estate markets, and a contraction in labor markets. This chain reaction challenged political authorities, whose experience with their own bounded jurisdiction did not provide answers to the question of how best to dial into globalizing processes.

The difficulties in the interactions between local banking systems and unregulated transnational finance manifest as the problem of how to find a balance between statist regulation and globalizing neoliberal demands. The conundrum is that the mercantilist strategy of self-insuring nationally by accumulating large reserves of foreign exchange is in conflict with the tenets of neoliberal globalization.

Closely related, higher levels of globalization, facilitated by technological advances, increase but do not necessarily cause the risks of contagion (Khan 2004, 173). With an outward orientation, regionalism can magnify these risks. Formal regionalism embodied in membership organizations may be either part of the neoliberal framework or a way to mitigate it. In comparison to Europe, regional groupings in Eastern Asia, such as ASEAN, hardly take the rough edges off neoliberal globalization. These Asian organizations are shallow, horizontal institutions linking states while barely touching civil society (Mittelman 2000). There have been few financial safeguards, and the deeper issues about a regional response to the insecurities visited upon Eastern Asia by the 1997–98 turbulence pertain to intersubjectivity (shared beliefs and a common identity) as well as networks that cut across territorial borders.

Perceptions came to the fore in 1997, when a domino effect in Eastern Asia resulted in panic among traders, investors, and holders of savings denominated in local currencies. To secure their interests, these players converted their funds into strong currencies on the worldwide market. Apprehensive about the future of certain economies in the region and an impending crash—in some cases, with the risk of default on international loans—they withdrew substantial sums from the real economy as well. Beliefs about vulnerability thereby contributed to large-scale capital flight from the most affected countries. Herd-like behavior influenced expectations among other actors. But to what extent and how?

Friends—former foes with whom they had competed—increasingly based their decisions on asymmetries in information and uncertainty. A collective psychology of exit among currency traders became a factor. Notwithstanding technological advances in sophisticated computer programs, emotion, including greed, no doubt played a part, though by itself could hardly be a decisive ingredient. It contributed to but did not bring about the 1997–98 debacle.

The contagion of fear had a basis in both actual and anticipated events. A number of Japanese banks declared bankruptcy. They could recall their loans from other Japanese banks, South Korea, and elsewhere. To prevent this cascade, the Japanese government infused funds into the banking system, and early in the slump, the IMF extended loans to South Korea, Indonesia, and Thailand. Malaysia and Taiwan adopted de facto SAPs, implementing reforms without signing formal agreements with the IMF. Nonetheless, failings in the financial system limited the possibilities for firms to boost their levels of production and exports. Improvements in the trade balances in 1997–98 reflected falls in imports, not an overall economic recovery (Kregel 1998, 52–60).

The contagious effects of this debacle were transmitted to transitional economies, palpably in the former Soviet sphere and the most vulnerable countries
in the developing world. For Africa, the narrowing of key markets in Asia immediately meant reduced exports. Overall, the leakage was multifaceted: lower
world commodity prices entailing a drop in demand for Africa's raw materials;
cheaper Asian exports increasing trade competition; and a decline in Asian FDI
in critical sectors, such as oil, minerals, and metal, in Africa (Harsch 1998). The
African Development Bank estimated the impact of the Asian imbroglio as a
slide in the continent's economic growth rate of 1.2 percent in 1998 alone, or
U.S. $6.2 billion, which was about U.S. $2 billion more than the annual average flow of FDI into the continent just before the fall (Hussain, Mlambo, and
Oshikoya 1999, 19).

Meanwhile, under great pressure, a small number of managers responsible
for emerging markets in Asia ultimately made vital choices on behalf of big
institutional investors, including pension and mutual funds. These firms had to
pay shareholders and to do so reduced holdings in countries such as Argentina
and Mexico. This breakdown in Asia also engulfed Brazil; thrust other parts of
Latin America (Chile, Peru, Venezuela, Ecuador, and Colombia), where commodity prices dropped, into a slowdown; and lessened confidence in the financial system in other areas of the world, including developed countries. Under
these conditions, the Asian economic flu infected various regions and became
a globalizing phenomenon.

The contraction in economies prompted political conflicts, induced shifts
in domestic coalitions, and sometimes entailed violence. The collapse of the
financial system in Indonesia, marked by clashes between central bank officials
and the president, aggravated the tensions that brought an end to Suharto's
thirty-year tenure as head of state. Vice President B. J. Habibie replaced Suharto
and, faced with severe economic pressure as well as a grave situation in East
Timor, yielded to democratically elected Abdurraham Wahid as president in
1999. The economic grievances in Indonesia took on other guises as well. Chi-
nese-owned shops and churches became a target of the Muslim poor; and in
a heavily Christian part of eastern Indonesia, resentment focused on Muslim
traders.

There was also political fallout in the Philippines. With signs of growing
unrest, President Fidel Ramos abandoned his attempt to amend the constitution to permit him to run for a third term in September 1997. Josef Estrada was
elected president largely on the basis of his promises to adopt policy reforms

that would address the effects of the economic collapse. Additionally, a shifting balance of forces defeated Thailand's Prime Minister Chavalit Yongchaiyudah in November 1997, enabling the Democrat Party, led by Chuan Leekpai, to take office. So, too, discontent with the South Korean economy allowed an opposition party to gain the presidency for the first time since the country democratized in 1987 (Lukauskas and Rivera-Batiz 2001, 12–13; Rivera-Batiz and Oliva 2001, 171–80).

Although Malaysian prime minister Mahathir Mohamad held on to power during the tempest, he faced vigorous resistance from within and outside the Barisan Nasional (National Front) government, culminating in the jailing of Deputy Prime Minister Anwar Ibrahim (also finance minister). Heir-apparent to the prime minister, Anwar disagreed with Mahathir about policy responses to the economic turmoil and, as widely reported, was mounting a political challenge to his mentor. The uneven impact of the economic downswing in a multiethnic country awakened memories of the Chinese-Malay riots, violent conflict experienced in 1969, temporarily threatening the political order and bringing a clampdown by Malaysia's authoritarian regime.

RECOVERY

Although Malaysia was not hit as hard as some of the most affected countries, its response to the 1997–98 convulsions is at the center of debates about recovery strategies. Analysts have compared national experiences and have drawn conclusions about the pros and cons of different policy adjustments.[2] Yet this exercise is fraught with methodological problems, or even inherently unfeasible, because the variables are too numerous: historical trajectory, cultural matrix, resource endowment, geostrategic position, social structure, size of the domestic market, type of political system, state capacity, tethering to the central processes of globalization, and so on. Although all of the most affected countries sought to restore confidence and relied on corporate workouts, restructuring, and retrenchment, there were overarching differences in their policies.

Better in this research to probe a single instance, the Malaysian situation, and examine the fine texture. Surely, with any case of recovery, the conditions are distinctive. But which case is without special circumstances? Or free from globalizing structures?

Unlike Asian countries that patently agreed to IMF and World Bank structural adjustment programs, Malaysia adopted capital controls to stem short-termism, that is, hot money that flows rapidly in and out of the country. To come to grips with this strategy, it is important to bear in mind the backdrop. By 1997, Malaysia had made impressive strides in economic development.

Forty years before, at the time of political independence, Malaysia relied principally on exports of primary products such as rubber and palm oil. In the 1960s and 1970s, it upgraded to labor-intensive manufacturing, particularly electronics production in low value–added stages and mainly for overseas markets; and in some sectors, capital-goods industries. By the mid-1990s, Malaysia's leaders aspired to leapfrog to a technology-intensive economy. For example, they laid foundations for the Multimedia Super Corridor, a competitive environment with advanced services and sophisticated infrastructure, where national and transnational corporations could operate. National economic growth was built around policies that embraced a market friendly framework: in the Malaysian experience, as in most of Eastern Asia, a combination of interventionist policies and opening to the global economy. However, export-oriented industrialization chiefly driven by foreign capital was not without its problems.

Malaysian social scientists have amply documented the country's considerable accomplishments in reducing absolute poverty, yet register concern about relative poverty (Abdul Rahman Embong 2002; Rasiah 1998). Increasing differences between the rich and the poor accompanied the rise of a new middle class. A shortage of detailed government statistics on income disparities causes difficulties in studying the specific distributional effects of economic growth (urban-rural, interethnic, and gender dimensions of inequality). Nonetheless, Ishak Shari analyzed the most reliable data and concluded, "while the rapid economic growth during the 1991–95 period has enabled Malaysia to reduce the incidence of absolute poverty, it has occurred together with growing income disparities as benefits of such rapid growth are unevenly spread across different strata/regions in the Malaysia society" (Ishak Shari n.d., 24). Moreover, declining rural wages certainly hurt households in the countryside, but subsistence agriculture helped to meet their basic needs. In the meantime, city dwellers were left highly exposed to economic volatility. Urban workers in the formal sector and the middle class were most vulnerable to declining income levels (Ishak Shari 1998, 7–15).

Also apprehensive about inequality, the IMF turned attention to the market-distorting impact of affirmative action programs for the *Bumiputera* community (Malays and indigenous peoples), economically disadvantaged at the time of political independence. The postcolonial state adopted policies to uplift Malays relative to Malaysia's Chinese, some of whom were well established in business, and to alleviate poverty. Indeed, not only the poor but also affluent *Bumiputeras* and civil servants benefited from special dispensations—including loans, scholarships, and differential criteria for university admission—established by Prime Minister Tun Abdul Razak's New Economic Policy in 1971 and maintained by subsequent governments led by the United Malays National Organisation. The results, according to the IMF, included inefficient enterprises, weak management structures, and government-crony alliances.

For its part, in 1997, the government sought to harness volatile forces by empaneling a high-level team, the National Economic Action Council, with government economic adviser and former finance minister Tun Daim Zainuddin as its executive director. Credited with having engineered Malaysia's economic "miracle," Daim could now override the more orthodox, free-market moves that sitting finance minister Anwar Ibrahim wanted to make. The task of the National Economic Action Council was to spearhead policy adjustments: specifically, to restore investor confidence, to maintain social policy so as to cushion the deleterious effects of the market, and to use public funds to stop the hemorrhaging of the economy.

Like the other most-affected countries, Malaysia adopted a multipronged strategy. Its components included retrenchment, a squeeze on bank loans, renationalization of some privatized enterprises, and a freeze on the wages of the middle and upper civil service. Avowedly looking to the Chinese model, Malaysia imposed exchange controls and pulled the ringgit from trading in foreign currencies. Actually, several countries, such as Chile and Taiwan, had long-established capital controls of different kinds, some taxing or requiring a deposit on capital inflows, not only on withdrawals. The government in Kuala Lumpur imposed a series of restrictions on the buying and selling of foreign exchange and converting the ringgit. Most important, Malaysia's capital controls were intended to regulate short-term flows but not to discourage FDI in general. This policy allowed holders of Malaysian ringgit to convert their money into foreign exchange only after they had retained the security for at least twelve months.

By all indications, the capital controls helped, even if they stirred controversies about the wisdom of this course. Clearly, the ringgit stabilized in value. The stock market climbed. Foreign exchange reserves mounted. By late 1999, Malaysia's economic growth ticked up, while Indonesia's continued to plunge.

Among the strategies to cope with the storm that struck Asia in the late

1990s, Malaysia's selective capital controls were the exception. But the exceptional instance throws light on conflicts over capturing control of transnational capital flows. It has broad implications for the rule, or the lack of rules, for globalization, as the debates surrounding assessment indicate.

ASSESSING THE STORM DAMAGE

There are different standpoints for assessing the storm. Appraisals center on either internal or external factors as well as scripts that straddle this inside-outside divide.

As early as 1994, Paul Krugman expressed misgivings about signs of supposed "exceptional efficiency growth" in the Asian miracle economies. He attributed their high rates of growth to "the effectiveness of sophisticated industrial policies and selective protectionism" as well as "deferred gratification, the willingness to sacrifice current satisfaction for future gain" (1994, 78). Four years later, Krugman and other economists directed their attention not to national savings rates but declining current account balances as a manifestation of a deeper malaise. This is the problem of the "logic of moral hazard," which arises when a government guarantees a financial institution's liabilities, lessening the incentive for the creditor to be sufficiently attentive to the risks of its investments. On the principle, "heads I win, tails someone else loses," a financial intermediary can take large risks and attempt to land a sizable profit without threat of incurring losses (Krugman 1998, 6). For want of financial regulation, owners are not risking their own money. With loans backed by the state, financial institutions could lend to high-risk borrowers without the expectation of incurring significant losses. Profits are then privatized while losses are socialized. Basically, the issue is one of presumed bailout: a no-lose situation wherein actors do not fully bear the consequences of their actions.

Part of this explanation is the homegrown weaknesses in national institutional structures. In the most-affected countries, oversight of the banking systems was lax. Domestic financial intermediaries extended loans that became nonperforming. National legal frameworks and prudential rules for banking were inadequate.

The diagnosis of the domestic side of the equation also probes crony capitalism. Neoclassical economists hold that unlike Western "free market capitalism," crony capitalism is a key feature of Asian economies. Cronyism involves collusion among economic actors that damages market competition. Cronies behave in different ways. One involves relations between government and business. The state backs banks that provide large loans to select firms, as with the *chaeböl* (conglomerates) in South Korea. Another practice goes beyond state intervention in the market and extends to interfirm networks. Firms invest in one another's shares and lend funds to each other (Hamilton 1999, 46–49). Webs of interlocking ownership and debt are based on *guanxi*, a frequently encountered Chinese term that means connections.

In the neoclassical narrative of firms and institutions, these cross-holdings founded on interpersonal, familial, or ethnic associations are regarded as market distortions. Surely there is ample evidence of the doling out of *rentier* opportunities by politicians and major businesspeople (Gill 1998; Jomo 1998). Privatization provided space for rent-fueled patron-client relations. A system of patronage and preferential rewards for generously financed government contracts is amply documented (see, for example, Gomez and Jomo 1997). Whereas the neoclassical story captures part of the picture in Eastern Asia, the telling question concerns its use: whether it is deployed to support a singular vision of globalizing free-market capitalism—one that does not allow for contestation over diverse forms without local control—or variants of capitalism rooted in different historical experiences.

The IMF's narrative focused on the most-affected countries' domestic financial-sector shortcomings: corruption and nepotism, nontransparent transactions between local policymakers and businesses, a lack of credit-worthy criteria for lending, substantial external borrowing, and excessive speculation. Defending the Fund, Stanley Fischer, its first deputy managing director, maintained that given the complex problems afflicting Eastern Asia in 1997–98, the IMF took the best course by providing incentives for reform: "attaching conditions to assistance gives policymakers incentives to do the right thing" (Fischer 1998a, 106). Subsequently, the Independent Evaluation Office of the IMF reviewed the Fund's role in Eastern Asia's 1997–98 emergency and launched a self-assessment process (International Monetary Fund [IMF] 2003). Although the IMF is often regarded as stubborn in its adherence to neoliberal formulations, the Fund's public self-criticism candidly acknowledges mistakes in its prescriptions. The findings of the evaluation note several limitations.

The appraisal of the IMF's decisions undertaken by the Independent Evaluation Office points out that in pre-1997 surveillance, the IMF was more successful at diagnosing macroeconomic vulnerabilities than in bringing to light the risks coming from the financial sector and corporate balance sheets and identifying the ways in which government added to those weaknesses. Another shortcoming, according to the report, was the IMF's reluctance to stimulate broad policy debates. In other words, greater transparency could have helped catch the burgeoning problems. While the scope of the financing project was too small in South Korea, the IMF's part in coordinating the involvement of the private sector, particularly in South Korea (and in other countries, such as Brazil), was constrained by the Fund's shareholder governments, which had reservations about nonmarket instruments.

In the Independent Evaluation Office's judgment, a larger difficulty was the failure to develop a comprehensive strategy and to communicate the logic of the program. Hence, a lack of focus on reforms in the banking sector resulted in diminishing confidence and nonimplementation of policies. The IMF's own operations suffered from inadequate staff resources and insufficient up-to-date knowledge. Finally, troubles emerged in efforts to collaborate with other international financial institutions, especially the World Bank. To learn from its mistakes, the IMF called for improving pre-emergency surveillance, making assessments more available to the public, and cooperating more fully with other international and nongovernmental organizations. The Independent Evaluation Office also recommended adjusting program design during a financial downturn, giving more emphasis to human resource development, and strengthening the Fund's role as a coordinator during times of distress (IMF 2003).

A more critical position is taken by Stiglitz (2002), a former senior vice president and chief economist at the World Bank and corecipient of the 2001 Nobel Prize in Economic Sciences. He contends that the IMF has repeatedly adopted misguided and hypocritical policies—a "one-size-fits-all" approach that reflects a dogmatic adherence to ideology. It follows that the problem is not just international economic institutions themselves, in which finance ministers, shareholders, and trade ministers purport to speak for their countries, but the dominant mind-sets about globalization. According to Stiglitz, the culprit is the ideology of market fundamentalism, and the international institutions suffer from a democratic deficit. Lacking transparency, the policy framework—from capital market liberalization to substantial bailouts—serves the rich and ultimately contributes to global instability.

He maintains that in effect, the IMF augmented rising rates of poverty in some countries and failed to achieve macroeconomic success. Above all, the Fund has been insensitive to inequality. Stiglitz claims that its remedies are ill-advised, for development must be homegrown. Unlike shock therapy, as in

Russia, a coordinated and gradualist policy of opening to the market, as adopted in China, has much to commend it. A balanced encounter with globalization must be negotiated and implemented as part of a multifaceted system of reform, including interventions to correct large externalities stemming from risks in the capital market, bankruptcy provisions, reduced reliance on bailouts, banking regulation, more-extensive safety nets, and a reconsideration of basic economic principles. Stiglitz calls for a social transformation, but his agenda is a medley of old and vague proposals for reform (Mittelman 2004a).

Similarly, Jeffrey Sachs (1997) complained about the IMF's lack of transparency, specifically the failure to document its decisions, except for brief press releases that do not provide technical information required for a professional evaluation. Unaccountable staff at the Fund, a group of policy economists in Washington—on average, around seven of them per country—decide on economic conditions for more than one billion people in developing countries. And why is it that these economists praised Thailand's strong economic performance and solid macroeconomic policies shortly before the onset of the financial calamity? Why did they then inflict a severe "economic contraction on top of the market panic"? Sachs concludes that under these conditions, it was rational for investors to join the pack of speculators and pull out of the most-affected economies. When short-term debts exceeded foreign exchange reserves, Asia felt the sting of investors who acted according to their own interests (Sachs 1997).

Joining this discourse, Mahathir charged that in just a few weeks, Malaysia lost the economic gains of forty years of political independence when currency speculators suddenly moved their money out of Eastern Asian countries. The background to this grievance is important: before the Asian downturn in 1997, billionaire investor, philanthropist, and speculator George Soros was often accused of having caused the fall in the value of the British pound in 1992. At that time, Malaysia's Bank Negara (central bank) bet that the pound would increase in value. Subsequently, as we have seen, the value of Malaysia's currency, the ringgit, tumbled by 40 percent in 1997, and the quake in the stock market resulted in as much as a 70 percent decline. Mahathir pointed to a lack of regulation and the ways in which global capital spun out of control. He assailed the "present rules in which we had no say in their formulation, i.e., if there are rules at all" (as quoted in Abdul Kadir Jasin and Syed Nazri 1997; also Mahathir Mohamad 2000). To curb hot money and the offshore trading of the ringgit, Mahathir's application of selective capital controls took effect on September 1,

1998; however, some investors negotiated around these regulations, which were lifted on February 15, 1999, when a more modest "repatriation levy" was introduced (Mustapa Mohamed 2000, 6–8).

Blaming Soros, Mahathir alleged that foreign currency traders targeted certain Asian currencies because ASEAN had admitted Burma/Myanmar into its ranks on July 1, 1997. This policy contravened the U.S. and EU position of denying ASEAN membership to the military government in Rangoon/Yangoon on the ground of human rights violations (L. Lim 1997, 80).

Soros, who had endorsed Washington's stance and funded groups opposed to Burma/Myanmar's junta, responded that he and other traders were being scapegoated for homegrown problems in the most-affected countries. While targeted by Mahathir in this rift, Soros preferred to focus on the global capitalist system as the locus of the problem. The difficulty is a defective market mechanism—that is, unstable financial markets, the failure of politics, and the "erosion of moral values" (Soros 1998, xxiii). Emphasizing the "universal idea" of fallibility, Soros lambastes conventional economic theory for its presupposition that the market, left to its own devices, tends toward equilibrium. He adds that the capitalist system is characterized by the defects of market mechanisms, as evidenced in Asia, Russia, and the overall reverse transfer of capital from the periphery to the center. The root issue is that market values have weakened civic values and that the political process has not controlled the excesses of the market. The inefficiency of the political process works in favor of market fundamentalism, which undermines democracy.

For Soros, the remedy is to reclaim the institutions of representative democracy and recapture civic virtue (Soros 1998, 200). Rejecting the ideology of untrammeled individualism and the imposition of market values, Soros wants to check the disintegration of the global capitalist system. He would reform globalization so that it becomes a socially oriented process. The way to do so, Soros believes, is by buttressing Special Drawing Rights (SDRs), so that developing countries have a more substantial reserve of foreign exchange, and by making international assistance effective for helping the poor. The antidote is not to dismantle international economic institutions but to fix them—for example, by establishing a special independent board to help implement SDRs and reorienting these bodies so that they are more socially responsible and geared to welfare. Soros's call is thus for a more effectual multilateralism and greater equity in the distribution of goods and services (Soros 2002).

These assessments by neoliberal reformers differ markedly from rival explanations by free-market economists. Like Stiglitz, Sachs, and Soros, proponents of a free market seek to stabilize capitalism. But they veer outside the standard neoclassical paradigm. Advocates of a self-running market express their unshaken belief that greater exposure to competition grows economies. The mobility of capital enables the market to break down the barriers to the gains of globalization and establishes the conditions for cross-border flows. Yet the actors who distort global capital flows are national governments and interstate institutions, which underwrite risk, impose regulatory measures, mint money, and lend as well as borrow funds. The only viable course is an open, global system in which each participant is liable for risk. The way forward is to unshackle market restrictions, dismantle regulation, and cut unsustainable deficits. From this perspective, power should not be tied to the erstwhile conditions of Bretton Woods in 1944, when the World Bank and the IMF were launched.

In this vein, Milton Friedman, a Nobel laureate economist, put it bluntly when he contended that if there had been no IMF, there would have been no crisis in the Asian economies in the late 1990s (as indicated in "Is It Doing More Harm or Has the IMF Cured Asia?" 1998). Claiming that the IMF and the World Bank had caused more damage than good, Friedman declared that these organizations worked against private business and averred that they should "disappear" (as cited in Gill 1998, introduction, n.p.). In fact, some champions of free markets draw the conclusion that international economic institutions cannot be reformed; they must be abolished if there is to be global economic stability and steady growth.

Not only purveyors of free markets but also other analysts hold that the developmental state had failed, that this prototype collapsed: the calamity that first struck Asia signified, in Fukuyama's sense, the "unabashed triumph" of and the "exhaustion of viable alternatives to" neoliberalism (Fukuyama 1989). At most, this form of state had helped to start infant industries and link domestic structures to the global market. But once established, local firms find opportunities and are less compliant to state directives. Bureaucratic agencies are unable to hold sway in long-term economic expansion and leapfrogging in the world economy. Rather, indigenous actors and sectors hook up with the world arena with changing reference to strictures at home. The policy tools used by the developmental state to guide national economies, and represented in the "national interest" in an earlier era, are less relevant when nationally based competition is joined by outside businesses with access to the domestic economy.

One need not endorse Fukuyama's triumphalism to recognize the shortcomings of the developmental state. Built on (often informal) administrative guidance to business and a close relationship between government and firms in Eastern Asia, this form of state was a product of historically contingent factors (Khan 2004, 76–81). Confronted by global forces, it, like other kinds of states, underwent major restructuring in order to adapt to globalizing structures.

Having shown the wide variety of ways in which the 1997–98 cataclysm is read, I suggest it is worth asking about the lessons that may be learned. This exercise is of course fraught with difficulty, given analysts' divergent commitments. Nonetheless, from my perspective, seven points emerge.

First, the free movement of short-term capital bears the risk of destabilization. Second, the lack of sufficient financial regulation may also have destabilizing consequences. Third, to engage globalization, balance and careful sequencing are in order. Fourth, the standard prescriptions, including the Washington Consensus of the 1990s, often compound the insecurities that emerge in a hypercompetitive world in the sense that they normalize risk. Fifth, as Mahathir found when he stridently complained about currency speculators and realized that a court of last resort does not exist, specific conflicts are embedded in global governance. The theme of who is in charge of globalization cannot be avoided in different contexts, an issue to be revisited in Chapter 8. Sixth is the need for protection against the jagged effects of the market: a relinking of economic reform and social policy. Finally, a part of the conflict addressed in this chapter is the neoliberal paradigm itself, the way of thinking and policy framework responsible for delinking economic reform and social policy. Not only was this paradigm implicated in the 1997–98 episode, but its impact continued to be felt during the aftershocks.

This paradigm drove states and firms in Asia toward an Adam-Smithian model of market-oriented capitalism. There was heavy pressure to take on more features of the U.S. economy and to open more fully to the forces of globalization. Yet Asians sought regional means to cushion the damaging impact of embracing markets and to avoid a recurrence of the 1997–98 downturn. For this purpose, in 1997, Japan proposed setting up an Asian Monetary Fund (AMF). Rising China also wanted to exercise leadership, partly to counter the Japanese position. Both Japan and China tried to find a way to establish an Asian system operated by Asians themselves. The objective was regional self-protection against disruptive currency fluctuations and volatile transnational capital movements so that this zone of the global political economy could build economic security and reduce uncertainty.

However, in the face of gathering momentum for collective self-reliance, U.S. Treasury Secretary Robert Rubin and Deputy Treasury Secretary Lawrence Summers scotched the initiative for Asian monetary measures, which they believed could compete with U.S. interests in the region. Using its clout as the lead power, the United States exerted pressure to block Eastern Asia's bid to act independently, underscoring the availability of existing institutional arrangements and preferring greater cooperation with the IMF, the G-7 framework, and the Asian Development Bank (ADB). Notwithstanding its moniker as the "Manila Framework," this approach had neither a new institutional component nor a regional structure (Lipscy 2003, 96, 100). Rebuffing Tokyo's support for capital outflow controls, Washington resolutely insisted on the primacy of the IMF, an organization in which U.S.-led hyperpower is readily applied.[3]

Hyperpower commanded tactical means of pressuring local actors, using international economic institutions as instruments of foreign policy, and drawing on the structural power of capital. And everyone knew that Washington had the option of military deployment to ward off "enemies" in exceptional circumstances. The discourses among U.S. policymakers and strategic planners offer insight into their calculations.

STORM TRACK

In the restless, disorderly climate of 1997–98, officials in Washington unequivocally expressed the need for a sustained U.S. security presence. Some narratives registered concern that the economic decline in Eastern Asia, including the political ferment in Indonesia and elsewhere, would reduce defense spending, weapons procurement, and cooperation with the U.S. armed forces for "military modernization."

In light of the unreliable balance of power in Asia, a view from the national security community in Washington maintained that "only the United States can provide a framework for cooperative and joint action and a security structure that other states can accept as legitimate" (Blank 1999, 19–20). Punching home this point, a military analyst, the author of a report on the 1997–98 economic collapse, issued by the Strategic Studies Institute of the U.S. Army War College, professed that "[t]he U.S. involvement with the area or our role as the ultimate financial and military guarantor of security and defense" will mount (Blank 1999, 20). Budget reductions for defense in the most-affected countries added to growing disparities within the region, particularly in military spending between China and its neighbors, making it imperative for Washington to revisit its role in the Asian security system. The IMF's prescriptions "have only globalized" the problem in "crisis-ridden Asia," where the links between economic competition and military-political power crystallized:

[T]his crisis confronts Washington with the necessity to reformulate its Asian agenda and stop relying simply on economics and free trade to work their magical charm. Washington must now actively lead in the resolution of Asian issues and the promotion of a new Asian order. It cannot evade the choices inherent in its position. [Blank 1999, 21]

So, too, Scott Snyder and Richard H. Solomon, president of the U.S. Institute of Peace (a former assistant secretary of state for East Asian and Pacific affairs, also a former director of policy planning at the Department of State), drew the connections between short-term assistance, such as Export-Import Bank credits for Thailand, and political capital (Snyder and Solomon 1998). The purpose of the loans was to protect the interests of American investors, to show U.S. leadership, and to avoid a "nationalist backlash" against Washington: "The Asian financial crisis thus far has demonstrated that the United States remains the essential economic, political, and security stabilizer in Asia" (Snyder and Solomon 1998, 2).

From the perspective of these policy intellectuals, the 1997–98 problems with the financial systems in Eastern Asia showed the risks of political instability in the region, the necessity for a "U.S. security presence" there, and one might infer, an opportunity to push for expanding the American military apparatus.

In the 1997–98 maelstrom, this strategic thinking was injected into policy. The language constructions noted above framed the issues. Washington exercised power through bilateral channels and multilateral institutions, both of them being policy tools. Reference has already been made to U.S. demands on Japan to abandon its proposal for an AMF. Washington viewed Japan, with the world's second-largest national economy, as both a competitor and an ally that could help pull the most-affected countries in Eastern Asia out of the doldrums. Yet policymakers in Washington knew that Tokyo had profound difficulty engineering its own recovery from a long period of stagnation. President Clinton and his top aides strongly advised Japan against dithering in the face of the demonstrable strengths of the American model of free-market democracy, the medicine prescribed for the economic flu. For other countries in the region, this message, delivered by senior members of the Clinton administration, including Treasury Secretary Rubin and Secretary of Defense William Cohen, came laden with material incentives and expectations of commitments for political and economic reform. These cabinet members recognized that international economic organizations as well conferred legitimacy on U.S. foreign policy goals.

Jeffrey Garten, undersecretary of commerce during Clinton's first term as president, candidly expressed the rationale for employing U.S. power when Asian countries had entered "a deep and dark tunnel. . . . [O]n the other end there is going to be a significantly different Asia in which American firms have delivered much deeper market penetration, much greater access" (as quoted in Hamilton-Hart 2000, 202).

Leverage could be used because of hyperpower's specific strengths in Eastern Asia. The U.S. dollar was the principal reserve asset in the region; the yen and the new euro had limited scope (Noble and Ravenhill 2000, 35). Japan produces no oil at home and, without an army of its own, relies on the U.S. military in areas such as the Middle East to ensure a large part of its energy supply. But American policymakers also had more cost-effective means at their disposal.

Wielding power in the Washington-based international financial institutions was seen as a way to uphold national security. Testimony to this understanding of the interests served by multilateral organizations is provided by Zbigniew Brzezinski, national security advisor to President Jimmy Carter:

> [O]ne must consider as part of the American system . . . the global web of specialized organizations, especially the 'international' financial institutions. The International Monetary Fund (IMF) and the World Bank can be said to represent 'global' interests, and their constituency may be construed as their world. In reality, however, they are heavily American dominated and their origins are traceable to American initiative, particularly the Bretton Woods Conference of 1944. [Brzezinski 1997, 27]

Brzezinski adds that "global cooperation institutions," that is, the WTO, the World Bank, and the IMF, have established abroad major features of "American supremacy" (1997, 28). To be sure, the United States has by far the largest voting weight of any single country in the IMF—17.8 percent in 1997 and 1998—to which support from its pro-market allies could be counted on to maintain the Washington Consensus (IMF 1997, 215; IMF 1998, 169). And the IMF itself did not want to temper its stance during the Asian debacle, as could have been the case if the AMF had been created.

Thus, in 1998, the IMF obtained a commitment from Suharto, famously represented in a photograph of the Fund's managing director Michel Camdessus,

Figure 1. IMF managing director Camdessus and Indonesian president Suharto (1998). Photo courtesy of Enny Nuraheni/Reuters.

arms crossed, standing over Indonesia's president as he signed the document containing the terms for emergency financing (see Figure 1).

Under heavy internal and external pressure, Suharto lacked options. In keeping with the Washington Consensus, Indonesia's economic reform package mandated deregulation, privatization, and liberalization, along with microeconomic directives for achieving macroeconomic targets. In its program for dismantling the local political economy of domination, penalties were levied for the lack of sound competitive pressures. Meanwhile, the IMF globalized liability for macroeconomic failures. Economic and moral responsibility for the SAP would spread over several states.

Pursuing this avenue of analysis, Wade (2000, 2001) notes that the U.S. decision to sever the link between the dollar and gold caused increased imbalances in the world economy. These resulted from a mismatch between the reserves of surplus countries and decreases in those of the United States, the major deficit country. The U.S. unwillingness to cut its external deficits coupled with its predilection for financing them by generating debt held by other countries in the form of foreign exchange assets brought a rush of world liquidity, excess capacity, and overall fragility. According to Wade (2000, 107), the 1997–98 bust in Eastern Asia may be chalked up to these aspects of structural power. In this matrix, international agencies in which Washington had preponderant power, including the World Bank and the IMF, championed a neoliberal world order, a system with interlocking institutions (corporations, households, pension funds, and so on) that organize themselves around the principle of free-market mobility (Wade 2001, 214–23).

A staunch defender of contemporary globalization, Jagdish Bhagwati (2004, 204–6) also argues that the U.S. Treasury imposed inappropriate policies on these economies. What he calls the "Wall Street–Treasury Complex," mindful of American interests, forced premature liberalization of financial markets and capital accounts in Asian countries. Bhagwati stresses close personal ties and shared ideology (cronyism) between Treasury Secretary Rubin, a former Wall Street currency trader who had worked at Goldman Sachs for twenty-six years, and managers of banks and hedge funds in the United States.

But some analysts are opposed to an explanation of the 1997–98 turbulence based on systemic processes, with the United States as the wellspring. Among them, Linda Lim (1998) dismisses "conspiracy theorists" on the ground that many different actors, including governments and currency traders, who competed with one another for profits, produced the turmoil. The United States did not want nor have the means to drive down the Asian economies. Their fall hurt U.S. businesses and national interests, which are varied and sometimes in conflict; they are by no means unified or coordinated. According to Lim, the source of the bust may be best understood in terms of the imperfections of global capital markets and states, namely, mismanagement of exchange rates, overinvestment, excessive lending, and miscalculation by financial players (L. Lim 1998, 18–19).

Yet are views that stress structural power and state-market imperfections incompatible? I think not. These are different emphases: the one concerns U.S. control; the other, fluidity in power relations. Both of them allow coercion and had drawn attention during the "miracle" years of economic growth.

In this surge, Malaysian prime minister Mahathir proposed forming an East Asian Economic Group, which would bind Japan, China, South Korea, Hong Kong, and the ASEAN members. He sought to establish an exclusively "Asian" alternative to the Asia-Pacific Economic Cooperation (APEC) forum. Advanced in 1990, the concept was unacceptable to the United States, which put pressure on Japan (some of whose officials favored Mahathir's proposal) and South Korea—ever dependent on U.S. security assurances for protection of their interests. The idea was therefore transformed into a modest East Asian Economic Caucus, or arena for discussion. Subsequently, a mechanism—ASEAN + 3, which comprises the ten nations of Southeast Asia plus China, Japan, and South Korea—was set up to facilitate intraregional trade and investment (Yip 2001).

For both the American and Asian wings of APEC, an incentive to deepen the regional structure was the potential gain from trade and investment. But which and whose deepening agenda would prevail? The Asian wing was wary that deepening would be a means for the United States to impose its notion of fair trade. The smaller, developing countries feared that the United States would seek to reshape tried and proven domestic economic policies that rely on large-scale state intervention, and insist on social issues—human rights as well as labor and environmental standards (though not necessarily the sort demanded by some NGOs). Plus, the effort to imagine or construct an Asian identity poses broad and nettlesome questions about conflicts between different value systems. Hence, Mahathir's call for an Asianization of APEC would bring together Japan, China, and ASEAN as a strong counterweight to the EU and a U.S.-centered regionalism; Australia, New Zealand, Canada, and the United States would be omitted. In other words, in comparison to the Pacific scenario, the Asian scenario called for a more exclusive membership. Wanting to maintain its lead power in the region, the United States played its trump cards—guarantor of military security, container of China, and sheer market size—to deflect the Malaysian authorities' frustration with the dominant script of globalization.

SOLACE

Noteworthy in this jousting are the debates surrounding the definitions of "we" and "they," Selves and Others. With trepidation over dislocation and combustible politics in some countries, identities were imagined and reimagined in a short time. By 1997, nationalist backlashes involved renewed efforts to delimit friends and enemies. Foreign workers were especially vulnerable. Some of them were undocumented migrants who competed with locals for jobs and represented the Other. Accurate data on intraregional labor flows covering both legal and illegal migration are hard to confirm. The figures given vary widely.[4] Undocumented workers came from within and beyond Eastern Asia. Among others, Indonesians and South Asians had illegally entered Malaysia, the Republic of Korea, and Thailand. The increasing feminization of labor flows, a major feature of economic globalization, accompanied the creation of jobs in manufacturing and services during the years of plenty and partly structured the composition of the workforce.

The contract labor system in Eastern Asia in 1997 was large, with considerable variation of registered and clandestine migrants by country, sector, and enterprise. The Philippines, Indonesia, and Thailand were major sending countries. There was a vast range in the number of foreign workers in receiving countries. In Malaysia, the size doubled after 1992, reaching, according to different accounts, between 1.7 million and 2.5 million in 1997. With a labor force of 8.6 million in a country of nearly 21 million people, migrants constituted almost 20 percent of the personnel. Singapore also had a high proportion, approximately 20 or 25 percent, of overseas workers. In comparison, Thailand's 1.3 million foreign workers made up only 4 percent of the total supply of labor in a country with a larger population, 61.8 million at the time (Skeldon 1999, 4, 7; Abella 2004, 5).

Rising unemployment in 1997–98 led to massive job losses. For example, the Ministry of Labor in the Republic of Korea reported that in January and February 1998, seventy firms laid off 7,500 workers, compared to seventy-seven enterprises that dismissed 10,500 workers in the entire year of 1997; unreported job destruction connected to bankruptcies and other factors, of course, do not enter these calculations. From January 1997 to February 1998, recorded retrenchments in Thailand amounted to 54,000 workers, with more women than men made redundant (International Labor Organization 1998, 15, 18). Disadvantaged in the labor market, women were concentrated in the most precarious forms of employment, underrepresented in decision-making, and disproportionately lacking access to safety nets (Chin 1998; ILO 1998, 27; Shao 2001). In this gendered division of labor, many women were let go from formal employment and faced the burden of poverty. For them, increased insecurity shifted to the informal sector. Expulsion from the hard-hit sectors pushed some women and children into prostitution, upping the number of sex workers trafficking across borders and through criminal networks.

At another level of abstraction, these phenomena may be read as biopolitics wherein power operates on bodily sites. In the Foucauldian conception, biopolitics is regulatory power that enters the biological, social, and economic aspects of human life. The workings of biopower on the social body are evident in the lives of trafficked, transnational workers who became disposable, subtracted from the system of sovereign nation-states. These sojourners emerged as what, in Agamben's terms, this system treats as debris, waste cast off from territorial spaces (Agamben 1999; Schütz 2000, 121–22, as cited in Rajaram and Grundy-Warr 2004, 38).

Indeed, when the economies of receiving countries contracted and unemployment grew, political pressure for the deportation of foreign workers mounted. Yet in certain niches, the Asian economies still required imported labor. The call to repatriate nonnationals, mostly unskilled laborers, to their home countries took on various tones, from reserved to pitched. In many cases, the private sector recruited, employed, yet barely protected foreign labor. In others, state agencies in receiving countries had sought to ensure the supply of a workforce. But the security forces clamped down partly in response to the demands of citizens who blamed immigrants for encroachment on forest reserve land and farms, rising unemployment, crime, and the spread of disease. The police and army raided areas in which clandestine newcomers resided, criminalizing them to show that the state would protect disadvantaged nationals protesting competition in the labor market and coping with shortages of food and water.

Accordingly, the extent of expulsions varied by sector and country. The deportations were selective because of the continuing need for migrant workers in certain segments of Eastern Asia's labor markets, and some migrants sent home subsequently found their way back to the host countries. In addition, the host states refrained from across-the-board expulsions inasmuch as the presence of foreign workers helped depress wages and thus benefited local entrepreneurs. The imported labor force, especially illegals, was more compliant than citizens, who could more easily seek political redress at home. Moreover, religious bonds (a Muslim *ummah*), regional identities, and international conventions may have been factors in political conduct regarding the repatriation of migrants from Asian countries (Skeldon 1999, 7–8). But these ties were often disregarded. Indonesia, for example, was lax to protect its citizens employed overseas and ignored many compatriots' pleas.

Even with local industrialists and TNCs resisting a ban on foreign workers, crackdowns in the labor-importing zones in Eastern Asia recurred. Thailand sent out Burmese/Myanmars, Cambodians, and Laotian workers, though it later eased some restrictions. In 1997 and 1998, Malaysia, which received more migrants than any other country in Asia, expelled Indonesians, Filipinos, Burmese/Myanmars, Thais, Bangladeshis, Indians, Pakistanis, Nepalese, and Chinese. Some sending countries—the Philippines being a premier source of emigration—sought to counter these measures to protect the human rights of migrants, who were subject to rape, extortion, unsafe and lengthy deportation procedures, and hazardous passage. Yet the home countries also had to calculate the fall in remittances as well as the large cost of resettlement (S. Jones 1998; Skeldon 1999, 8–10). So, too, the involuntary movement of people included internal migrants, many of them food vendors, petty traders, and maids. Thus, large numbers of women in their home countries were compelled to leave the jobs that they had found in a globalizing economy.

In some cases, coercion took the form of displacement to overcrowded detention centers. Security forces rounded up migrants and held them in camps, often for unspecified periods, in Australia, Malaysia, and Thailand (Rajaram and Grundy-Warr 2004). These wards of the state are in addition to the prison populations, which harbored numerous nonnationals. In Malaysia, where the number of migrants deported from detention centers doubled between 1996 and 1998, protests in three internment sites turned into violent riots, culminating in nine fatalities (Fauza Ab. Ghaffar 2003, 285; Syarisa Yanti Abubakar 2002, 27).

Ikatan Relawan Rakyat Malaysia (RELA), or People's Volunteer Corps, founded as a dedicated security force in 1972 to assist the government in maintaining peace and security, helped police migrants during the 1997–98 turmoil.[5] RELA's mission includes "[p]utting the Ministry of Home Affairs at the highest standard at national and regional levels" and "[e]nsuring that the directions and implementation of the policies of the Ministry of Home Affairs are in line with the objectives and visions of the country at all times" (People's Volunteer Corps online). This armed auxiliary police force identifies its roles as follows:

- Area defence using the concept adopted by the Home Guard, ie to maintain peace and security of an area until relieved by the security force. This role covers. . . . psychological warfare duties in terms of monitoring parties suspected to be fifth columnists in areas of responsibility. . . . [and] [c]rime prevention duties in areas of responsibility until relieved by the police.
- RELA manpower can also be mobilized for various purposes according to the skills available. Among [them] . . . are . . . [w]eapon skills.
- Although RELA was formed as a security apparatus to help the country in times of emergency, in times of peace, it focuses its attention on: Security matters . . .
- During times of peace, its security duties encompass the concept of the

EYES AND EARS OF GOVERNMENT, which functions as follows. . . . Collecting and providing important information to the relevant government agencies such as the police. . . . [c]onducting crime prevention patrols . . . . making citizen's arrest of undesirable persons. [People's Volunteer Corps online; capitalized words in original]

Added to this, RELA holds that it is empowered in community development so that it "can produce beneficial effects in terms of psychological action or warfare" (People's Volunteer Corps online). To this end, RELA offers training courses for its recruits. The topics include psychological warfare and shooting skills, taught along with an "Excellent Family Course" (People's Volunteer Corps online).

Now numbering 313,847 members, including 26,679 women, serving in 9,178 platoons (People's Volunteer Corps online; compare nearly half a million members more than the country's military and police, according to Mydans's report 2007), RELA has been granted wide latitude to act on its own accord. In 1997–98, this group deployed its forces in national crackdowns on illegal migrant workers from Indonesia, Burma/Myanmar, Pakistan, Bangladesh, and elsewhere. Migrants escaped and claimed that if repatriated, they would be imprisoned or executed at home (for example, by the Indonesian military in Aceh). The armed contingent in Malaysia consequently faced, or helped provoke, fierce resistance in the detention centers, from where deportees were to be taken by their home countries' navy vessels. Some migrants say that from these centers they are flushed out to an area along the Thai border, where for a fee, human traffickers will smuggle them back to Kuala Lumpur; if payment is not forthcoming, they may be sold to work on fishing boats or in the sex industry (Mydans 2007). Complaining that they have been terrorized by RELA, migrants are subject to health screening, including random checks, by the Foreign Workers' Medical Examination Monitoring Agency, established by the Malaysian authorities in 1997 (Kanapathy 2004, 387).

In response, human rights groups such as Tenaganita, Aliran, Suara Rakyat Malaysia (known as Suaram), the Women's Aid Organization, and the All Women's Action Society called for monitoring RELA, disclosing abuses, and assisting unlawfully held migrants (Gurowitz 2000, 872).[6] International NGOs like Human Rights Watch spotlighted international human rights law and the constitutional guarantees for suspected criminals in Malaysia and neighboring countries. Yet under its Internal Security Act, introduced by the British colonial authorities to curb communist rebellion in 1948, and the Emergency (Public Order and Crime Prevention) Ordinance, adopted as a temporary measure in 1969, the Malaysian government identified unwanted migrants as an exception to its own professed principles and authorized the detention of suspects without charge, evidence, or trial. The minister of home affairs subjected detainees to torture and held them without access to legal counsel. By all indications, recourse to the legislation constitutes a state of perpetual emergency.

At bottom, the mobilization of a home guard, the clash with migrants, cordoning many internees off in camps, and the invocation of coercive laws mark the link between security compulsions and identity politics. Together, they signify the assertion of identity against the Other and the growth of a militarist consciousness. In these moves, the representations themselves are striking. To drum up loyalty to place, the "home guard" was first introduced in the early 1950s in the fight against communists. Like the term *Bumiputera* (literally, "son of the soil"), it reflects orientation to a land. In the political authorities' construction of political and economic order, this language evokes overtones of attachment to place in Carl Schmitt's sense of *nomos*.

In a classic Schmittian manner, a world historical event in Eastern Asia then entailed enclosing aliens, building fences, and drawing lines. The Other was both within and without, a friend who could serve practical economic purposes yet an enemy excluded in camps and an exception from general rules. In detention centers, the Other was silenced, denied political rights, and consigned to a depoliticized life as an alien. Noteworthy then is the construction of a nonthreatening Other, recruited to fill certain niches in the national economy, and a threatening Other, relegated to detention camps and for export. Though solid evidence is unavailable, it may be hypothesized that Othering took place not only between a dominant community of friends and subalterns, but also among the migrants themselves.

Establishing a public enemy, an enemy from within, became a vital component of nationalist discourses—"Malayness" or *Bangsa Malaysia* ("Malaysianness")—that added to narratives about interethnic rivalries in Eastern Asia, especially when some groups of Asians were threatened by the dominant community. These threats helped the superordinate group to cohere and bolstered its political identity. The sovereign securitized and outlawed the enemy and, when convenient, decriminalized and readmitted him and her, a gesture of peace and regional solidarity with neighbors in Asia.

The system maintains itself by stoking fear, establishing exclusion, and delimiting exceptions. Only in this instance, the enemy is unlike the Schmittian Other, an assimilated citizen identified by a religious identity that the sovereign sought to destroy. Rather, like Agamben's alien, Asians warded in the detention centers originated from outside the sovereign's spatial territory and were transferred inside "zones of exception." And redolent of both Schmitt's and Agamben's analyses of strangers, Asian migrants were dispatched in extraordinary circumstances to the space where the law is exempt, represented as a site of contamination.

IN SUM

The Asian debacle contextualizes the affinity between elements of hypercompetition and hyperpower. Globalizing forces generated instability, hence insecurity, with leakage beyond the zone in which the proximate conflict first erupted. In this case, conflicting interests among competing investors precipitated political unrest. The infusion of funds from overseas fueled asset bubbles in a region with severe weaknesses in governance. In response, the United States adopted a policy of containment to curb actual and potential unrest. In Indonesia, for example, the boom and bust sparked increasing ethnic tensions, putting minorities in jeopardy.

Another aspect of this cycle was a spike in intraregional labor migration to augment global competitiveness, followed by detention and deportation of surplus laborers. Legitimized by the Malaysian state on the ground that the country's security was at risk, a civilian armed force assumed police and prison duties. Securitizing immigrants and representing them as "enemies" of law and order, this home guard, an agent of the state, has hunted foreign laborers, required them to undergo bodily inspections, and stirred fear among the general populace. The result is conflict within the domestic arena, along the borderlands, in relations with other states, and with international NGOs that have responded to allegations of state-sanctioned terrorism visited on foreign workers.

Alarmed by mounting signs of economic fragility and political turbulence, the United States relied on bilateral channels to thwart Asian initiatives to find a regional solution. Some American strategic thinkers, noted earlier in this chapter, viewed the cataclysm in Eastern Asia as an opportunity to expand U.S. armed forces, already arrayed in a network of military bases in the region. Also, the U.S. government availed itself of multilateral instruments in order to secure its agenda, embodied in the Washington Consensus. The United States thus acted in tandem with the IMF to contain the effects of the fallout, namely, a growing loss of confidence, unemployment, and retrenchment.

The restructuring that followed set in train new forms of inclusion and exclusion in Eastern Asia. These processes culminated in solace, assuaging the sufferings of some citizens. Yet the aftershocks of the 1997–98 downswing are felt in the application of coercion. They are experienced as continuing displacement and fear among subjects—evident, for example, among the three million overseas workers presently in Malaysia, about half of whom are illegal residents.

At this point on the path of hyperconflict, a series of both old and new narratives about friends and enemies altered the mix of order and disorder. This shift in the balance of forces oriented and disoriented actors who encountered the risks that globalization normalizes, subject to backlashes and protectionist moves. At this rendezvous, the Asian debacle helped set the stage for the 1999 WTO talks in Seattle, an effort to govern the liberalization of markets.

6 CONFLICT 3: BATTLES OF SEATTLE

(Coauthored with Jacob Stump)

Following the unraveling of the MAI framework in the OECD and the collapse of a group of Asian economies, the major powers launched a "Millennium Round" of international trade negotiations in Seattle in 1999. This WTO Third Ministerial meeting sparked resistance by social movements and proved to be a staging post for transnational activism surrounding globalization. The original agenda set for trade talks among the ministers of the WTO's 135 member states was soon submerged in the varied demands of protestors who took to the streets to disrupt the proceedings. The police could not maintain control, violence erupted, and the conflict rippled to cities on five continents. Subsequently, protests accompanied international summits on different aspects of globalization, drawing public attention to the uncertainty and contention over its uneven and often jarring effects. The Battles of Seattle became the insignia of this strife and the ways in which it pushed deeply into the crannies of daily life.

As a metaphor, the Battles of Seattle signifies a layering of stories. Not only do these narratives travel across borders, but also the issues that gave rise to them may be understood as elastic accounts: texts that open to different interpretations. From this perspective, the rules of globalization may be read as contingent inasmuch as they encounter resistances from localizing and fragmenting elements. Allowing for this pluralism, we will explore patterns of discourse.

While methodologically eclectic, previous chapters have picked up on the production of discourses and the ways in which they are employed. This chapter and the next one do so even more explicitly by scrutinizing written and spoken texts as sets of interaction and situating them in historical context. When embraced by a clientele, a lexicon convincingly shapes power competition. Both the meanings constructed around the power of hypercompetition at Seattle and the resistance to them may be thus seen through filters colored by class, gender, race, and language. It follows that meanings are jointly produced by material power and word use. In this sense, assigning significance connects material structures and their ideational representations.

Ostensibly, the issues vetted in Seattle pertained to the promised benefits of trade liberalization and economic reforms to secure them. The ministerial meeting sought to address problems surrounding increasing openness of the global economy. Concretely, between 1950 and 1998, production on a world scale multiplied sixfold; the volume of exports, by a factor of eighteen. During this period, output increased ninefold; and exports of manufactures, thirty-four-fold ("Trade Expansion Remains the Engine of Growth" 1999). By the late 1990s, the world's large economies were more tethered to trade than ever before, but developing countries remained particularly sensitive to openness, for the benefits flowed primarily and disproportionately to developed countries—70 percent of wealth generated from trade liberalization just before the Seattle summit, according to a UN publication (Fleshman 1999, 1). However, undergirding these flows are deep structures of global governance based in hypercompetition and hyperpower.

To reveal the intricacy of these processes and the mechanisms, we will probe the meanings of the Battles of Seattle. The objective in this chapter is to examine the ways in which the conflict at the 1999 ministerial meeting manifests in diverse narratives: civil society versus the WTO, developed versus developing countries, and developed versus other developed countries. Threading analysis of these narratives through this chapter shows how the Seattle episode embodies the forces of hypercompetition and hyperpower.

To foreground the themes that follow, it is helpful to explore the origins of the metaphor Battles of Seattle. When did it first appear? And how did it become an emblem for globalization? We venture that since the advent of this metaphor in the nineteenth century, the media, the Internet, and film have disseminated the Battle of Seattle (initially in the singular). More than nomenclature for a set of events, it is a historical practice that delimits social boundaries between communities of friends and enemies. The Battles of Seattle (plural) is used as an image for transforming identity communities by transnationalizing them.

THE LINEAGE

Metaphorically, the phrase Battle of Seattle was first employed on January 25, 1856, by Rear Admiral T. S. Phelps, an officer on the sloop-of-war *Decatur*, anchored in Elliott Bay to provide military support for the village of Seattle against a possible assault by native Americans. Writing in his diary, Phelps described a daylong skirmish that reportedly took the lives of two white settlers and one hundred "savage Indians" and called it the Battle of Seattle.

The 1856 battle fit in a broader, historical course of U.S. economic and political expansion. The growth of the capitalist market, the ideology of manifest destiny, and military technology generated deadly imperial encounters that shored up an evolving American identity (Stephanson 1996; Drinnon 1997). In recounting tales of violence on the frontier, Phelps introduced the image of the Battle of Seattle into popular vocabulary. He published excerpts from his diary, including about the battle, in *The United Service: A Monthly Review of Military and Naval Affairs* (Phelps 1881). Although this magazine reached only a small audience, it was the earliest venue for the circulation of the expression "Battle of Seattle" on a national scale.

But evidence suggests that it was in currency in Seattle and not limited to Phelps's use of it. Emily Inez Denny, the first white woman born in Seattle, was three years old at the time of the 1856 battle, when her mother carried her to the community blockhouse for protection. Later, as an accomplished artist, Denny painted a work titled *The Battle of Seattle* (see Figure 2). The painting's name indicates that this turn of phrase was becoming known, and the picture projects fear of a coming onslaught on that cold January day when white men, women, and children ran toward the blockhouse, with the *Decatur* looming offshore (Denny circa 1890). The attackers are conspicuously absent from the painting, but the action betokens peril. Perched at water's edge, the security structure marks the place to make a heroic last stand, a site where the settlers and the protective arm of the national military commune in the face of danger. The constitution of a security community, a circle of friends at war with a threatening enemy, denotes a social boundary.

At a deep cultural level, the 1856 attack on a homeland signifies how settlers were terrorized in conflicts—Indian wars—and lived in a state of perpetual emergency. The trauma of the Battle of Seattle reveals the insecurities of the colonial political economy and the vulnerability of a way of life. The legacy of the 1856 ordeal is about borderlands, with domination at issue. And the emergency concerns changing frontiers, threats, and reigning myths conveyed in narratives.

The Battle of Seattle metaphor is thus not simply an innocent description. Rather, it is a historical practice that engraves a divide between "we" and "they."

Figure 2. *The Battle of Seattle*, fought in 1856; painted circa 1890 by Emily Inez Denny. August 6, 1986, photo courtesy of the Museum of History & Industry, Seattle.

From its inception, it etched a manner of differentiation and adumbrated the politics of fear.

The metaphor again appeared in 1892, when the *New York Times* revisited the story of the 1856 Battle of Seattle and conveyed it beyond the *The United Service*'s readership to a sizable audience ("The Battle of Seattle" 1892). This article recounted the daylong fight and used many of the same racial and national categories as had Phelps, but situated the conflict in a broader national and historical context. Thereafter, stories in the *Chicago Daily Tribune* ("Princess Angeline Dies at Seattle" 1896), the *Atlanta Journal-Constitution* ("Relic of Battle of Seattle" 1906), and the *Los Angeles Times* ("Battle of Seattle" 1906) were published. All of these are major urban and regional newspapers with extensive distribution networks.

Hence, by the turn of the century, the Battle of Seattle metaphor circulated widely in the United States. The key mechanism for dissemination and in the shift in scale was the newspaper or, in a more general sense, print capitalism, which not only propagated a metaphor but also infused it more fully with national and racial signifiers so as to secure boundaries between friends and enemies.

In the midtwentieth century, with the onset of the Cold War and an image of a potent Soviet adversary and mounting conflict ensconced in the public mind, the valence of the Battle of Seattle allusion increased. Newspapers employed it in sports columns to describe heated rivalries in athletic competition as well as in the business and politics of sport (Dyer 1951; Heisler 1984; Nidets 1976). In-text narratives frequently became intertext. In one iteration, State Attorney General Slade Gordon and Seattle mayor Wes Uhlman vied with each other to land a major league baseball franchise while City Councilman Tim Hill fought the multimillion dollar deal. The metaphor covered a three-way struggle involving state versus local politicians and sports promoters. A historically recurrent sports/war intertext applied sports phrases to war contexts and war phrases to sports contexts (Shapiro 1989). This intertext drove the Battle of Seattle metaphor across the inside/outside, domestic/foreign distinctions, though its usage was initially limited to the United States.

However, shortly after the collapse of the Soviet Union in 1991, the Battle of Seattle metaphor appeared in newspapers outside the United States. They popularized talk about sports and related issues in Seattle. For example, the *Calgary Herald* published an article titled "Battle of Seattle: Why Is Baseball Afraid of Japan, Land of the Rising Sum?" (McDermott 1992). Although the newspaper bearing the metaphor is located in the vicinity of the U.S. Pacific Northwest, the narrative extended across national borders and, with globalizing processes, is an instance of the mobility of a galvanizing symbol.

Specifically, the *Calgary Herald* noted that Japanese entrepreneurs wanted to buy the Seattle Mariners, a baseball team in dire financial straits. But the U.S. owners refused to sell because the potential buyer was foreign. Notwithstanding the offer, they were unwilling to allow nonnationals to purchase part of the national pastime. In this situation, the Battle of Seattle metaphor encapsulated a double movement of rising hypercompetition and the counter of local resistance imbued with national differences. By 1999, then, the battle metaphor was already interspersed with sports and business talk in the United States and Canada, plus the United Kingdom, thereby providing discursive space for constituting heightened cross-border competition between owners and among fans.[1]

DISSEMINATION

Against this background, the WTO ministerial meeting scheduled for November and December 1999 was supposed to be a pivotal phase in the spread and deepening of neoliberal economic practices. Myriad organizations assembled.

Some, like the AFL-CIO, concerned about protecting jobs and more aligned with the commitments of hyperpower, had a nationalist outlook. As the gathering approached, other local, national, and transnational civil society groups, such as the Ruckus Society, Earth First, Jubilee 2000, Teamsters, Black Bloc, and the Women's International League for Peace and Freedom, planned strategies and tactics to challenge officials' claims, collected and shared information, and mobilized for what was increasingly called the looming Battle of Seattle.

Ever more frequently, this phrase was splashed in newspapers in the United States, Canada, Australia, Ireland, Hungary, South Africa, the Philippines, and the United Kingdom. Along with the print media, the Internet played a key role in producing the 1999 Battle of Seattle (Klein 2000; J. Smith 2001; Reed 2005; Tarrow 2005).

Both electronic and print channels disseminated the Battle of Seattle metaphor across national borders. Together, they effected both a momentary stabilization and desynchronization of transnational actors: a globalizing community of elites and heterogeneous resistance movements. Information technologies spread the meaning-making and knowledge-producing power of the metaphor to constitute the events surrounding the ministerial meeting. So, too, a cleavage between friends and enemies implanted in the imagery configured multiple story lines, concerns, hopes, and desires in an ensemble for audiences far removed from the city on Elliott Bay.

Yet, after the 1999 events, the trajectory of the metaphor changed. It was decentered. Projected from several places in the world, the Battle of Seattle no longer referred solely to what had transpired in the city of Seattle but to similar sets of conflagrations in diverse contexts. The Battle of Seattle became the Battles of Seattle, which could be constituted almost anywhere (Lichbach 2002). Thus, in January 2000, the metaphor was used to describe a demonstration in Davos, Switzerland, an echo of the Battle of Seattle that had transpired the previous month. Recurrently over the next seven years, the Seattle metaphor encompassed protests in Bangkok, Hong Kong, Washington, D.C., Melbourne, Prague, Doha, Gothenburg, Genoa, Evian, Geneva, Seoul, and elsewhere, where critics targeted the IMF, the World Bank, the WTO, the WEF, and the Group of Eight (G-8). The information channeled by the media and the Internet enacted the plot of an unfolding story line, with implications for how communities and resources are organized and engage in collective action on a transnational scale. The Battles of Seattle metaphor thereby re-formed around the problematic of neoliberal globalization.

Print and electronic media also circulated stories of a film project known as "Battle in Seattle." A documentary-style action drama that focuses on a series of characters and their relationships to the protest events in Seattle in 1999, this movie itself is a global venture. Directed by Stuart Townsend, an Irish actor, it stars the Oscar-winning South African Charlize Theron along with Americans Woody Harrelson and Ray Liotta. The making and global marketing of this movie (primarily shot in Vancouver, Canada, so as to lower production costs) represent facets of hypercompetition: the intensification of rivalries among capitalists, in this case featuring celebrities playing their roles.

Released in 2008, this picture (so to speak) tacitly harks back to Denny's image painted in the nineteenth century. At local theaters, battling in Seattle again represents the split between friend and enemy, the contemporary content enacted by a new cast. Along with newspapers and the Internet, the film produces transnational identities, an important practice of cinema and the cultural industry since the 1920s (Sieg 2008). The three technologies transmitting the metaphor transnationally are central to the globalization of neoliberal practices and resistance against it. Indeed, deploying the Battles of Seattle metaphor is a means of restructuring conflict on an increasingly global scale. The cinema-graphic representation, supported by a $10 million budget, is a cultural crescendo for the metaphor and its long history, bringing the Battles of Seattle to an even larger consumer market.

IN THE STREETS

This genealogy must be considered in conjunction with the record of the WTO, which was ushered in by the 1994 Marrakesh Agreement and formally launched as the successor to the GATT in 1995. At that time, newspapers carried critical op-eds and probing news articles about the WTO. The main concerns centered on sovereignty, democracy, the environment, human rights, and labor. Clearly, many vexing issues that arose in the 1999 protests had already been vetted. Building on a seedbed of criticism, sixteen demonstrations against the WTO and other international economic institutions took place between 1994 and 1999 (Lichbach 2002, 10). These involved thousands of people and were amplified by symbolically charged actions, such as when Taiwanese farmers hurled pig dung to express their opposition to Taipei's accession to the WTO and when an environmental activist threw a pie in the face of its director-general, Renato Ruggiero.

In October 1998, Boeing chairman and chief executive officer Phil Condit and Microsoft chairman Bill Gates asked the WTO site selection team to hold the Third Ministerial meeting in Seattle (Gorlick 1998). Then, during the nine months after the team decided to make Seattle the venue, nearly fifty thousand people and more than seven hundred organizations assembled to attest that the WTO had harmed large swaths of citizens. Demonstrations targeted the WTO in twenty-four cities in the United States; an additional fifty cities in sixteen other countries in the global North; and twelve cities in seven countries in the global South (Lichbach 2002, 16).

Effectively, the meaning of the WTO crystallized as a transnational symbol of difference and Otherness that evoked critical interpretations. Articulating multiple narratives, swarms of individuals and organizations cultivated counterdiscourses.[2] By all indications, these were inchoate, fragmentary, overlapping, and sometimes competing formulations, not a single set of alternatives.

Print and electronic technologies, particularly flyers and the Internet, were key informational mechanisms for disseminating stories that buffeted the WTO. Meanwhile, U.S. and WTO officials attempted to negotiate this contestation and define the situation on their own, albeit differing, terms. The result was that the 1999 battle became emblematic of a hypercompetitive struggle over meanings, the rules of global governance, and control of resources.

The discourse centering on natural resources resonated with longtime residents of Seattle and its hinterland, a vast territory reaching Alaska and the Rocky Mountains. (In fact, the University of Washington was founded as the Territorial University in Seattle in 1861, only one decade after the arrival of the first white settlers.) Locals and history buffs know that Seattle had served as a frontier town and provincial capital for the region, that its first large business was the steam sawmill built on Elliott Bay in 1853, and that economic development has been linked to the exploitation of natural resources. Historically, prospecting for gold, logging, and fishing have provided mainstays of the economy. The environment itself is promoted as the source of a vital industry for enthusiasts of recreation: skiing, hiking, mountaineering, kayaking, and sailing (Raban 2007).

Seattle's influential families, such as the Boeings, and Bill Gates's large network pioneered start-up companies (software companies and spin-offs in Internet-related enterprises), attracting highly educated and entrepreneurial newcomers. By 1999, Seattle had become a globalizing city, a hub with substantial links to rising Asia-Pacific and other world regions. But beyond its urban sprawl, greater Seattle has left behind many manual workers and marginalized people. In the timber towns and rural areas, people who have not reaped globalization's benefits and are unable to gain from virtualized space are sometimes nostalgic for the olden ways. Mindful of such transformations in their daily lives, disgruntled citizens strung a banner on a freeway leading to the Third Ministerial. The streamer graphically displayed two giant arrows. The southward arrow pointing downtown read "WTO"; the northward one, "DEMOCRACY." To the north are the outlying blue-collar towns, Canada, and the Arctic region (Raban 2007). This symbolic representation of the 1999 ministerial conference suggests a deepening conflict between the old city and the new ways, winners and losers in the tide of globalization. A part of this tension manifests as rootedness versus an inflow of values and waves of people seeking to sink roots in a globalizing region. These dynamics are a local variant of an evolving narrative, an inflection added to the juxtaposition of the WTO and democracy.

In the 1999 Seattle mêlée itself, individuals lacking Internet access were disadvantaged. In fact, relatively few poor people and members of minority groups of color participated in the events. One factor that helps account for how the Battle of Seattle was racially constituted is the local demographics (a relatively small African American population in Seattle, King County, and the state of Washington). According to Elizabeth (Betita) Martinez, an activist and writer, another reason that an overwhelming number of protesters in Seattle were "Anglo" was that many minority peoples did not have Internet access and failed "to see how the WTO affected the daily lives of U.S. communities of color" (Martinez 2000, 77). For people without informational ties to counternarratives and symbols, the Internet-dependent mobilization of the Battle of Seattle was, then, a movement constituted in relation to the internal Others of race and class. The dominant face of civil society during the 1999 battle looked white and middle class, partly owing to the technological disparity and knowledge divide that enabled rather privileged people to organize against the WTO.

But some local marginalized groups, such as the Brown Collective and the Basement Nation, were linked to the Internet and could partake in evolving transnational structures. Denise Cooper, a student and member of both groups during the 1999 protests in Seattle, termed the Internet, especially e-mail, a valuable means of communication: "the Internet is a big tool" for organizing against the WTO (D. Cooper n.d., 14). Yet, "we still have to rely on those old ways of mass mailings and flyers" and not get "too comfortable" with electronic technologies, because the poor and minority groups often lack Internet access (n.d., 14). For Cooper, mobilizing against the WTO is a matter intimately tied to globalization, as it in turn relates to disadvantaged groups in various parts of the world. In this civil society narrative, the WTO is again a key organizing symbol. Members of the Basement Nation and the Brown Collective pitted their mobilizing efforts and resources against this institution. Their activities inserted more critical voices in the controversy and thrust out transnationally.

Unlike the Basement Nation and the Brown Collective, the Rainforest Action Network (RAN) is a well-established group connected to transnational organizations (J. Smith 2001, 11). According to Jennifer Krill, a RAN staff member during the protests, RAN rented an apartment in Seattle and assigned a full-time media person there before the demonstrations started (Krill 2000, 1–2). From this locale, the agent issued press releases and helped link RAN spokespersons to media outlets for interviews and press conferences. Krill notes that RAN increased understanding of the stakes by circulating electronic action alerts, gathering signatures for petitions, mounting demonstrations, providing experts, holding teach-ins, and conducting training sessions.

Krill maintains that RAN became involved in the Seattle protests because the WTO's stance toward "global logging" would "hasten the decline" of various species of trees in old growth forests, pollute the water, and open areas to deforestation wrought by powerful corporations (Krill 2000, 1). The impact is "bad for the environment and it's bad for species and it's very bad for Labor" (2000, 2). Again, the WTO serves as an organizing symbol: the "bad" Other against which RAN legitimates the mobilization of its members and formulates a critical and interest-constituting story line. The "bad" Other also helps forge a coalition of organized labor and environmentalists (groups that have frequently not aligned with one another). But the 1999 battle produced solidarity between them, at least temporarily.

Like Krill, Jason Adams, a member of the Industrial Workers of the World (IWW), produced information and knowledge for the 1999 battle. He used popular graphics already in circulation, combined them, and creatively added words and stories. Variations of this design were then printed on about one thousand stickers and twelve thousand flyers for dissemination in Seattle. Adams also set up listservs with announcements about protest events and used the Internet to collect data from other organizations, such as Peoples' Global Action. He compared the WTO to a "global union of the richest corporations and the richest people in the world ... [while] we're like the global union of workers and the people that work for these corporations" (Adams n.d., 7). For

Adams and the IWW, the WTO is a symbolic Other, their "exact opposite" (n.d., 7). The WTO is the target of IWW protest efforts and the constitutive reason for mobilization. Adams thus artfully wove together electronic and print technologies to produce a multimedia story line that framed the WTO as a global rallying point for dissident workers.

There were also ideological differences among the social movements. On November 29, small scattered groups of protestors wearing scarves over their faces began overturning newspaper containers and trash cans; wielded baseball bats, hammers, and other implements; and demolished corporate property, including at Starbucks, Old Navy, GAP, and the Bank of America, in Seattle's downtown business core. A communiqué explained that attacking "property is not a violent activity unless it destroys lives or causes pain in the process" (ACME Collective 2002, 118). For their efforts, Black Bloc anarchists were criticized and marginalized, not only by fellow protesters, some of whom tried to stop the assault on property, but also in news accounts, editorials, and government and WTO statements.

Responding to the disruptions, the WTO director-general's press statement released on November 30, 1999, asserts that the "[c]onference will be a success" (Moore 1999a). Notwithstanding this optimism, Director-General Mike Moore framed November 30 as "a very sad day" because of the actions of a small number of protesters who resorted to "violence and destructive behavior." He nonetheless sanctioned a "peaceful protest" that would allow the WTO meetings to proceed smoothly (Moore 1999a). On the same day and in a similar tone, President Clinton condemned the "non-peaceful" demonstrators who "tried to block access and to prevent meetings" as "wrong" and "illegal" in their efforts and lauded protestors with "peaceful purposes" as "healthy" actors in a democratizing global economy that is no longer the sole "province" of a corporate elite (Clinton 1999c). Moore's and Clinton's narratives draw a common boundary. On one side are protesters who respectfully allow WTO meetings to take place. They are portrayed as the legitimate, healthy, and peaceful activists. On the other side are the protesters who disrupt the officials' assemblies and damage corporate property. They are pronounced violent, undemocratic, and unacceptable critics who legitimate aggressive policing tactics.

On November 30, with pressure from the Clinton administration and following a recommendation from the police, Seattle mayor Paul Schell declared a state of emergency and a curfew over a fifty-block downtown area. Meanwhile, arrests began at Sixth Avenue and Pine Street, where Secret Service agents escorted President Clinton. Governor Gary Locke also deployed three hundred state troopers and the National Guard to assist the Seattle police force. By midnight on the first day of the WTO's Third Ministerial, sixty-eight demonstrators had been arrested, and the police procured supplementary supplies of tear gas from the nearby towns of Auburn, Tukwila, and Renton as well as King County and the State of Washington law enforcement agencies. On December 1, the Seattle city attorney issued an emergency order that prohibited the possession of chemical masks (except for police and military forces), while teams of plain-clothes police officers were deployed to thwart vandalism. Mayor Schell established a no-protest zone in the central business district and hundreds of demonstrators were arrested ("Timeline" 2001).

These sanctions established a hierarchy demarcated by boundaries. Ringed by the multitude excluded and gathered outside in the streets, political and corporate elites were enclosed in a heavily fortified security area. By citing the need for public order and security, officials sought to justify this enforced border line.

The effort to control the distribution of space in Seattle may be construed as a means to discipline the body politic and maintain stability so that negotiations over neoliberal policies could continue without further disruption. From this standpoint, the contour between friend and enemy, the state and civil society, is perceptible in the configuration of police and demonstrators. Unmistakably, this corporeal representation constitutes an inside/outside schematic.

The U.S. government aimed to avert what it viewed as a perilous situation and convert it into an opportunity (Grimaldi and Anderson 1999). President Clinton sought to link official discourse to criticisms voiced by protesters. On December 1, in remarks to farmers, students, and trade officials, Clinton said,

> When I see all these people in the streets here, I'd like to point out that among a lot of people who are peacefully protesting here in the best American tradition, are protesting in part because the interest they represent have never been allowed inside the deliberations of the world trading system. And I went all the way to Geneva last year to talk to the WTO to tell them we had to change that, we needed to open this system up. [Clinton 1999b]

In effect, Clinton embraced the peaceful protesters' argument that the global trading system generally and the WTO in particular are insufficiently democratic and opaque. His speechifying was to distinguish Washington from the WTO and simultaneously incorporate the narratives of the critics under the auspices of hyperpower. This oratory could also sap the appeal of the activists' case. By assuming this demeanor, Clinton crafted a self-image as an engaged and democratically minded leader who listens to his constituents' shouts of dismay. The persona is that of a populist of sorts. Moreover, in this discourse, the WTO is a site of difference against which Clinton is pitted.

At the same time, Clinton wanted to distance himself from the unlawful and violent protesters who devastate property and interrupt WTO meetings, but not from the law-abiding reformers in the streets who respect the process of international summitry. His move was to exemplify the American tradition of championing nonviolent democratic representation and liberal inclusive politics, a sharp contrast to the passion and belligerence in the streets that excludes incompatible participants. For hyperpower, this gesture would legitimate one mode of protest (peaceful), one type of protester (patriotic), and one kind of economic system (free market).

Notwithstanding Clinton's tactics, civil society groups charged that the WTO suffered from a democratic deficit. To defend the trade organization, Director-General Moore maintained that members of the WTO are in fact accountable to their governments and the citizens of their countries, and that is the way it should be (Moore 1999c). He traced a line of accountability directly from individual voters in their national states to the WTO. In other words, Moore held that the WTO is linked to each citizen in a chain of representation. Implicit in his thinking is an unshakable belief in an overall harmony of interests: a concord of advantages for market citizens, national collectivities, and the entire world. The economic and political good of the individual and the collective concatenate in a totality of economic exchange and increased wealth for all partners.

In this account of the Seattle events, Moore similarly intervened on the matter of the relationship between trade and labor. Recall that Adams framed the IWW and the WTO as arch rivals—the WTO is the enemy of the IWW. Contravening this view, Moore told international trade unionists that "I have never seen a contradiction between trade and labour because I don't believe one exists" (Moore 1999b). According to Moore, the globalization of trade and the opening of markets bring "jobs, opportunities and security" to workers and their families (Moore 1999b). In this narrative, trade and the institution charged with managing it, the WTO, are framed as beneficial to labor. Moore thus stood critical discourse on its head and posited a concurrence of interests between trade and labor. The position against which Moore set his discourse is a closed economic system and the protectionists who sustain it. This manner of speaking wove together a global-scope story line that situates trade and labor in a relation of integration and identity, a depiction at odds with the views articulated by Adams of the IWW, Krill of RAN, and other protesters mobilizing against the WTO in the streets. But not all Battles of Seattle were fought in the streets.

INSIDE THE MINISTERIAL MEETING

Alongside clashes in the streets between demonstrators and police, disputes arose within the Third Ministerial meeting. Division and competition emerged between the developed and more numerous developing countries and among the developed countries themselves. Trade ministers and their delegations enacted story lines constitutive of identity communities and interests. Officials seated at the table were supposed to represent peoples and territories throughout the world. There were those who *define* and those who *are* defined: the elites *inside* the WTO meeting and the masses *outside*, some of their ranks in the streets. Among the latter, certain groups, but not all of them, were invited to participate in the Seattle Symposium on International Trade Issues in the First Decades of the Next Century, an official WTO forum established to facilitate dialogue between member states and accredited civil society organizations. Yet the symposium's detractors claimed that it excluded vehement critics of the WTO and was no more than a public relations display (Zoll 1999). This variation in representation shows that at Seattle, inside *and* outside became more complicated than an either/or distinction. Indeed, the narratives were intertwined. There was a mesh of narratives within narratives.

That said, the categories of environmental and labor standards delineated the relationships between major trading powers and developing countries. The most powerful states pushed for the incorporation of these items on the agenda of trade negotiations, and developing countries wanted to separate them. This debate brings to light conflicting logic and interests in the negotiations.

President Clinton's address to the trade ministers exemplifies the more comprehensive, or globalist, view. With the 2000 presidential elections approaching, and Vice President Al Gore named as the nominee of the Democratic Party, Clinton took a position that would appeal to environmental and labor groups in the U.S. domestic arena. He proposed the formation of a working group within the WTO to deal with labor issues (for example, child labor standards and workers rights). Exhorting developing nations to "not avoid this labor issue," Clinton intoned that "we must work to protect and to improve the environment as we expand trade" (Clinton 1999a). A number of Northern countries and regional groupings, including the Commission of the European Community, supported this stance. Political and economic elites in the global North wrought trade, labor, and environment in a whole in which the meaning of one issue hinged on the others.

In contrast to this integrative narrative, trade ministers from the global South expressed a logic of differentiation. They framed the idea of tying trade to labor and environmental standards as a protectionist measure. Thus, India's minister of commerce and industry, Murasoli Maran, described the multilateral trading system as having "been designed to deal with issues involving trade and trade alone" (Maran 1999). To include "non-trade issues" such as environmental and labor standards in the Seattle negotiations, he insisted, would exceed the "competence" of the organization, and "open the floodgates of protectionism" (Maran 1999). Brazilian minister of foreign relations Luiz Felipe Lampreia advanced a similar argument. Affirming that protesters had "genuine concerns" about labor and environment, he held that these critics were being "used as a disguise" by major trading nations and that developing countries thus should treat them with "suspicion." The basic point, according to Lampreia, is that "[p]rotectionism in developed countries is on the rise" (Lampreia 1999).

Joining forces with Maran and Lampreia, Pakistani minister of commerce, industry and promotion Abdul Razak Dawood viewed the developed countries' attempts to introduce the "completely extraneous" issues of labor and environmental standards as "disturbing" (Dawood 1999). Insisting that these are not altruistic efforts, he avowed that the "clear objective" is to impose "market restrictions on competitive exports from developing countries." Furthermore, peoples' "genuine concerns" are "being manipulated to serve protectionist ends" (Dawood 1999). In short, a chorus of ministers from the global South used "protectionism" as a refrain to vie with their Northern counterparts and delegitimate the latter's initiatives for shaping globalization.

Another disputed item was implementation. Agreements hammered out at the 1986–94 Uruguay Round were to be executed by WTO members over the next five to ten years. These included accords on textiles and clothing, antidumping, and trade-related aspects of intellectual property rights. But shortly after the founding of the WTO in 1995, implementation became a vexing matter. Developing countries recurrently brought it up at WTO ministerial meetings in Singapore in 1996 and Geneva in 1998 but to no avail, for the major trading

powers generally dismissed this issue (Raghavan 2000). In Seattle, however, this
pattern changed. Despite efforts by the United States and the EU to keep implementation off the agenda, the chairman of the General Council incorporated
it in the Third Ministerial meeting program (Raghavan 2000, 6). This decision
came after the General Council received nearly one hundred written proposals
from developing countries in the previous year; many of the suggested policies
dealt with implementation (Watal 2000, 72–73). In this instance, trade ministers used implementation as a narrative resource to confer meaning and define
an encounter as well as the relationships enveloped in it.

Hence, at the opening plenary sessions in Seattle, Bangladeshi minister for
commerce and industry Tofail Ahmed declared that the thrust of the Third
Ministerial conference should be "implementation issues" and "built-in agenda issues" (Ahmed 1999). Implementation served to justify his stand, which
conflicted with the U.S. delegation's push for new trade talks. Advocating the
completion of the Uruguay Round agreements, Ahmed implored, "[t]here is
therefore no need for holding a 'new or comprehensive round' of multilateral
trade negotiations" (Ahmed 1999). Implementation became a stratagem for securing an effective border between the global South and the United States on
the part of the global North.

Speaking for the European Commission (before he became director-general
of the WTO in 2005), Pascal Lamy framed implementation in a similar way:
"Our friends in developing countries are in general worried. They have raised
a number of issues concerning implementation" (Lamy 1999). In this instance,
too, the narrative of implementation works to differentiate "we" and "they," the
global North and the global South. The putative relationship is not one of en-
mity. Indeed, the poor countries are constituted as "our friends"—close associates and partners, some of them neighbors, but not kith and kin with special attachments. Lamy thereby constructed an inclusionary logic that stopped short
of Self-identity. He posited a familiarity that allows an openness to Others: "we
should listen to them and we should take their concerns into account" (Lamy
1999). Still, this inclusionary orientation had its limits, for ultimately the issue
of implementation marked the difference between "us" and "them."

The point is that implementation worked as a means of differentiation. This
expression served as a cog in the production of separate groups of elites at the
Third Ministerial meeting.

Among those represented was the Quad of the United States, Canada, Japan,
and the EU. Their relations were not entirely harmonious. In fact, tension be-

tween the United States and Japan materialized in Seattle. Before 1999, Washington and Tokyo had clashed on issues surrounding agriculture and industrial imports and exports, with each government accusing the other of protectionism. And in February 1999, the WTO Dispute Settlement Mechanism decided against Japanese efforts to restrict apple and cherry imports from the United States. These bilateral quarrels were but one strain within the Quad.

When Japanese minister for foreign affairs Yohei Kono backed the developing countries by affirming that implementation was an urgent issue worth addressing in Seattle, he effectively widened a fissure among developed countries. He wanted to do more than just listen to developing countries, as Lamy had more conservatively suggested. Kono sought to broaden the scope of the negotiations. As he put it, "the Japanese Government attaches particular importance to reviewing the rules on anti-dumping" (Kono 1999).

The Japanese and U.S. delegations engaged in a pitched debate over antidumping. Although Minister Kono and U.S. Secretary of State Madeleine Albright met for nearly one hour before the start of the Third Ministerial meeting, they refused to budge on this issue. Just as Japan continued to push for inclusion of antidumping on the agenda, the United States doggedly fought this initiative. And the tension was never really overcome at Seattle. The divergence was not only a matter of incompatible views on trade policy but also conflicting interests. For example, unlike the other Quad countries, Japan had a lower trade ratio in the 1990s (17 percent of GDP) than it did in 1910 (30 percent) or even 1950 (19 percent) ("Trade Expansion Remains the Engine of Growth" 1999). This difference illustrates the recurrent friction. Cross-boundary ties among trading powers in the Quad could not withstand all the pressure brought to bear during the Third Ministerial meeting.

A measure to counter these disintegrative tendencies is the narrative of integration in the WTO framework. After all, the organization's raison d'être is coordination in a manner that aligns the economies of its members, as well as those of states seeking accession to the WTO, with the global trading system. Additionally, integration is represented as a way to alleviate poverty. The image of "the poor" is the internal Other in the global economy and the justification for certain trade rules adopted to facilitate efficient integration.

A joint statement by the chiefs of the IMF, World Bank, and WTO, released on November 30, 1999, epitomized interlinking the narratives of integration and poverty. As they put it,

Poverty afflicts an intolerably large proportion of the world's population. The evolution towards a more open, integrated and competitive global economy offers great potential for fostering growth and the economic and social development needed to eradicate poverty. [Camdessus, Wolfensohn, and Moore 1999]

Trade ministers from both the global North and the global South embraced this sentiment. Speaking on behalf of the developing countries, Bangladeshi minister Ahmed framed the challenge as marginalization "from the mainstream of the world economy" (Ahmed 1999). For impoverished countries and regions, integration into the global economy is regarded as the key to development. Or in the words of Minister of Foreign Affairs Didier Opertti of Uruguay, the Seattle negotiations "must achieve the objective of fully integrating agricultural trade into the same rules" as for other goods in the WTO (Opertti 1999).

On December 1, 1999, U.S. secretary of agriculture Daniel Glickman offered to find common ground with trading nations in the global South. He held that the WTO and its member states must take advantage of "the opportunity to fully integrate the people of the developing world" into the global economy (Glickman 1999). Together, this double rhetoric of integration and poverty, one theme reinforcing the other, structured relations among sometimes discordant officials so as to add meaning to efforts to legitimate and liberalize the global economy. At the ministerial meeting, these practices gave impetus to the quest for consensus among the trade ministers.

However, the partial inclusion of NGOs in the ministerial disturbed internal consensus-making among WTO members. The aforementioned Seattle Symposium on International Trade Issues in the First Decades of the Next Century began its deliberations on November 29. No longer barred from taking a seat in the WTO forum, some NGOs could voice their positions to delegations and trade officials, though of course this framework had its own parameters.

Representing the International South Group Network, Zimbabwe, at the WTO NGO symposium in Seattle, Yash Tandon called attention to the necessity of maintaining international economic institutions. "I am not in favour of abolishing the WTO. Nor for that matter am I in favour of abolishing the World Bank or the IMF" (Tandon 1999). Unlike many demonstrators in the streets, he framed the WTO not as an enemy but a victim of the forces consolidating transnational capital. Expressing popular discontent inside the symposium, Tandon quoted statistics that Clinton had called up and then attested that the

WTO is "one of the most non-transparent and undemocratic organs of global governance" (Tandon 1999). In his view, the enemy is the "over-consumptionist demands of Western populations and the profit imperative of their corporations" combined with a "collective" of powerful "individual states" that enables them to "over-exploit the rest of the world" by controlling the rules of the WTO (Tandon 1999). Tilting against the niceties of conventional diplomatic talk, Tandon submitted that multilateralism enshrines the "rule of the jungle" that supports a "democratic and ethical deficit" between rich and poor people and regions of the world. Not really helping the masses of impoverished and disenfranchised citizens, the WTO is basically "killing itself" by stoking the fires of mass "Rebellion."

Tandon thus advocated assisting the WTO to effect genuine and fundamental change for the sake of institutional adaptation. The new system of global trade would embody just and egalitarian relations among member states and a greater voice for citizens. Excluded from this story is the power politics of the "jungle." Yet integral to this reformed structure of trade is a global surveillance mechanism operating in the name of civil society. Beckoning civil society in the global North, Tandon appealed to his listeners "to monitor your governments who are imposing on our weak governments agreements that are iniquitous, illegitimate and forced by means of bribes, threats, and decisions reached in 'green room' secretive talks" (Tandon 1999).

This story line was meant to facilitate interventions by member states and the WTO to save and enhance human life. As a biopolitical instrument that would secure well-being through economic policy, the WTO is reaffirmed as a vital part of the global social body as long as the power relations that sustain it are transformed.

THE OUTPOURING OF DISCONTENT

To sum up, the 1999 Third Ministerial meeting broke into conflict and dashed hopes for flattening trade barriers and affording greater access to world markets. This clash was partly about the ascendant narrative of a flat world without unrelenting hierarchies, an order that holds out prospects for rapid upward mobility through trade, for peaceful intercourse among nations and economic betterment for all.[3] But this story conveyed an antiseptic, depoliticized imaginary about world order. It also worked to efface counternarratives about the barriers to independent, auto-empowered communities seeking to control their own fate in a globalizing world.

Against this backdrop, within the ministerial meeting, the definition of trade broadened, extending to basic problems of globalization and different notions of what it would mean to govern this set of processes more democratically. But the original causes of the strife became lost in the escalating conflict and the demands of protestors and civil society organizations. Seattle marked the rise of a backlash against top-down globalizing summitry, tête-à-têtes besieged by resistance from citizens' movements.

As these groups spun narratives within narratives, much of the discord concerned the business of hyperpower. A champion of free trade, save in select sectors of the economy in which the government subsidizes domestic producers, dominant interests in the United States were and are principal beneficiaries of expanded globalization; Europe has followed closely; Japan has gained large advantages, too, along with elites in some other Asian countries, especially China and India.

Indeed, trade is a major aspect of hypercompetition. The chief negotiators in Seattle were steadfast in promoting it. Hence, Barshefsky, the head of the U.S. delegation, issued a stern warning about her determination to secure Washington's position. "I reserve the right to use a more exclusive process," she declared, "to achieve a final outcome" (as quoted in Fleshman 1999, 31). In the fiery conflict with Barshefsky over their exclusion from negotiations in the green rooms, ministers from developing countries voiced their indignation. The Africa Group, later joined by the Caribbean governments, stated, "There is no transparency in the proceedings and African countries are being marginalized and generally excluded on issues of vital importance to our peoples" (as quoted in Fleshman 1999, 31).

The U.S. delegation drew on reserves of hyperpower to try to build the consensus that it wanted among elites and to incorporate moderate groups in civil society. This effort nonetheless encountered quandaries of hypercompetition: a jam of different interests, agendas, and belief systems.

As indicated, after these difficulties came to the fore at the 1999 Battle of Seattle, they catalyzed the subsequent Battles of Seattle. By staging a symbolic drama of rage over the underside of neoliberal globalization, the 1999 battle prepared the ground for the ensuing events in other cities. Quite clearly, it signaled resistances not only to the WTO but also, more broadly, to globalizing processes promoted by hyperpower and taking the form of hypercompetition. Joined over trade issues in Seattle, these structures signaled rising hyperconflict.

In this chapter, we have traced the coalescing of these processes. In our evidence of this blending, the resemblance between the 1856 and 1999 battles is striking. Interlocutors represented both of them as morality tales without history and devoid of hierarchical provenance. But each battle has its own history tunneling into the macrodynamics of power and competition. These structures entail resilient hierarchies that constrain choice and circumscribe policy space. Also, the stories told about these epic contestations are not on the same footing. There is no moral equivalence among the values asserted by the protagonists in any of these battles. The claimants embraced different principles. And as the next chapter shows, the struggle over the norms inscribed in globalizing processes, as well as who is authorized to securitize them, arose anew when a nonstate actor struck lethally at prominent sites of hyperpower and hypercompetition on September 11, 2001.

7 CONFLICT 4: 9/11 AND THE "GLOBAL WAR ON TERROR"

(Coauthored with Priya Dixit)

September 11 turned a shared sense of security into insecurity. The image of airplanes attacking the World Trade Center and the Pentagon, symbols of American economic and political might, is a threshold in the minds of ordinary citizens. Most of them, at least in the West, had not been particularly worried about transnational threats to physical security in their daily lives. Suddenly, many people experienced sorrow and horror. To be sure, the perpetrators' objective on 9/11 was to sow fear and insecurity. Although terror is not a new tactic, the arena is now global; its parts, increasingly interconnected; and the weaponry, ever more destructive.

The very words used to mark this phenomenon—"war" and "terror"—are an aspect of intersubjectivity that places people in categories. For neoconservatives, war is the ultimate way to force change. It is a means to impose the hegemony of values and, especially after 9/11, define relations among people. To this end, neoconservative thinking and policies construct meanings about Others. The language takes the form of narratives that represent Selves and Others as opposed to one another. Discursive power employs violence as an element of strategy. As in President George W. Bush's fillip for endless war—"Either you are with us, or you are with the terrorists"—this framing is a mode of constituting hyperconflict. Thus, in the same speech, President Bush declared, "Our war on terror . . . will not end until every terrorist group of global reach has been found, stopped and defeated" (U.S. President 2001).

It is not simply that a narrative, such as Bush's pronouncement, automatically becomes dominant, but there are battles over which stories to tell until one of them prevails, at least for a time. This combat takes place on a hyper-competitive landscape, forming a discursive economy of networked narratives. And the contestation among them is not only within global space and single countries but may even occur in an individual's mind.

A striking feature of 9/11 is the way in which power holders, the mass media, and security intellectuals honed in on the perpetrators' acts and crafted a broad historical narrative about a global conflict, cultivating a culture of fear. Washington and its allies transformed terror into a moral abstraction, joining diverse groups that employ similar tactics, and defined their actions not as a specific problem or method but as a war of global scope (Appadurai 2006). Waging what it regarded as a campaign for freedom and against terrorism, which must be met by force and supplanted by democracy, the U.S. state called for eternal war for perpetual peace. Using the terrorism filter, Vice President Cheney often proclaimed that this war against a network of enemies who know no rules would continue indefinitely. He predicted that it "may never end. At least, not in our lifetime" (as quoted in Kolko 2006, 103).

Ratcheting up fear about a "global war on terror" built on one dreadful incident, in which 2,689 U.S. citizens were killed, and elevated it above other tragedies that afflicted America.[1] In 2001, the death toll in the United States from malnutrition was 3,500 people; HIV/AIDS, 14,000; pneumonia, 62,000; heart disease, 700,000; suicide, 30,000; traffic accidents, 42,000; firearm-related fatalities, nearly 30,000; and homicides, 20,000 (Abbott, Rogers, and Sloboda 2006, 16). And the use of narratives has steered government spending to fighting terror, $48.5 billion on homeland security in 2005 compared to $2.6 billion to combat HIV/AIDS globally in the same year (figures taken from Abbott, Rogers, and Sloboda 2006, 16).

Yet the dominant discourse about 9/11 is one among a cluster of competing narratives. Unlike studies of 9/11 that primarily explore its "hard" dimensions, this chapter directs attention to five narratives of global conflict and depicts them in the tide of history. The other accounts are incomplete without appreciation of the roles of rival stories, each of them with their putative plots and actors. Our contention is that there is more to 9/11 and emergent global conflict than the personalities of the protagonists, the history of foreign policy, and military-strategic interests. We want to examine ways in which hypercompetition and hyperpower are intertwined and the extent to which they incline toward hyperconflict.

Offering close textual analysis, we will scrutinize five narratives: 9/11 as a binary opposition of the nation and its enemies; an identity rooted in religion; a representation propped up by states and their adversaries; a symbol of economic power; and an image of masculinity that subordinates women. These are remarkably diverse stories. But they all involve the coercive aspects of power relations. They are, for the most part, told by officials and public intellectuals who create and disperse discourses, which are more than encrusted debates among academics. The point is that the identity of the Other is not limited to foes but pertains to alternatives that stem from Self-reflection in the process of Othering. That is, the Other is about both representing enemies and producing strategies of interpretation and responses, as indicated below (Falk 1997, 44).

NATION

Resting on a binary distinction of opposition between Selves and Others, Samuel Huntington's *Who Are We?* (2004) examines threats to American national identity mainly from large-scale immigration from Mexico. Worried about weakening nationhood, Huntington faults transnational elites who develop cross-border identities and adopt cosmopolitan attitudes. By neglecting challenges to the state and the values of the general public, they betray their homeland (2004, 138).

One of the world's most influential public intellectuals ("The Top 100 Public Intellectuals" 2008), Huntington describes a core culture, or "American Creed," buttressing American identity. This creed stems from Anglo-Protestant values and a strong work ethic that settlers brought to the United States (Huntington 2004, 37). Its principal ingredients are the English language, English-based rule of law, Christianity, and individualism (Huntington 2004, 37–58). Although previous waves of immigrants readily absorbed American culture and are now part of this Protestant-based creed, new immigrants, especially those from Mexico, deviate from American national identity, and basically differ from their predecessors. Newcomers from Mexico maintain close ties to a nearby homeland, are lax in applying for U.S. citizenship, retain the Spanish language, and do not easily assimilate (Huntington 2004, 243). In this narrative, Huntington frames Mexican immigrants as risks for national identity and security.

By claiming that an Anglo-Protestant culture formed the American Creed, Huntington disregards the diverse backgrounds of the early settlers from Europe: the immigrants from many countries who shaped American culture while being incorporated in it. Troubled about, or merely dismissing, the hybridity of cultures in America, Huntington probes the impact from outside on a solid American Creed and, by extension, the American state. For him, at issue are threats to an Anglo-Protestant culture and the ramifications of a divide between Spanish- and English-speaking America.

Although Huntington's 2004 book does not attempt a detailed analysis of 9/11, it submits that the attacks on the twin towers and the Pentagon provided a new enemy, "militant Islam," against which Americans could coalesce (2004, 264). Yet how does this notion of the United States, galvanized by Al Qaeda and terrorists in general, mesh with Huntington's view of the enemy within—Mexican immigrants, who he alleges are not readily becoming part of American culture?

The element that links Mexican immigrants and terrorists is the appeal to nationalism as a way to bind a community. Much like Carl Schmitt ([1932] 1996, [1950] 2003), who in another era and a different context, sought to justify exclusion of an enemy as an adhesive for the political identity of friends, Huntington turned his attention to the impact of putative foes: to be exact, a "clash of civilizations" at home. This time, Mexicans are the Muslims, the local aliens who clash with American values and who rankle anticosmopolitans like Huntington himself (Sennett 2004). A binary identity is established. Immigrants from Mexico are the equivalent of Muslims who threaten U.S. national security. This imagery is implicated in the policies of building fences along the border between the United States and Mexico and dispatching the National Guard to curb illegal immigration.

Huntington's *Who Are We?* illustrates the extensive use of binary identities, a practice not at all limited to the United States, as indicated by the controversy over cartoons construed as depicting the prophet Mohammad as a terrorist. Many Muslims regarded these representations as blasphemy. First published in the Danish newspaper *Jyllands-Posten* in 2005, then republished in newspapers elsewhere, and posted on the Internet, the cartoons prompted street protests in the Middle East and South Asia. Nearly 150 demonstrators died, and the Danish embassies in Damascus and Beirut were set aflame (Brun and Hersh 2008, 15). In addition, boycotts of goods produced in Denmark, an ally of the United States in the "war on terror," and other countries where the images appeared also brought into sharp relief the power of representations over purportedly conflicting values.[2] The ensuing debates in many parts of the world centered on the free press versus the sanctity of Islam. Widely contested, this issue pivoted on the question, Is freedom of expression a Western construct, and do religious beliefs take precedence over it?

In the "cartoon riots," sometimes also called "Muslim cartoon riots"—terms widely employed in the Western media—framings of "us" and "them" may be readily discerned: in Europe and the United States, the West was portrayed as composed of open societies that protect free expression and are in stark contrast to closed communities constrained by adherence to a strict religion. Meanwhile, in majority Islamic countries, Western nations were often described as peopled by nonbelievers shorn of ethical values and unlike the faithful who lead pious lives. This polarization of identities parallels a Huntingtonian framework of Selves and Others perilously counterpoised. Yet unlike Huntington's narrative of we-and-they national identities, the "cartoon riots" were framed by religious identities wherein Muslims and non-Muslims are Selves and Others locked in both symbolic and violent conflict. The shift is from twofold national identities to dual religious idioms.

RELIGION

Exemplars of framing in terms of religion and identity are books that have received extensive public notice, including in the mainstream media. Authors Mahmood Mamdani (2004a), Olivier Roy (2004), and Mark Juergensmeyer (2003) share a concern about the link between religious identities and violence. They want to bring to light the differences between people who are observant in their faith and live peacefully, and the believers who invoke religion and use violence in their efforts to transform world order.

Mamdani calls attention to the practice of categorizing "good" and "bad" Muslims. He claims that imposing this sharp division is a misconceived attempt to try to understand what is seemingly incomprehensible: manifold reasons why people commit varied acts of violence in the name of religion, as on 9/11. In several other instances, the perpetrators of organized violence—say, against Nazi Germany—sought to justify their actions as waging war for perpetual peace (Chapter 1). But when applied to 9/11 and the "war on terror," this rationale for protracted war has produced doubt and resistance. Hence, Mamdani contends, talk of culture and religion may be partly understood as a way that the powerful address particular audiences. Politics is expressed as "Culture Talk," wrongly in Mamdani's view, because history is represented as static and lacks reference to the intricate conditions to which political terror responds (Mamdani 2004a, 18; 2004b, 11).

Although Culture Talk is flawed, it is unlike Huntington's reductive formulation of binary identities. In Culture Talk, the Other is not only deemed an enemy but contains within it a potential friend. Culture Talk thus consists of a double claim: the first is that premodern Muslims trail on the path to modernity and cling to an unchanging culture; the second, that their politics are antimodern and antithetical to progress (Mamdani 2004a, 18; 2004b, 11). The first imagines an identity of the Other as the needy requiring assistance in the

quest for modernity; the second conjures up fear, possibly violence, and annihilation. While the two identities pertaining to culture and politics are oppositional, these narratives point to different responses. Mamdani insists that both
narratives stem from a limp concept of culture, which presumes immutable
traits and a linear process rather than socially and historically constituted phenomena.

Punctuating his point, Mamdani contends that Culture Talk pays little notice to the history of the United States' role in supporting violent movements
that eventually adopted terrorist tactics. According to him, the events of 9/11 are
partly traceable to past American actions in Afghanistan, Iraq, and elsewhere.
U.S. policies contributed to the rise of a specific form of political Islam that
employs the weapon of terror. But this response to external conditions must be
grasped in conjunction with the history internal to Islam itself. In other words,
political Islam is not merely an "American invention" (Mamdani 2004b, 11).

Mamdani mainly locates terror, particularly the roots of Islamist terror, in
state-centered, not society-centered, movements. He is thus able to claim that a
"*political* encounter" rather than Culture Talk is key to understanding Islamist
terror (Mamdani 2004a, 61; emphasis in original). In this political engagement,
particular institutions, especially the Central Intelligence Agency (CIA), have
enacted Washington's "embrace of terror," paving the way for proxy, and later,
direct, wars. The impact is growing disenchantment and resentment among
those who have suffered on account of American military adventures (Mamdani 2004a, 118, 163). In Mamdani's view, these aspects of U.S. foreign policy
must be explained with reference to "Protestant 'fundamentalism' . . . and neoconservatism" as well (2004a, 202).

In short, Mamdani emphasizes that Muslims should not be slotted into
boxes of "good" and "bad" people. Debunking the notion of a premodern culture with a timeless essence, he shows the consequences of the politicization
of culture and explicates the complex intersections of identity formation and
politics.

Certainly, the political culture of the United States itself exhibits considerable diversity, including myriad resistance to government policies at home and
abroad. It can be debated whether Mamdani's indictment of CIA involvement
in external and covert wars gives sufficient scope to the heterogeneity in the
U.S. political landscape. Taking into account dissent, surely various positions
on compelling issues range widely. Additionally, it would be worth investigating
the extent to which Islamic political and religious leaders themselves employ the

language of "good" and "bad" Muslims. More important, Mamdani's incisive critique of U.S. actions raises telling questions about the actual ways in which local phenomena and globalizing processes interact and produce violence.

Globalization, its link with deterritorialization, and the rise of "neofundamentalism" are core concerns in O. Roy's *Globalized Islam* (2004). A French researcher, he joins Mamdani in rejecting a "culturalist" view of Islam wherein religion itself is deemed to be the main force driving violence (2004, 9–12). Whereas Mamdani notes parallels between the ideological language used by Osama bin Laden and George W. Bush in their attempts to justify defeating terror with weapons of terror, thereby rendering ordinary citizens as collateral, O. Roy maintains that in the post–9/11 period, "neofundamentalism" and antiglobalization are both routes for radical protest (2004, 8–9, 49). O. Roy submits that "[n]eofundamentalism is both a product and an agent of globalization" (2004, 258). With globalization, Muslim communities are increasingly spread across the world. Many Muslims are members of diasporic minorities in the states in which they reside and must continually negotiate their identities (2004, 18, 109).

According to O. Roy, owing to a rise of migration, re-Islamization coincides with the ongoing deterritorialization of Islam and a declining state, at least in some regions (2004, 99). Other analysts have also argued that what lies behind the 9/11 attacks is the emergence of armed groups—secular nationalists as well as Islamists—in West Asia, ever more connected across borders. These militants ultimately seek to oust the regimes at the helm of repressive and corrupt states in the Middle East (Halliday 2001). Likewise, O. Roy describes how the "global war on terror" retains a focus on the state, though with the emergence of terrorist networks like Al Qaeda, the state is increasingly contested (2004, 338).

Unlike Mamdani, who locates the problem of political violence in past state-led activities, O. Roy claims that Islamic resurgence is associated with a worldwide community of Muslims but not tied to a particular state or states. His argument is that the relations of societies and persons to religion are in flux inasmuch as globalization disperses communities around the world, albeit within territorial states, even as the principle of territoriality is subject to increasing pressure (O. Roy 2004, 29). This reterritorialization reinforces identification with the ideal of a global Muslim community, or *ummah*, rather than with, or in addition to, a locality.

Distinct from O. Roy and Mamdani, Juergensmeyer posits a rise in worldwide "religious violence," though the concept itself is not clearly defined in his

2003 book. Juergensmeyer provides several case studies as instances of this violence, including the 1993 attack on the World Trade Center and bombings of
abortion clinics in the United States. He claims that the roots of religious conflict lie in "the current forces of geopolitics and in a strain of violence that may
be found at the deepest levels of religious imagination" (Juergensmeyer 2003,
6). Drawing on interviews with leaders and spokespeople of religious movements, Juergensmeyer scrutinizes the logic of the architects and perpetrators of
religious violence. He probes the concept of a "cosmic war" and the reasons that
individuals are willing to kill and die for the sake of their faith (2003, 148–66).
In his account, religion is above all a means to find order among the many uncertainties in the contemporary world (2003, 151).

By linking religion and violence, Juergensmeyer does what both O. Roy and
Mamdani are wary of, namely, tightly connecting these two phenomena. While
there are different types of violence used as political strategies in myriad contexts, Juergensmeyer's religious terrorist is presented as socially marginal. But
still, under similar conditions, why do some people firmly embrace religious
values yet are unlikely to adopt violent measures, whereas others are also pious
and prone to violence? In Juergensmeyer's 2003 book, these thorny questions
remain open.

In the abovementioned analyses of religion and 9/11, violence is a strategy
employed on the margins: for Mamdani, a political response, with an autonomous history in Islam, and used by the weak in the teeth of direct and indirect
U.S. actions; for O. Roy, "neofundamentalism" driven by the deterritorializing
tendencies of globalization and the failure of the state; and for Juergensmeyer,
a religious force in quest for certainty in a geopolitical age of increasing uncertainty. Extrapolating from these accounts, one may read terror as a combination
of phenomena. These are diverse forms of resistance to hyperpower enmeshed
in globalizing forces and deployed by social movements as well as states. But
terror is constructed with different idioms in the state's own representations
and by the actors with whom it engages in combat.

STATE

In the case of the United States, the 2006 National Security Strategy portrays
the "terrorist enemy" as a threat to human rights reminiscent of dangers posed
by adversaries in earlier eras. It likens the "war on terror" to the Cold War. In
both instances, the enemy is said to be totalitarian ideology, which menaces humanity itself (U.S. President 2006, 1). According to George W. Bush, "winning

the war on terror means winning the battle of ideas, for it is ideas that can turn the disenchanted into murderers willing to kill innocent victims" (2006, 9). For the U.S. state in its role as protector of both its own citizens and the public elsewhere, the adversary's ideological commitment to "Islamo-fascism" is the peril to be defeated.[3]

As expressed by the U.S. Office of the Coordinator for Counterterrorism, "it ['the terrorist enemy'] threatens the United States, its allies and interests and the world community" (U.S. Office of the Coordinator for Counterterrorism online). Beating this enemy requires "sound policies, concerted U.S. Government effort, and international cooperation." This mission entails "disaggregation" and "attacking all levels of the threat simultaneously." "The [terrorist] enemy" is defined as a "three-fold threat complex" of leaders, safe havens (including physical sanctuary, cybersanctuaries, and ideological sanctuary), and underlying conditions. In other words, "[t]he enemy is a federated terrorist threat complex with the character of a global insurgency" (U.S. Office of the Coordinator for Counterterrorism online).

This framing of the Other appears repeatedly in government officials' daily statements and written communiqués. For example, in a speech to the U.S. House Armed Services Committee on "Improving Interagency Coordination for the Global War on Terror and Beyond," Coordinator for Counterterrorism Henry A. Crumpton held that "Al Qaeda and affiliated forces" constitute "the greatest threat to the United States, its allies and partners" (Crumpton 2006, 2). The strategy for routing this enemy is to use "calibrated application of all the elements of United States national power: diplomacy, information, intelligence and covert action, economic power, military power, and the rule of law" (2006, 4). Furthermore, the United States must "build trusted networks that undermine, marginalize and isolate the enemy, displace terrorist networks from the societies on which they prey, and empower legitimate alternatives to extremism" (2006, 4). A key component of this strategy is "flexibility," for "our terrorist enemy is highly adaptable" (2006, 7).

Enlisted in this effort are academic institutions that have established courses, certificates, and degrees in homeland security. The Department of Homeland Security and other government agencies offer incentives for these programs and funding for a consortium to coordinate their efforts. For instance, the National Consortium for the Study of Terrorism and Responses to Terrorism (START) is "a center of excellence of the U.S. Department of Homeland Security based at the University of Maryland" (National Consortium for the Study of Terrorism and Responses to Terrorism online). Similarly, the National Academic Consortium for Homeland Security is housed at Ohio State University. The stated goal for Ohio State's Program for International and Homeland Security is to "help improve the security of the nation, while preserving our values, freedoms, and economy" (Ohio State University Program for International and Homeland Security online). There are other such centers, including Syracuse University's Institute for National Security and Counterterrorism (Institute for National Security and Counterterrorism online). The U.S. Department of Homeland Security envisages that "the academic community will play a key role in securing America" (U.S. Department of Homeland Security online; U.S. Department of Homeland Security Office of University Programs 2003).

In this amalgam of knowledge and power, the Self is embedded in academic institutions that maintain a symbiotic relationship with the state. The academy forms part of the complex Self and is engaged in Othering those alleged to mount threats to national and international security. This is acknowledged in the Ohio State program's avowed objectives, namely, to "help align the university's capabilities and resources with the requirements of people and organizations responsible for America's national security" (Ohio State University Program for International and Homeland Security online). Whereas Ohio State calls its course of study "homeland security," universities adopt varied language for similar initiatives; for example, George Mason University offers masters and doctoral degrees in "Biodefense" (George Mason University Molecular and Microbiology Department online).

In fact, there are efforts to harmonize the panoply of academic curricula, think tanks, and training programs on homeland security. This task is assigned to the United States coordinator for counterterrorism and, effective in 2004, the National Counterterrorism Center, which is supposed to bring together all U.S. counterterrorism activities, including military and intelligence-gathering efforts (U.S. National Counterterrorism Center online).

Yet it is not only states that engage in Othering, influence curriculum, instruct personnel, and assemble intelligence. In a training manual, allegedly belonging to a Qaeda cell, found in a house in Manchester, England, in 2000 and entered as evidence in the trial of suspects for the 1998 bombings at the U.S. embassies in Nairobi and Dar es Salaam, the frontispiece bears a picture of a globe with Africa and the Middle East featured prominently in the center and a sword passing through the globe itself (Al-Qaeda 2000, 3). The manual claims that this image is a "declaration of jihad against the country's tyrants" (2000,

3). The Other is framed there not only in opposition to the West and against Western states but also against local "apostate" rulers who took over "the Islamic nation" after 1924, when the "orthodox caliphates" are said to have fallen. These rulers are condemned for jailing young people and trying to eradicate the Muslim nation's identity in an attempt to produce a "wasted generation" of youth—wasted in the sense that this cohort followed only the rulers' way of life (2000, 9–10). Thus represented, the Other is not only the Western countries or even a different religious group but also Muslim rulers corrupted by non-Islamic ideas and who are deemed nonbelievers.

According to the Qaeda manual, the way to respond to the Other parallels the measures called for by states that seek to repel terrorist threats. Al Qaeda urges confronting nonbelievers, both within states and outside them, in "godless and apostate regimes" (Al-Qaeda 2000, 10). In this definition of the Self, or potential members of its ranks, a qualification is that a person must be truly Muslim, not an "unbeliever" (of Christian or Jewish faith), "a secular person," or a "communist" (2000, 15). The member "has to be willing to do the work and undergo martyrdom" (2000, 15). Additional criteria include "listening and obedience," "keeping secrets and concealing information," "patience," and "caution and prudence" (2000, 15–20). Not surprisingly, the text incites "brothers" to act together against "the enemy" (2000, 138). Teamwork is required to defeat the Other, whose identity is based on its role as the initiator of violence.

But there is a fourth 9/11 tale, widely told, about economic resources and who controls them.

ECONOMY

Economic reasons are frequently cited as part of the rationale for waging war. Unlike the three clusters of narratives recounted above, discourses of economy do not take the form of binary distinctions. Rather, given their strategic importance in the "war on terror," material resources are framed as multiple sources of power. This story line plays a vital role in the effort to legitimate war and present the pursuit of conflict as a cause that benefits the world community. In this rendering, violence is linked to market forces. Hence, marginalized areas become pivotal in the quest for energy security. Selves and Others are cast in the guise of economic well-being.

Not only is the discursive economy a key element in the hypercompetitive landscape, but also the panorama of economic resources encompasses wellsprings of hyperpower.

Studies by Harvey (2005) and Bernard Porter (2006) on 9/11 and the aftermath examine the interlocking of hypercompetition and hyperpower in the run-up to hyperconflict, though they do not use this vocabulary. Harvey (2005) investigates how, after 9/11, "new imperialism" relies on both military and non-military means to extend its reach. At the apex of this structure, the United States seeks to not only control oil flows but also optimize its position with respect to reterritorialization—the time and space compression embodied in globalization. Violence is instrumental in these processes. It is manifest in "accumulation by dispossession" wherein capital itself becomes an agent in the acquisition of spaces and territories ("A Conversation with David Harvey" 2006). This form of accumulation is implemented through privatization (of social security, public utilities, and education), the depletion of the global environmental commons, the commodification of culture, and biopiracy ("A Conversation with David Harvey" 2006). As a means of diffusion of power, biopiracy is crucial because it vests knowledge taken from local resources in TNCs, usually without disclosure to the local stakeholders in the contractual relations.

While Harvey emphasizes power over flows of natural resources, Porter traces the historical links between the British empire in the nineteenth century and the era of U.S. "superempire" after 9/11 (B. Porter 2006, 8). He maintains that the U.S. "superempire" has surpassed the British type of empire and has acquired an identity that is *more* than [an empire]" because its cultural, military, and economic reach is increasingly spreading throughout the world (2006, 162; emphasis in original). Moreover, Porter argues that claims to American exceptionalism are without merit if one takes into account the ties between past and present versions of imperial power. Like Harvey, Porter peers into the discourses of global economy to explain how neoliberal support for the expansion of capital and neoconservative relish for the ideals of freedom and democracy are aligned. Both authors arrive at the interconnectedness of neoliberal and neoconservative positions in the "global war on terror."

Although these prisms cast analytical light on 9/11 and the "war on terror," there are limitations. If the concept of imperialism and its "neo" variant suggest straight administrative control, they should also be robust in disclosing indirect and more subtle mechanisms. Additionally, the notion of empire is West-centric insofar as it fails to make known non-Western forms, as in the history of China, Japan, parts of Africa, and elsewhere, where hierarchies of power were organized differently. By comparison, the multidimensional concept of hyperpower, which includes intersubjectivity, is more compelling than a hard-nosed notion of imperial rule. The construct of hyperpower has the advantage of joining relational and structural forms of power. Hyperpower is a more fluid and flexible approach than imperialism or empire. It allows for the ways that political and economic forces seek to expand networks of coercion, and opens to interactions with hypercompetition, which cheapens the production of weapons as well as their transportation and requisites in communication.

That said, it is worth extrapolating from Harvey's and Porter's looks at 9/11 and the "war on terror" to see that the rise of hypercompetition along with a plunge in energy security imbue oil reserves with the symbolic meaning of strength. Control of oil resources is a staple of hyperpower. Fierce competition for oil is for the sake of fueling production and economic growth, and to bolster the symbol of hyperpower.

Hyperpower thus relies on both direct and indirect forms of power. Among the indirect forms are those that operate through international institutions. Many IMF and World Bank programs, for example, have purchase over natural resources, in some instances leading to privatization and vertical integration in agroindustrial corporations. On the margins, this move transforms daily life, as with small family farms.

The margins are not only outside the Self of hyperpower but also inside it. The Other is denied. There are efforts to silence her voices. Yet differences are integral to the Self insofar as they provide resources and spaces for the expansion of hyperpower. Building on this notion of the Self and Others, let us now turn to gendered constructions of 9/11 and the "war on terror."

GENDER

The four sets of narratives scrutinized above are mainly about the acts performed by men. Women are largely sidelined or rendered invisible. Hence, Juergensmeyer forthrightly identifies the social groups in his research: "What they have in common, these movements of cowboy monks, is that they consist of anti-institutional, religio-nationalist, racist, sexist, male-bonding, bomb-throwing young guys" (Juergensmeyer 2003, 210).[4] He submits that women have not traditionally played a major role in militant religious organizations (2003, 199). Similarly, men are typically portrayed as the ones who commit violence, and women are those who suffer from it. But this framing fails to capture multiple identities among both men and women during times of conflict and in the "war on terror."

In waging the "war on terror," U.S. government officials justify military policies as serving the cause of women's liberation. Mediated images of Afghan women clad in *burqa* (an all-enveloping outer garment with a small opening for the eyes covered by a net) and Iraqis in *hijab* (headscarves) signify sharp cultural differences. Featured prominently in these representations are the bodies of Muslim women. Pictured are the ways in which Islam reputedly debases women. The claim to liberate oppressed Muslim women from the Taliban and Sadaam Hussein's barbarity validates the military invasions and occupations of the U.S.-led "coalition of the willing." In this representation, veiling symbolizes pervasive threats from both the faith-based and secular Other, thereby homogenizing Muslim women (Zine 2006).

This issue has sparked controversies in Europe over the cultural practices of migrants and the successor generations. In an anticipation of this contention, Frantz Fanon (1965) and Edward Said (1979) disclosed ways in which veiled Muslim women are inscribed in the Western imagination as particular kinds of subjects and objects of desire. Subsequently, the "war on terror" revived Orientalized discourses about women and casts them as victims of the machinations of Islam.

Supposedly showing the way forward are strong Western women, liberated professionals in top policymaking positions. Women who exercise power, like secretaries of state Hillary Clinton and Condoleezza Rice and, before the "war on terror," Madeleine Albright, respect male hierarchies and really want peace. But they do not shy away from hard decisions about the use of force and help socialize other women into their roles as soldiers and civil servants. Women have thus become an integral part of the U.S. armed forces. In fact, Rice was characterized as "Bush's secret weapon," "the one who is always in the room when George W. Bush makes the tough calls" (*Newsweek*, December 16, 2002, as cited in Chenoy 2004, 30). And in encouraging partners to strengthen their positions in military globalization, Rice counseled, "The United States invites—indeed, we exhort—our freedom loving allies, such as those in Europe, to increase their military capabilities" (Rice 2002, 6, as quoted in Chenoy 2004, 29).

Distinct from this masculine-themed standpoint, feminist narratives of 9/11 and the "war on terror" divulge the tendency to render women indistinct except as victims or passive beings that need to be rescued from the scourge of war. Marginalizing female voices and reflecting the argument that an invasion and occupation would liberate women, U.S. political authorities and the media alike offer gendered images as a means to legitimize war, a fight to save these victims from lifetimes of suffering. The U.S.-led "coalition of the willing" are saviors whose ranks include their own warrior women (Hawthorne and Winter 2003; Hunt and Rygiel 2006).

Another theme in feminist narratives of 9/11 is the emphasis on the masculinized character of U.S. foreign policy itself. Thus, Cynthia Enloe (2003) delineates the increasing militarization of Washington's approach to foreign relations and takes it to task for giving little attention to feminist questions about war and violence. She claims that America often advises officials in other countries about remaking their cultures without acknowledging that its own political culture is based on masculinized presumptions that shape its foreign policies (Enloe 2003, 288). Other observers, too, evince ways in which George W. Bush relied on tropes and badges of masculinity, such as cowboy expressions of speech and military attire, in order to demonstrate that the United States is strong and will stand up to its foes (Ruby 2003, 177; Shepherd 2006, 21–25).

Arundhati Roy (2004, 71–72) also considers the masculinity of the United States in the ways in which the state commits violence directed at women and ethnic minorities. Unlike Huntington, who views the margins as sources of violence and destabilization, A. Roy notices the means by which the most powerful state itself can perpetrate violence. She blames imperial powers (Britain and the United States), along with the media and international organizations, for producing insecurities worldwide and paving the way for 9/11. Further, A. Roy seeks to elicit voices that cannot be heard on a global stage and calls for protests against U.S. "neo-imperialism" (2004, 93). Yet in this account, it is not clear what actions precipitate these protests and who will organize them. Her plea that "we" have to challenge imperialism through collective action is vague about the unitary "we" (2004, 94).

An additional aspect of feminist analysis of the framings of 9/11 is the effort to shed light on calls by U.S. authorities for a "state of emergency." These rallying cries respond to a momentous and tragic event but deflect attention from the insecurities suffered by men and women in their daily lives (MacKinnon 2003). Hence, Catherine MacKinnon depicts gendered ideology as follows: "acts of violence against women are regarded not as exceptional but inevitable, even banal, in an unexceptional context, hence beyond no pale" (MacKinnon 2006, 3). The providence of battered wives, forcibly recruited sex workers, and low-wage earners who face myriad dangers is obscured in the general, largely undifferentiated image of women on offer to the public during the "war on terror" (Shepherd 2006, 25). While it is being fought, women in many parts of the world encounter arduous problems finding jobs and surviving in zones of pervasive poverty and amid local conflicts; but these difficulties are eclipsed in representations of the exceptional nature of terrorist violence. In this setting, women are framed as "passive objects and orientalized victims" while the hardships in their daily toil do not appear in the structure of analysis (Youngs 2006, 12).

As discussed in Chapters 3 and 5, Schmitt ([1932] 1996, [1950] 2003) and Agamben (1999, 2005) contend that during severe conflicts, sovereign states convert exceptions into the norm and then, with the onset of peace, maintain the provisions implemented in exceptional times. Extending beyond this argument to include diverse actors, feminist narratives show that the reverse proposition applies to the fate of many women: the very basis of normal life is itself exceptional in its potential for violence.

Feminist narratives of 9/11 restore layers of complexity in men's and women's identities, stripped away in mainstream representations. For example, feminist writers explore the gendered account of 9/11 and "terror" directed *at the West*. Occidentalism portrays the West as replete with permissiveness and moral decay. Inasmuch as the lack of control of womanhood debases Occidental society, heroic warriors in the Islamic world are incited to violence to rectify this rampant depravity. For their courageous acts, male martyrs are assured that they will receive sexual recompense in paradise. Thus, narrative and counternarrative alike construct gendered representations of 9/11. It is posited that on opposing sides of the conflict, patriarchal hierarchies are driving gendered contentions. In feminist accounts, 9/11 and the ensuing "war" signify the clash of gendered orders and reflect a "globalization of gender politics" (Tickner 2002, 338–39, 348).

Various streams of feminism also center attention on agency, seen not merely in terms of a stark division between the powerful and powerless but as a more complex series of interactions among people. For example, Judith Butler's concept of agency includes transformative potential within itself, thus providing a site for critique and resistance (Magnus 2006, 81). Butler (2004, 2005) views agency as a liberating force and not merely an effect of oppressive power. Her conception of transformation denotes an "ethics of responsibility" wherein social conditions and subjects are interrelated (Magnus 2006, 92). She indicates that subjects are products of the societies and cultures in which they are embedded (Butler 2004, 45). Thus, social beings are always oriented toward a "you" (Butler 2004, 45). Ethics are neither simply symptoms of social conditions nor values that transcend these conditions. They are part of the everyday order and arise out of daily practices. Responsibility to the Other becomes a collective action and not only a personal matter. The Other is therefore required to make sense of Ourselves and societies. Butler argues that the "I" needs a "you" to come into being, and adds that this "you" is also dependent on a set of sociocultural norms that allow each to recognize the plurality's existence (Butler 2004, 45).

Reading sovereign power as a constellation of tactics, Butler calls for an ethical answer to alleviate the plight of those whom the state categorizes as different and dangerous. Linking ethics to the exigencies of the "global war on terror," she urges her audience to rise to the challenge of an ethical intervention and proposes an understanding and practice of ethics in the face of increasing violence and mourning (Butler 2004). But for Butler this appeal is social, not only individually based: "Our responsibility does not pertain merely to the purity [of] our souls, but to the whole of the commonly inhabited world" (Butler 2003, 114, as cited in Magnus 2006, 94).

Precise details may not be found in Butler's ethical aspirations for a peaceful order. Specificity about the "ethics of responsibility" is elusive, likely because readers themselves are agents responsible for determining the content—the "you" that is necessary to recognize the existence of the subject. Serving as an interlocutor exhorting an ethical answer to Otherness, Butler attempts to elicit an active intervention grounded in norms distinct from the values encoded in predominant policies.

By enjoining mindfulness of ethical responsibility toward Others, Butler shuns oppositional identities. She emphasizes interdependence among subjects. This nuance in reasoning and the ability to pose questions silenced by mainstream discourses, whether focused on binary choices or grand narratives, are among the contributions of feminist analysis of both 9/11 and the ensuing "war on terror."

THE MARGINS AND VIOLENCE

Striking then is the extraordinary range of narratives of 9/11. Yet common to them are the contentious issues of marginalization and violence in a globalizing world. Should the margins be regarded as spaces of encounter and confrontation? Should they be tolerated, absorbed, or eliminated? Are there alternative ways to deal with differences? To answer these questions, let us briefly revisit each of the five stories about 9/11 and draw out the pertinent points.

National identities of the Self and Other render the latter as opponents or menaces. Difference is seen as pernicious, and Othering has a noxious quality, threatening the safety and security of the national Self. This optic accommodates division as a policy option. Hence, Huntington justifies the need for enemies as natural—it is rooted in the "human condition and psychology" (Huntington 2004, 27). He claims that growing numbers of new immigrants change the relationship between state and society and may produce disorder. His narrative locates an oppositional identity within the territorial state, jeopardizing the unity of the state. The enemy is a presence not like "us." In this duality, each identity—American and Mexican, the equivalent of American and Muslim—is deemed homogeneous. The margins are perilous, disruptive, and potentially violent. Nonetheless, they enable the dominant majority to affirm its Self-definition.

In the construction of religious identity, whether the Other is nurtured or targeted for annihilation, difference remains at issue. As indicated, both Mamdani (2004a) and O. Roy (2004) delimit the political and historical conditions that marginalized Islam in Western minds (and conversely, sometimes the West in Islamic perspectives). The narrative scorned by Mamdani and O. Roy—Islam as an enemy animated by premodern elements, to be contained by a mix of coercion, dialogue, and friendship—is prevalent in the post–9/11 period. By using Culture Talk and the refrain that firmly links religion and violence, this narrative builds the image of political Islam as hostile to world order and as evil. This latter framing is especially evident in George W. Bush's mantra about "Islamic fascists" as adversaries of the United States.

In this vein, Juergensmeyer dwells on actions said to be driven by religion, thus framing religion as an autonomous force that offers an enemy for war (2003, 174). An enemy is needed, and if one is not obviously present, then it must be produced (2003, 174). The margins of exclusion are invented. Sovereign power can either incorporate or eradicate them. Like the identities in the first narrative, the margins in the second one are sources of danger, disorder, and insecurity.

The margins figure prominently in counterterrorism programs. In the United States, an institutional framework of think tanks, institutes and centers at universities, and the Department of Homeland Security forms a weblike structure. It constitutes a network that has a contagion effect, disseminating images within the United States and overseas through instruments such as public diplomacy, radio and television, and the Internet, all of which identify threats, name them (read "terror"), and downgrade other challenges.

This manner of describing the margins, as well as the discursive machinery that enables it, are both inside and outside the territorial boundaries of the Self. Both states and terrorists themselves frame threats. Violence is purportedly fostered by those who threaten: for the United States and its allies, it is terrorists abetted by rogue states; for Al Qaeda, it is a decadent West and nonbelievers. For opposing forces alike, the means to counter threats is through confrontation, often involving violence. The contagion thus operates as meanings diffused in the form of reinforcing narratives propagated by both states and terrorists. While differences are fluid and cross borders, they are increasingly met by similarity in the form of cooperative ventures among allies who seek to eliminate enemies by relying on armed violence.

In an extended formulation, another state narrative casts the margins in terms of the imperial Self. The margins are arenas where imperial identities form, locales where "accumulation by dispossession" must be secured. But generally missing from this lens is how Others see the United States (and Britain) as an imperial Self. The margins, in this prism, are used for the expansionary aims of the Self. Relatedly, the conception of violence itself, while broadened from focusing on military violence or violence based on religious identities, is centered on capitalist accumulation. Margins, in this narrative, are pivotal in that they are sites for spatial enlargement and objects of coercion by the imperial Self in the "global war on terror."

Finally, feminists look at the margins not wholly as anomalies, antitheses, or candidates for obliteration and compulsion into sameness. Rather, their narratives allow for multiple identity formations and caution against homogenized versions of Selves and Others. As with national identity and religion-based representations, feminism locates the margins in relation to conflict. But for feminists, the distinction is that the margins also have the potential to become agents of transformation. In addition, feminism stresses that margins are not separate and outside states. Rather, daily lives encompass violence.

Thus, Butler holds that feminism is able to call up resources to understand and contend with vulnerability (2004, 42). The impact of this ability lies in transforming relations between Selves and Others in both the operations of sovereign power and daily life. But which resources are enlisted in this process? To extend Butler's analysis, they would be the capacity to see Ourselves in the Other and, conversely, to discover and recognize the Other in Ourselves (Der Derian 1987, 209).

This point qualifies earlier writings on friends and enemies. For instance, in his extension of Schmitt's concept of the state of exception, Agamben offers keen insights, and his lens takes in elements of the margins. He focuses on "man," a symbolic figure of all humanity, without explicitly focusing on women (Edkins 2000). Agamben's analysis is furthered by feminist scholars who write about the exclusion of the feminine from the military sphere (Pin-Fat and Stern 2005, 33). They note a specific conception of the feminine, namely, that protection is necessary and constitutive of war and military spheres, both of which are depicted as mainly masculinized activities (Pin-Fat and Stern 2005).

By simplifying gender relations in such ways, sovereign power portrays the feminine as an Other that maintains the masculinized image of the state and its military power. At the same time, the masculinized identity of the military itself is unstable and must be constantly reinforced, as in a patriotic moment in 2003 when U.S. Army Rangers and Navy Seals stormed into enemy territory in Iraq to rescue injured, nineteen-year-old Private Jessica Lynch (Pin-Fat and Stern 2005). Saved by male heroes, Lynch provided a feminized image incorporated in the governing narrative of the "war on terror."[5]

The story about Private Lynch points to the ways in which military power and social relations are interrelated (Chapter 3). As noted, Foucault claimed that power relations in society are established through force and that politics continues war through other means (2003, 15). In his view, war takes place in everyday life and is a regular feature of society. The state militarizes war, and war becomes the space where states define themselves. So too for Schmitt: the political ever entails violence. A perpetual possibility, war is a means to secure order. Sovereign power requires militarized violence. This pattern is explicitly evinced in state and terrorist narratives on violence and in the diffusion of official views of security. Both states and terrorists seek to use instruments of power to ingrain their own meanings of the "global war on terror."

However, for Foucault, insecurity is also part of the production of ongoing relations between power holders and subjects. Insecurity arises within relations of power, where those who are deemed dangerous, different, or terrorist are categorized and disciplined. Biopower is exercised at the individual, societal, and sovereign levels.

While Foucault adopts a perspective from below (2003, 96), Schmitt is concerned with maintaining order. Yet Foucault and Schmitt alike reject universalized representations of friends and enemies, call for contextualized analysis, and concentrate on changing relations among state, society, and violence. And Foucault, like feminists, Butler included, views the margins as positions within power relations where Others are encountered. The margins are more than sites of insecurity but bear potential for critique, resistance, and transformation. They are spaces where agents may craft political strategies. In these arenas, translations of conventional lifeways are made; new meanings, forged.

The meanings of marginalization and insecurity are inextricably bound up with gathering hyperconflict. The narratives of 9/11 assessed in this chapter variously represent the margins as threats, vulnerability, and sites of potential transformation. They constitute a changing *nomos* of disorder and reorientation. Do these stories about terror, a kind of riposte to and of stateless attackers, then become a metaphor for the dark side of globalization? This question cannot be answered with certitude. But the uncertainty itself is without an end in sight and conjures images of perpetual war for perpetual peace. In thinking about what lies ahead, let us now reflect further on the junction of hyperpower and hypercompetition: hyperconflict and its implications for the world at large.

8 POSTNATIONAL SECURITY

This conclusion revisits key scholarly literature, traces the book's main themes, and indicates what the concepts developed in the preceding discussion capture that others have not. In so doing, the task is to consolidate responses to the questions that guide this research: What are the relationships between globalization and security or insecurity? What are the implications for future world order? And is the idea of perpetual peace more compelling or less so in a globalizing world order?

The basis of my answer to each query is that the economic spearhead of hypercompetition and the political spearhead of hyperpower point in the direction of hyperconflict. Grounded in case studies, this proposition leads to a layered explanation of the interactions between globalization and insecurity.

The cases show evolving combinations of hypercompetition and hyperpower whose ingredients are incorporated in a conceptual map of hyperconflict. Not a singular phenomenon, hyperconflict is a dynamic formation of multiple kinds of insecurity. Although both hypercompetition and hyperpower involve concentration and hierarchy over expanded space, these structures touch down in varied ways so as to provoke resistance from a host of actors.

Let us now turn to how this reframing and evidence may be used to set forth scenarios for world order.

THE ROSY VIEW

The approach presented here draws on the rosy view characteristic of empirical studies of war and peace.[1] While presenting an optimistic picture, scholars in this tradition offer gradations of interpretation. They differ on methodological issues: time frames, subcategories of conflict, thresholds of deaths, and coding procedures. The strengths of this genre of research are sophistication with quantitative techniques and subtle analysis of data within its given parameters of inquiry. By all indications, these data-collection activities are a growth industry in the "scientific discipline of the study of war" (Sarkees and Singer 2001, 3). Following is an overview of and commentary on a sample of them.

The Correlates of War (COW) project, established by J. David Singer in 1963, provides a database on the incidence of war from 1816 to 1997. In an update of the earlier categories in this project, Sarkees, Wayman, and Singer (2003) constructed a typology of interstate, intrastate, and extrastate wars. (Whereas the first two forms are self-evident, the latter takes place between a territorial state and a nonsovereign actor outside the state.) Considering one thousand battle deaths per episode as the threshold, the authors conclude that since the time of Napoleon, the risk in battle is trending neither upward nor downward, though the frequency within the three categories fluctuates (Sarkees, Wayman, and Singer 2003, 65). Nonetheless, the unit of reference for all these categories remains the territorial state in its different dimensions (2003, 59).

Other scholars specializing in the incidence of armed conflict quarrel with the COW definitions and findings. From the vantage point of the International Peace Research Institute, Oslo (PRIO) as well as the Uppsala Conflict Data Program (UCDP) and its associates, the COW dataset incorporates incompatible costs in deaths in its categories. The number of deaths in *interstate* conflict accounts for direct battle deaths (combatants and civilians who perished in the fighting), whereas the *intrastate* grouping records total deaths, including those caused by famine, disease, and genocide (Lacina, Gleditsch, and Russett 2006).

In their own data-gathering and analysis, Lacina and Gleditsch conclude that "[b]attle violence has declined significantly over the past 50 years due to a decline in major interstate conflict and large internationalised civil conflicts" (Lacina and Gleditsch 2005, 146). Yet their optimism is tempered by the fact that the number of fatalities caused by humanitarian crises exceeded the lives taken in armed combat (2005, 158).

Using the UCDP dataset, Harbom, Högbladh, and Wallensteen, scholars based at Uppsala University who work in collaboration with PRIO, classify conflicts as intrastate, international intrastate, or interstate. The levels of intensity are designated minor, intermediate, or war. Their survey of armed conflicts around the world also provides sanguine findings: "In 2005, there were 31 ongoing armed conflicts in 22 locations. The highest number of armed conflicts was recorded in 1991 and 1992, with 51 conflicts active. Thus, the overall trend since the early 1990s has been that of a marked, steep decline" (Harbom, Högbladh, and Wallensteen 2006, 617).

Also in this genre is the Political Instability Task Force (PITF), a panel of analysts and methodologists originally formed at the invitation of the U.S. government.[2] The PITF focuses on the post–World War II period and employs a two-level threshold to measure armed conflict: a mobilization benchmark of one thousand or more people (armed agents, demonstrators, troops) and a conflict intensity threshold of at least one thousand direct conflict-related deaths with a minimum of one year when the number of conflict-related fatalities exceeds one hundred (Marshall, Gurr, and Harff 2001).

In the PITF *Peace and Conflict 2005* report, Marshall and Gurr share PRIO and UCDP's rosy outlook: "Despite the prevailing sense of global insecurity, the positive trends traced in previous editions of this report have continued in early 2005" (Marshall and Gurr 2005, 1). While hailing the decline in interstate and intrastate conflict, the authors caution that the "globalization of conflict processes" includes new threats, especially from terrorism and weak states (2005, 28). Linked to this report is mention of "systemic strains" brought by global inequality (Marshall and Goldstone 2007, 12).

An even rosier view is found in the *Human Security Report 2005*, which derives data from the UCDP/PITF datasets. This study documents that the number of armed conflicts involving a government fell by more than 40 percent between 1992 and 2003. The deadliest conflicts, defined as at least one thousand battle deaths, plummeted by 80 percent during this period. War-exacerbated diseases and malnutrition caused the largest death tolls (Mack 2006). By delving into both direct and indirect deaths in armed conflicts, this report thus provides a helpful source for policy-oriented research.

Undoubtedly, empirical studies of the magnitude of worldwide conflict and the trends are valuable, up to a point. The main emphases in this type of inquiry are rigorous measurement and quantifiable evidence. Taking another step, the PITF project registers concern about the trajectory in a "globalization era." And the COW research includes an autocritique: "given our preoccupation with inter-state war engaging the major powers plus the minor powers belonging to the central system (largely European), it was natural that our system membership criteria would be not only state-centric, but to a considerable extent, Euro-centric as well" (Sarkees and Singer 2001, 7).

In addition, what needs to be taken into account are contraindications: signs that a flat or downward trend in armed conflict may not actually exist or is discontinuous. For one, the World Bank's Independent Evaluation Group (IEG) offers less-than-rosy findings. Although its categories are open to challenge (Chapter 2), especially when hybrid actors of statelike and nonstate groups such as Hezbollah render the basis of the taxonomies themselves increasingly problematic, the IEG reports that the number of poorly governed "fragile" states grew from seventeen to twenty-six between 2003 and 2006 (World Bank Independent Evaluation Group 2006). These countries are said to be characterized by "weak security" and represent major threats to peace and stability. Misrule, a breakdown in law, corruption, and a lack of legitimacy can cascade, spreading risk and conflict to other countries.

Another less-than-sanguine analysis emerges from the 2007 Global Peace Index, mounted by the Economist Intelligence Unit in collaboration with an international team of experts (Vision of Humanity 2007). They explore the texture of domestic and international peacefulness on the basis of twenty-four indicators, such as a country's level of military expenditure, relations with its neighbors, and the degree of respect for human rights. Conspicuous is the position of the lead power: the United States ranked 96, between Yemen and Iran, among 121 countries on this scale (Vision of Humanity 2007). Rated highest were Norway, New Zealand, Denmark, Ireland, and Japan; and lowest (from the bottom up), Iraq, Sudan, Israel, Russia, and Nigeria. From the standpoint of this book, the figure that stands out is the score of the United States, given the impact of hyperpower, especially with the rise in U.S. and global defense spending.

World military expenditure topped one trillion dollars in 2005, representing a 34 percent increase during the period 1996–2005, when the United States alone was responsible for 80 percent of the spike (Stockholm International Peace Research Institute [SIPRI] 2006). At 4 percent of GDP in 2006, U.S. defense spending came in ahead of the United Kingdom's (2.6 percent), the next highest, and China's (2.1 percent) (SIPRI 2008, 178). The worldwide figure reached $1.339 trillion in 2007, with U.S. expenditure, including its supplemental spending for Iraq and Afghanistan, up 59 percent since 2001 (SIPRI 2008, 175). This rise is linked to an arms race under the banner of the "war on terror," American plans to establish a missile defense shield in parts of Europe, and sustained military buildups in China and India, though in percentage terms commensurate with these two countries' economic growth.

In addition, the question of texture arises when one considers qualitative studies that allude to violent currents at odds with social scientists' quantitative descriptions. Eric Hobsbawn (2002) and Niall Ferguson (2006, xxxiv), distinguished historians of very different persuasions, straightforwardly state that the twentieth century was the most lethal in modern history, and they do not foresee a reversal. While statisticians and other international relations scholars may dispute their claim and query the sources of data (compare Levy 1983), the point is that there is hardly cast-iron evidence or firm agreement to sustain the happy view.

The numbers clearly matter but do not tell the whole story. While armed conflict bears tangible and supreme consequences, it is important to highlight problems in accounts centered on tallying it. Indeed, the data are coded with layers of perception and meaning.

Through dark-tinted rather than rose-colored glasses, one might express misgivings about the standard interpretations of the trend line. The empirical projects on armed conflict cited above recycle large amounts of information. As helpful as the quantitative data are, descriptive statistics have their limitations. They treat conflict in so objective a manner that they silence thorny issues. Apart from the frequency of different types of conflict are the matters of the depth of conflicts and structural shifts. The databases noted above leave out crucial elements, including some forms of violence, such as rape as a specific instrument of war, and the intersubjective side of insecurity. It is vital to open to genres of qualitative research that probe the interplay between the objective and subjective dimensions of globalization and security. After all, in our times, how can one assess these phenomena without bringing in the role of ideational frameworks such as neoliberalism and neoconservatism?

Debates about the threshold of armed conflict—one gun fired, one hundred people wounded, one thousand people lost in direct battle or battle-related deaths—should be joined to countervailing analyses of world order. The evidence adduced in the "scientific discipline of the study of war" is telling but, as noted, linear. It would be mistaken to jump straight from these kinds of data to the future. Let us now shift to the central theses of this book as a point of departure for thinking about future world order.

THE CONCEPT OF HYPERCONFLICT REVISITED

The term "hyperconflict" captures what other vocabulary has not, namely, the dynamics of acute insecurity. This approach brings to light the production of insecurity. It directs attention to questions about why it happens and how its mechanisms operate. These issues not only join structure and agency but also identify winners and losers in globalizing processes. Hyperconflict thus encompasses much more than conflict as conventionally understood.

Held together by the mutual attraction of hypercompetition and hyperpower, hyperconflict is an evolving galaxy containing social power relations and historical narratives. As argued, mistaking its parts for the whole frequently occurs because of the urgent life-and-death matters at stake in quelling specific conflicts. It is worth stepping back and recognizing the range of traps and confusions: being blind to hyperconflict, exaggerating the concept, or being drawn into a refrain of "War Talk" in lieu of crafting a sober analysis.

Hyperconflict first arises when the interstate balance of power is unsteady and a medley of nonstate actors both accommodates and more assertively resists state initiatives. Merging with local conditions, hyperconflict is given to various permutations in different locales, and globalization renders it increasingly pervasive in the twenty-first century. Expedited by technological innovations, lowered barriers across national frontiers, and the cheapening of weapons, globalization multiplies the risks of, and enlarges the market for, coercion, even when it does not take the form of armed conflict. Consequently, hyperconflict is much more than an episodic condition.

In this milieu, Kant's concept of permanent peace must be considered in light of evolving structures. The balance of forces favors perpetual competition, induces a state of perpetual emergency, and sows perpetual fear. Nontraditional threats, including climate change, pandemics, transnational crime, and cross-border terror emanate from above and below the nation-state. Thus, there cannot be a neat separation between national and global security. Nor is there a sharp division between internal and external security. Sundry threats at home have extraterritorial dimensions. Among them are financial flows and other mobile connections between diasporas and homelands, as well as between the environment and humankind.

Uganda's president Yoweri Museveni gave voice to this point when he described climate change as "the latest form of aggression" by rich countries against Africa (as quoted in Kristof 2007). He referred to the amply documented facts that emissions—in the form of greenhouse gases—and other environmental harms from affluent nations, as well as from countries closing in on their ranks, cause crop failure and famine, the spread of deserts, and the contraction of lakes. The shrinking of glaciers in mountainous regions could be cited as well. As a result, it is vulnerable, impoverished populations that starve.

They have little or nothing on which to fall back. Their insecurities can result in intensified competition over scarce resources, in some contexts leading to death and escalating into war.

With the transcendence of borders and the blurring of temporal and spatial boundaries, the categories of war and peace are not clear-cut. They blend, calling to mind an Orwellian dystopia in which these conditions are hard to distinguish. Without completely conflating war and peace, it is possible to note a convergence of their elements. Likewise, national security and global security, often regarded as counterpoints, are becoming a single stream. This rapidly evolving configuration may be best described as *postnational security*.

Although the holders of state power doggedly try to monopolize the legitimate use of force, or to authorize their agents to employ it, they encounter several forms of resistance from nonstate actors and gradually suffer a loss of control. In the quest for national security, a double gap emerges in security and credibility. To fill it, heads of state attempt to reassert sovereign power. But how can statesmen and stateswomen restrain opponents whose threats do not conform to their logic and who challenge the state system itself? As Beck poignantly asks, By deterring suicide bombers with threats of death? By deploying the means of power to conquer a territory when the perpetrators of attacks are stateless and not rooted in a particular territory (Beck [2004] 2006, 139)?[3] All the while touting their unremitting devotion to freedom and peace, the agents of state power suspend certain laws, trespass civil liberties, and use the bully pulpit to refashion the supposed identities of friends and enemies. Increasingly, a state of exception becomes unexceptional. Ontological security is drastically diminished.

Insecurities are rife. They pertain to military and nonmilitary aspects of conflict. Irregular forms of fighting (such as suicide bombing and the use of satellite and cellular phones and handheld navigation devices) are prevalent, and nonmilitary means such as cyber and space warfare expand conflict beyond the conventional battlefield (U.S. National Intelligence Council 2008, 71). Hyperconflict turns into a seemingly chronic condition.

Alerting people to this situation may jerk them out of their complacency and delusions. This awareness is potentially unsettling because they are conditioned to think differently. After all, enormous intellectual and political power has been trained on micro conflicts, especially the conflicts *du jour*. Focusing on such discrete events rarely catches a glimpse of the big picture. Many policy analysts have framed questions about instantaneous time, the here-and-now, without adopting a longer historical and structural perspective. This shortcoming is acute when it comes to grasping the problems of (in)security in what defense planners and some scholars view as the connections between liberal democracy and the "fringes" of world order.

For example, when the United States and its allies named a welter of states as failed or failing on the grounds that they do not control the use of force, deliver basic services, or maintain legitimacy, Washington promptly bracketed quite dissimilar situations, such as Somalia, Iraq, Sudan, and Venezuela, in a supposedly ordered whole. Analytically, the category became hollow (as elaborated in Chapter 2). The figurative term "failed state" identifies failure as the weakness of the state itself, not the linkages between local dynamics and external support for authoritarian and corrupt regimes, the political role of TNCs, the global arms market, the policy framework of neoliberalism, the mandate of structural adjustment, or the debt trap. Locating the cause of ills in certain countries as state failure, weakening, or warlords and leaving it at that is a means to validate state-building and, in the case of Iraq, invasion and occupation. This state-centric view diverts attention from state-society dynamics (Simpson 2007). It also neglects the global shift in temporal and spatial boundaries. Compared to the woolly construct of "failed states," the notion of "margins" better captures multiple relationships between globalizing tendencies and insecurity.

INTERACTIONS

A fresh perspective may thus be summoned by analyzing large-scale processes. These must be seen in conjunction with the ways in which they connect to local conditions to form an archipelago of conflicts. Without doing so, the effort to focus on broad patterns is fraught. The task is to comprehend the structures in play and their interactions with varied dynamics on the ground in different zones. This requires multisited research so as to take into account diverse historical and cultural roots.

The place to begin such work is at the more general level and with the proposition advanced at the start of this book: the combination of hypercompetition and hyperpower inclines toward hyperconflict. This conception views hypercompetition as a structure that is more aggressive and destabilizing than the benign economic force depicted in mainstream thinking. Meanwhile, hypercompetition's counterpart in geopolitics is derived from French post–Cold War thinking. But as illustrated in Chapter 1, hyperpower goes beyond the reductive notion that a sole state itself is capable of dominating the global political economy.

Distinct from the French usage of this word as X having power over Y, hyperpower is better understood by melding the Gramscian sense of hegemonic power as including ideational factors and Foucauldian biopower as politically bridging public and private space (for example, in regard to bodily sites, as illustrated in Chapters 3 and 7). The United States is the dominant locus of hyperpower but not synonymous with it. Elements of hyperpower, such as an extensive network of overseas military bases, a coterie of allies, and cultural resources, notably the widespread use of the American version of the English language, enwrap large swaths of the globe.

Although both Gramscians and postmodernists might object to this synthesis, I stake my claim on the ground that the categories and arguments in this book elucidate what others do not. And to avoid misunderstanding, it is well to underline that "hyper" is neither a rhetorical flourish nor a mere extension of prior conditions. It is an analytical tool that provides insights into political and economic transformations constituted in and by globalizing forces.

The synergy between hypercompetition and hyperpower manifests in four ways. First, both processes involve transnational concentration and hierarchy stretching over global space. Second, the ideologies of neoliberalism and neoconservatism are employed to legitimate them. As indicated, they also overlap, forming neoliberal conservatism, which is in flux. Third, the impact of this combination of forces is felt keenly in marginalized zones. Deepening poverty in these regions spurs a displacement of population that aggravates conflict within and across national borders, as in Darfur, Sudan, and the neighboring countries of the Central African Republic and Chad. With demographic pressure and a shortage of resources, violence offers one of few opportunities for material gain. In some impoverished countries, youth experience life as a cauldron of violence absent other options. For the young and adults alike, this path may lead to criminality, which in a globalizing world comprises networks that span national frontiers. Transcending national space, too, are feelings of indignity and fatalism characteristic of not only the poorest countries but also certain diasporic groups residing in the West.

Fourth, then, this convergence of forces deeply affects developed countries. Some transnational criminal elements do business with terrorists targeting the West as well as its citizens and allies overseas. Terrorists are a clientele for criminals, whose aim, after all, is to make a profit. Plus, there is a chasm between the rich and the poor within the West, where conflict is increasingly apparent among classes. In the United States, this gap is growing so rapidly that it may be unbridgeable. Between 1990 and 2002, every additional tax dollar earned by the bottom 90 percent of Americans was matched by $18,000 received by each taxpayer in the top bracket (Herbert 2005). Tax cuts enacted after 2002 under President George W. Bush primarily benefited taxpayers with the highest incomes. Meanwhile, heightened globalization has encompassed American workers. The effects include rising competition with workers overseas in the form of outsourcing of jobs, an increased presence of immigrant workers at home, a drop in manufacturing, and the weakening of trade unions (Herbert 2005). Fewer Americans are sufficiently insulated from these insecurities.

In aggregate, the impact of insecurity can be wrenching. The mix of factors is volatile, though the eruptions need not emerge in one volcanic explosion.

Having argued that there is a convergence phenomenon, I want to say emphatically that it would be wrong to engage in any kind of reductionism or determinism. There are multitiered encounters between the macro elements and micro dynamics. The connections are intricately bound up with a particular time and place. Rather than producing an inflexible formula for delimiting the interactions of hypercompetition and hyperpower, the four cases presented in this book are historical markers and portents of a brewing storm. They are harbingers of hyperconflict.

Conceivably, conflicts could simply follow or simultaneously parallel one another, seemingly without interconnections. However, with new technologies, information and ideas about conflict easily jump across frontiers and are swiftly diffused (Lake and Rothchild 1998, 27). Combined with flows of people, finance, and weapons, heightened awareness of rising conflict among transnational networks and other parties to discord can then multiply risks and increase vulnerability, with the result of a global bandwagon. In this sense, conflicts are additive, not unrelated episodes. Of course, there could be a broad recognition of conflict resolution as well. But the burden of evidence—say, for the spirit or means of reconciliation spreading from South Africa to Zimbabwe and north to central Africa—for lasting peace as a result of this kind of demonstration effect is not established. Rather, a succession of conflicts occurs within a globalizing environment and its strategic context, as the case chapters suggest.

EVIDENCE

These empirical studies are meant to examine the hypothesis that hypercompetition plus hyperpower vector toward hyperconflict. Just as the salience of hypercompetition and hyperpower varies according to time and place, so does the weight of different forms of security and insecurity (energy, food, and so on).

The following brief sketches of the cases highlight the correlations between hypercompetition and hyperpower:

- Launched in 1995, the proposed MAI's aims were to instill hypercompetition by accelerating the globalization of investment and making markets more competitive. Specifically, this initiative would transform the meaning of "fair" competition and expand the conditions of globalizing capital. The MAI's provisions, such as guaranteed national treatment for foreign investors, would signal major restructuring in the infrastructure of a globalizing order. A champion of this treaty, the United States regarded it as a vehicle to promote the unrestrained flow of arms. At the core of hyperpower, Washington could use the MAI as a way to foster national defense industries and armies so as to secure the militarization of globalization. But negotiations in the OECD flared into conflicts among member states and with nonmember countries, partly along the lines of global North and global South, and involved TNCs and transnational civil society organizations. This attempt to securitize global investment flows not only posed vexing questions about foreignness and borders but also triggered stiff resistance.

- Even before the tamping down of these flames, sharp competition practiced by currency traders in the unregulated financial markets of Eastern Asia set off blazes in 1997–98 that engulfed stock, real estate, and labor markets. Retrenchment in the most heavily affected economies brought shifts in domestic political coalitions and in some cases ignited violence. Hyperpower sought to arrest the growing turbulence. While scotching an Asian regional initiative to cope with the ordeal and adopting a policy of containment, Washington made clear that it would maintain a strong military presence in the area. Defense planners and strategic thinkers trumpeted the U.S. role as the "essential . . . security stabilizer in Asia." In this case, hyperpower manifested as well through multilateral governance agencies such as the IMF and the World Bank in which the United States plays the dominant role. In concert with its allies, Washington used leverage to normalize the risks of neoliberal policies in Asian economies.

- Prior to the Asian economies' rebound from their predicament, the WTO sought to establish rules to liberalize global trade as a modality for open-

ing the world economy. The 1999 Seattle Ministerial was an effort to secure conditions of hypercompetition in the realm of global trade. The
lead power backed this project and tried to build consensus among elites
and with the moderate wings of civil society. Yet street violence erupted,
and the unrest spread to other cities, sites of global summitry, on five
continents. Conflicts emerged along several axes: civil society versus the
WTO, globalization's winners and losers in Seattle, developed versus the
more numerous developing countries, and among the developed countries themselves.

- While the alterglobalization movement continued to mount protests
  against the partisans of neoliberal globalization, a transnational network
  of Islamists attacked the World Trade Center and the Pentagon, emblems
  of American-oriented hypercompetition and hyperpower, in an effort to
  stir pervasive fear. The United States and its "coalition of the willing" responded by waging a "war on terror" represented by a global enemy. A
  key factor is the discursive machinery that produces narratives for this
  "long war," as the George W. Bush administration called it. For example,
  in the discursive economy, the dominant story lines imbued energy security, crucial for sustaining hypercompetition in other sectors, with the
  symbolic meaning of strength. Meanwhile, the Department of Homeland
  Security offered incentives to think tanks, institutes, and universities to
  propagate stories and securitize the issues at stake. This symbiotic relationship and American foreign policies themselves roused resistance
  from very different quarters: inter alia, globalization protestors and networks of terrorists.

All these cases are about rule-making, norms, the mobility of capital and
people, and power. And in every one, the underlying and proximate causes lin-
ger. Not a single one of the nominal issues in the four instances—the institutional framework for global investment, a world trade regime, the volatility of
currency, and terrorist attacks—has been actually resolved. The conditions that
spawned the conflicts are still afoot.

For example, despite all the fanfare about recovery from the 1997–98 turbulence in Eastern Asia, the five worst-hit countries have never fully regained
the economic growth rates of the mid-1990s. According to the ADB, at 4 to 7
percent, the average annual growth in these countries from 2000 to 2006 was
2.5 points lower than from 1990 to 1996 (Asian Development Bank 2007, 1). Of

course, it could be argued that 1990 to 1996 were the "bubble" years that ought not to be repeated.

After the economies overheated in 1997 and 1998, nonperforming bank loans, corruption, and close ties between political contractors and tycoons persisted. Political instability also continued to rock certain countries. The instances include Indonesia, with the 2002 Bali bombings and the lasting effects of the overthrow of the Suharto government; Thailand, which experienced a military coup in 2006 and political violence in the south; the Philippines, insurgencies; and Malaysia, disquiet over cronyism among political leaders and opposing forces as well as unrest sparked by ethnic tensions. Unquestionably, the roots of the 1997–98 predicaments remain in place. Taking a ten-year perspective on recovery, Rajat M. Nag, the ADB's managing director-general, noted as much: "The losses we have suffered are really . . . permanent" (as quoted in Bradsher 2007).

That said, the four cases in the preceding chapters influence one another. The linkages vary but may be broadly charted:

- a changing balance between the global market and states, evinced in the agenda for formal negotiations over the MAI and at the WTO ministerial meeting in Seattle
- objections to a democratic deficit, epitomized in innumerable calls for good governance in strategies for recovery from the Asian debacle
- avowed democratic ideals accompanied by the use of the exception, invoked by countries such as Malaysia during the turmoil of the 1990s and the United States in response to 9/11—in both instances involving the suspension of laws and reliance on detention centers where internees are subject to abuse—raising the prospect of a perpetual emergency
- a reclassification of friends and enemies so as to elevate the threat level, whether, for example, from protestors at the Battles of Seattle or 9/11 terrorists

This trajectory differs from the course in prior epochs. Distinctive are the specific conflagrations, attempts to mitigate them, the structure of the globalizing order in which they take place, and the ways that a single individual or a group may spread mayhem.

More than I had expected before undertaking research on these cases, the evidence shows the fitfulness of hypercompetition and hyperpower. Up to a point, they move in the same direction and reinforce one another; however, irregularity in the matrix is apparent. Not surprisingly, the lead power is bold or more restrained under different conditions. Even so, the patchiness in the overall pattern diverges more than I had expected from my initial hypothesis about the arrows pointing toward hyperconflict. The capriciousness of political actors such as Mahathir and George W. Bush is particularly noticeable in the findings, warranting a relaxation, though not a rejection, of the strong formulation advanced at the beginning of this book.

My point about the evidence is that agency—the ability of individuals and collectivities to shape the world—is shot through the four case studies and joins with labyrinthine structures in diverse ways. In a hypercompetitive world, the state is but one actor pressured by many: international organizations, regional entities, corporations, civil societies and social movements, global cities, and individuals. Superimposed on this list of overlapping categories are cultures, networks, and the environment. All are engaged in multilevel global governance.

BETWIXT EPOCHS

The parametric forces that structure peace and conflict in this interregnum of the old and a new order are mapped schematically in Table 2. The old *spatial order* is based on the principle of territoriality and thus has linear boundaries. In the new framework, the territorial form is preserved, but the borders are partly erased and appear as dotted lines. Spatial relations are increasingly expanded and networked.

The old *political order* primarily consists of formally sovereign states. But states now operate in a multilevel environment in which states' freedom of action is more constrained. In some cases, Europe chief among them, sovereignty is being pooled, partly as a defensive measure against globalizing pressures and as a way to secure aspects of sovereignty (for an opposing interpretation, see Krasner 1999).

The old *economic order* is mainly composed of national economies and multinational corporations. Now, there is an expansion and deepening of markets and much greater concentration of capital, epitomized by cross-border mergers and acquisitions. In a manner that does not necessarily contradict this centralization, the distribution of stock ownership has spread to some core workers; their funds are channeled to large institutional investors.[4] While capital is highly mobile, the transfer of human resources is segmented by occupation, skill level, and political constraints.

TABLE 2

Changing World Order

World Order	Old Order	New Order
Spatial	Principle of territoriality	Borders partly erased; spatial relations increasingly expanded and networked
Political	Primarily sovereign states in a bipolar world	Multilevel environment
Economic	Largely national economies and multinational corporations	National economies along with transnational concentration of capital and wider distribution of stock ownership
Legal	Formal equality among states and, ideally, constitutional protections	National and international jurisdictions as well as acts that fall between or outside these realms
Normative	Professed liberal freedoms and declining legitimacy	Rival belief systems that increasingly challenge neoliberal conservatism
Social	Evolved hierarchy, mainly national and local in orientation	Increasing distance between the top and bottom in terms of wealth and access
Military	In theory, to secure the other orders by warfare between states and within them	Hyperpower enmeshed in assorted violent conflicts accompanied by the spread of weapons and as part of a globalized arms market

The old *legal order* rests on formal equality among states and, in principle, constitutional protections. Emergent are sharp disagreements about the basic rules that constitute this system. With contemporary globalization, certain acts, such as cybercrime, fall between or outside national and international jurisdictions.

The old *normative order* of professed liberal freedoms experiences declining legitimacy. Emanating from the West and always contested, these beliefs are arrayed against a bevy of different religious and secular values as well as combinations of them. Rival normative systems increasingly challenge the ideology of neoliberalism and its neoconservative coupling.

The old *social order* is a hierarchic structure, mostly national and local in orientation. With evolving clusters of privilege at a world level, there is greater distance between the top and the bottom in terms of wealth and access; between new superrich and middle classes; and between elites and the marginalized, who despair, sometimes triggering violence. This can spill over to other locales, given the broadening of ties to extranational groups.

The old *military order*, its raison d'être being to secure the other orders, is permeated by wars between states and within them, as well as partial safeguards with rules to manage them. This complex is partly supplanted by hyperpower enmeshed in assorted violent conflicts, but the most flagrant conflicts defy military solutions. In fact, the application of more and more coercion inflames tensions, emboldens unconventional enemies, and inspires recruits for their causes. And the spread of weapons—nuclear proliferation (with some warheads in the hands of the former Soviet republics) and light weapons as part of a globalized arms market—continues apace.

In Schmittian terms, the coexistence of the old and the new is constituting a distinctive *nomos*. The correlation of order and orientation is rapidly shifting. Just as the concepts of perpetual peace and "perpetual peace for perpetual war" emerged in prior eras, perpetual competition is a hallmark of contemporary globalization. But as the four case studies indicate, the rise in competition is accompanied by states of emergency that seem to give it permanence. Power holders invoke them as a means to control backlashes of diverse types against newfound enemies: among Others, civil society groups that protest state, interstate, and corporate actions; migrants encamped in detention centers and perhaps repatriated; and terrorist suspects who are interned and, in some circumstances, subject to extraordinary rendition.

Although these are deemed exceptions under the law, they become normal aspects of self-professed lawful societies. To the extent that exclusions are normalized, a state of perpetual fear is induced. If one civil society group, migrant community, or political rival that uses unsavory tactics is targeted, so can another be defined as an exception.

THE PRODUCTION OF SECURITY FEARS

But what lies behind the production of fear? From whence does political fear crop up? Who arouses and shores it up?[5]

These themes are explored compellingly in Philip Roth's novel *The Plot Against America* (2004). In the opening passage, Roth poignantly observes, "[f]ear presides over these memories, a perpetual fear" (Roth 2004, 1). The memories are feelings of terror that developed during the post-1929 Depression years in the United States. In Roth's fictional and prescient account, Franklin Delano Roosevelt failed to secure an unprecedented third term as president of the United States in 1940. Instead, the Republican nominee, Charles Lindbergh, an aviation celebrity and Nazi sympathizer, was elected. His supporters organized rallies, controlled major newspapers, and used radio broadcasts to redraw lines, demonizing the "Jewish race" as an enemy in and outside the United States. Collaborators, including a prominent rabbi, participated in relocating Jews to remote sites or facilitating their emigration. Roaming the streets, vigilante groups turned violent. Assassins murdered the Jewish newscaster Walter Winchell, well known for his public attacks on Hitler and American Nazis. This story line plays out to show how the public was mobilized, manipulated by a political elite, and stayed in thrall to the fear of demons.

Indeed, fear is more efficient and less costly than brute force. Fearmongering is an instrument for altering intersubjectivity, the collective consciousness of a people (Robin 2004). By naming the enemy and determining which threats to address or neglect, political officials responsible for the dominant group's security can obscure the forces at the root of growing conflict.

As seen in Chapters 2, 6, and 7, they drum up a clientele and maintain a climate of fear. In the construction of identities—for example, as regards ethnic minorities (Chua 2004)—strangers are represented as a threat to a way of life. The purveyors of these discourses include public intellectuals, political elites, and civil society organizations. In some cases, watchdog and vigilante groups report, intimidate, and favor relaxing legal restraints, as at the detention and deportation centers discussed in Chapter 5 on the Asian debacle and Chapter 7 on 9/11 and the "war on terror." In fact, some of these organizations are adjuncts to the state. In a form of state substitution, members of civil society are put on the public payroll (Robin 2004, 230). In this manner, the political economy of fear throws analytical light on the production of convictions about security, understood in this context as a way to perpetuate insecurity. Today, these insecurities increasingly become global fears about interrelated problems over expanded space.

STABILIZERS AND DESTABILIZERS

An alternative to straight-line projections is to bring to mind the balance of stability and instability in world order and then present credible scenarios. Since the theme of sources of stability and instability is threaded throughout this book, here I will sum up as concisely as possible.

One stabilizer is the emergent web of global governance. Certainly, this multilevel system of states, international organizations, civil society groups, networks, and norms and values is ill-defined and even ramshackle. Whatever the shortcomings, it has nevertheless been able to limit a number of conflicts and tensions as well as step up efforts for postconflict reconstruction and recovery. Within this framework, it is hyperpower that ultimately manages and maintains a neoliberal world order. Heretofore, the United States has kept the lid on some conflicts and served as a guarantor of aspects of economic security for major allies. For instance, Chapter 5 called attention to the dependence of Tokyo on the U.S. military presence in the Middle East to safeguard a large part of Japan's oil supply. But stabilizing conflicts may freeze a situation, enforce a cease-fire or truce, and prevent hostilities from erupting anew while not tugging at the roots of the conditions needed to win a lasting peace.

Thaws may be short-lived because power asymmetries abound. In a hyper-competitive world, they are increasingly breeding a politics of resistance. As evident with the MAI and the Battles of Seattle, local civil society groups and transnational social movements protest vehemently at summits and other international meetings. And in part, the rise of religious radicalism, the reassertion of identities, and strikes by terrorists are expressions of discontent with neoliberal globalization. They coincide or in some cases merge with other backlashes against hyperpower and anti-American sentiment.

Another source of instability is the sheer magnitude of inequality on a world scale. Analysts disagree about whether inequalities are becoming greater or if globalization is flattening them irrespective of structural obstacles. Many debates surround which measures to use and the types of data employed. Whereas certain studies rely on national income accounts, others treat the world distribution of household wealth as more telling. Then there is the question of whether the results are skewed by the rapid economic growth of only two countries, China and India, the world's most populous. According to the World Bank (2008), 75 percent of the drop in poverty in the developing world for the past twenty years has occurred in China alone. Surely, interregional and intraregional variation is vast. As documented by David Rothkopf (2008), although globalization helped raise the bottom level in certain societies, inequalities have increased within and among countries such that the benefits of global economic growth accrue to a smaller percentage of people. All that said, the main pattern is unmistakable, namely, the high concentration of world income and the persistence of abject poverty (as detailed in Mittelman 2008).

Reflecting sensibilities for these trends, Eurobarometer and Financial Times/Harris polls in six rich countries (Britain, France, Germany, Italy, Spain, and the United States) show the depth of concern over mounting inequality accompanied by a popular backlash against free-market globalization ("Six Nation Survey Finds Little Enthusiasm for Free Market Capitalism in Western Europe or the United States" 2007; Giles 2007). Janet Yellen, president of the Federal Reserve Bank in San Francisco, pointed to the repercussions of such trends: "There are signs that rising inequality is intensifying resistance to globalization, impairing social cohesion, and could, ultimately, undermine American democracy" ("Another Item on the Fed Worry List: Inequality" 2006). Her statement and these indicators, taken from the *Financial Times* and the *Wall Street Journal*, reflect a swing in the mainstream press and among the public in wealthy countries as regards growing insecurity about the future.

Mindful that it is only in conjunction with agency that these fears generate political shifts, I venture that globalization is altering the balance of stability and instability. Since geoeconomics and geopolitics are deeply intertwined, these forces help define possibilities and constraints for the future.

SCENARIOS

Alternative futures may be envisaged by projecting scenarios. These are neither predictions nor imaginary conditions. Rather than engage in wishful thinking, it is most useful to anchor scenarios in history and practice. The tendencies form varied patterns. Scenarists seek to grasp them and recognize the plausibility of multiple futures. But the methodology is not to extrapolate from frequency among categories to which a large number of cases are assigned—a dataset—and reason that the future will be more of the same. On the contrary, there are real alternatives shaped by structural pressures and the choices made by agents. History remains open-ended.

In appraising the prospects for the macro dynamics of peace and security, the place to begin is with the globalization syndrome: a complex of interlocking transformations in economics, politics, and culture (Chapter 1; Mittelman 2000). The ways in which it is spanning geoeconomics and geopolitics and extending to the geostrategic sphere are being played out as three world-historical scenarios. While analytically distinguishable, they can coexist. And each one turns on the course of globalization: its *persistence*, *decline*, or *renewal*.

The first scenario is a *neoglobalization syndrome*. It is not a replay of the present. Rather, while maintaining the Westphalian logic of sovereignty, political leadership comes not only from the United States as the hub but from Europe, Japan, the so-called BRIC countries (Brazil, Russia, India, and China), and perhaps South Africa. Similarly, there is diversification of global economic leadership, some of it organized in regional formations. The forces behind regionalism use it to ride globalization and fend off some of the deleterious effects. Liberal reforms in global governance agencies are numerous. Hypercompetitive capital and competitive states extend over the same time and space, propelling increasing contestation in the form of Othering—"we" and "they"—and a high level of insecurity. This Othering is an ideological phenomenon shaped by growing globalizing processes, as when migratory flows are securitized as threats in receiving countries.

Second, a *nonglobalization syndrome* is reminiscent of the Great Crash in 1929, the tumultuous conditions for remaking world order. In its wake, there was a reconstitution of global capitalism, wars, and a revamped system of governance charged with the formidable tasks of mitigating conflict and bringing peace (Chapter 1). So, too, there are signs that the current order, driven by hypercompetition and hyperpower, is imploding beyond the economic turmoil and armed conflicts underway in the early 2000s. Under this scenario, the tensions will be most acute in the heartland of globalization, the United States, the country with the greatest income inequality among Western democracies and Japan, with rising insecurity, and with declining albeit fluctuating civic involvement in politics (Putnam 2000; Skocpol 2003). In this case, world order would be a form of "neomedievalism": multiple layers of authority in a crisscrossing pattern, with sovereignty shared not only among states but with entities below the state or beside them, as with the Vatican in the Middle Ages (Bull 1977). In the twenty-first century, this kind of fragmentation could not maintain a balance of power for long but would result in a coil of conflicts of varying intensity. Although foretelling the exact pathways to this scenario would be mere conjecture, detecting the portents is feasible. They include predatory risk-based lending by banks and securitizers that wreak havoc in unregulated financial markets; the volatility of the U.S. dollar and its far-reaching impact on worldwide money flows; the sustained rise in energy prices and other commodities that strains industries such as airlines and automobile manufacturers; escalating costs for food; a global inflationary spiral, which sparked riots across the developing world in 2008; and an endangered biosphere.[6] Evidently, the globalization of risk is outpacing practices of normalizing risk.

Finally, an *alterglobalization syndrome* would be a polycentric world order. Promoted by various transnational civil society movements, such as the Association for the Taxation of Financial Transactions for the Aid of Citizens, or AT-TAC, and without the backing of states, this project's aims include a diffusion of power and a tolerance for different value systems. It also allows new venues for experimentation in governance and diverse formulas for relations among the market, state, and society. This scenario is an effort to redefine political life, to expand space for nonstate politics. The objective is to re-embed market forces in democratic politics. Toward this end are attempts to assert, relative to globalizing forces, greater autonomy: a political and moral concept employed by ancient Greek writers, Kantian ethics, and social contract theory. The core of autonomy is self-determination—a precept that resonates with contemporary liberalism, as in aspects of Rawls's theory of justice (1993). Yet from the standpoint of achieving global security and building lasting peace, this third course would require vast mobilization by popular movements, coalitions among them, extensive public education and awareness about neoliberal globalization, and keen analytic and strategic planning. Under current conditions, this path seems to be more of a potential than an actuality. In the near term, it is nevertheless a useful alternative for stimulating critical reflection and pressuring for the expansion of policy space.

A combination of systemic drivers, the actions of political agents, and contingency will resolve which scenario wins out. But the question immediately arises, Is there a profound shift in hyperpower?

As the key node in hyperpower, the United States continues to hold a preeminent position. Even after the withdrawal of most of its troops from Iraq, it will be the dominant military power in the Middle East and throughout the world. However, the U.S. military is stretched thin, and Washington's ability to enforce its decisions is diminished. Economically, the United States' capacity remains formidable. It is nonetheless the largest debtor nation and relies on external finance to buoy its GDP. A low savings rate and credit-funded overconsumption are hard to sustain. How the United States addresses global climate change, the quest for energy security, pandemics, and traditional security problems like nonproliferation will be crucial. These crisis management issues are ultimately matters of political will and legitimacy.

Hyperpower is lessened on account of a series of strategic misadventures. Neoliberal conservatism stokes anti-Americanism and is frayed. The Washington Consensus model of globalization has fallen into disfavor. This blueprint resulted in policy failings, especially in Eastern Asia and Argentina; and shock therapy led to ill effects in Russia and Eastern Europe. In the twenty-first century, there is a lack of coherence, a void in organizing principles for approaching world order. Global competitiveness stays as a prevailing byword.

The Washington-based international financial institutions, the IMF and the World Bank, emphasize the importance of increased competitiveness and point to "successful globalizers" in ascendant Asia, especially China.[7] Having sustained an annual growth rate above 9 percent in GDP for the last three decades (up to the contraction in the global economy that began in 2008), China has broadened the worldwide competitive playing field and is gaining an edge. China, of course, commands unique assets, including 26 percent of the world's population (more than the combined total of Latin America and sub-Saharan Africa) and thus a huge domestic market as well as a massive, inexpensive labor force. Whereas nearly all studies project that the Chinese economy will surpass that of the United States as the biggest in the world by 2025, as calculated in purchasing power parity, the country's per capita income reached just $2,000 in 2006 (World Bank 2008). It is below midpoint on the IMF's World Economic Outlook Database. Moreover, more than five hundred million people in China are living on less than $2 per day.

There is a series of severe weaknesses in China's economy and grave uncertainties about how an authoritarian regime will adjust to a changing world order. One source of vulnerability stems from demographics. With an aging population and a longer life expectancy (from thirty-five years on average in 1949 to more than seventy-three in 2008), China faces heightened labor costs. Second, given a high level of internal migration and worldwide economic restructuring causing more layoffs in China's factories, unemployment is on the rise. Third, China's weak social security net must cope with escalating expenditure for elder care and public health. Fourth, political unrest—reportedly more than ninety thousand protests annually (Economy 2008)—is linked to chronic corruption and widespread environmental abuses. All told, these structural problems challenge political authorities to alter the policy framework and devise new ideas for doing so.

At the global level, the Chinese set of ideas for guiding policy is often called the Beijing Consensus. This paradigm consists of "bleeding-edge" innovation (such as fiber optics) to start change more quickly than the emergence of problems caused by change; avoidance of large-scale contradictions by stressing contemporary quality-of-life concerns and chaos management; and new security priorities to avert the ill effects of hyperpower (Ramo 2004, 11–12). However, there are also rival policy agendas in China, infighting within the state and with civil society, and coercion that accompanies the effort to forge a new consensus.

In assessing foreign policy, many Chinese strategic thinkers contend that globalization can be used to democratize U.S. hegemony by restraining its unilateralist impulses and making Washington increasingly rely on sources of legitimate authority. Thus, if additional countries, including a strong China, are more tightly interlocked, globalization may serve as an affirmative force for democratizing U.S.-dominated world order. Pursuing this logic, Chinese think-tank and other policy analysts argue that globalization boosts competition in a positive-sum game; different actors may win, though not equally, through multipolarization (Deng and Moore 2004). Beijing's strategy of multilateralism is supported by growing military might and "the new security concept": a proactive approach extending beyond the historical weight of being victimized by outside powers to greater pragmatism in international affairs.

The trope "peaceful rise," widely employed by the leadership in Beijing until early 2004, is no longer in vogue in China. An undercurrent in China is that without wanting to appear hostile, political authorities are not willing to relinquish the sovereign state's prerogative to use force, as in hotspots like Taiwan or in territorial disputes with neighbors. Whereas the discourses in China do not altogether discard the word "peaceful," the other component of the phrase "peaceful rise" fails to resonate in Mandarin, for "rise" translates as "surge," which could be an abrupt phenomenon. In a nation that values stability and order, the insinuation of rupture is to be avoided. Discursively, hints of chaos are off-limits. Dialing into globalization in a sequenced manner is the favored course for pursuing peace and development.

Although China is ascendant in world affairs, it is not near to commanding hyperpower. China does not presently qualify for this position because hyperpower involves substantially more than a lead state. As we have seen, it draws on a weblike structure, including a net of overseas military bases, a clutch of allies, aspects of ideological appeal, and an educational system that widely propagates values associated with those at the epicenter of globalization.

Another consideration is that stories of the *imminent* decline of the United States have been told before without properly accounting for countervailing patterns. The declinist themes, as in Paul Kennedy's book *The Rise and Fall of the Great Powers* (1987), circulated widely in the 1970s and 1980s. Rise and demise is also a subject of inquiry in the work of world-systems theorists, who trace the spiral of hegemony over many centuries, even thousands of years, and compare historical periods.[8]

Careful scholars like Susan Strange (1987) argued that in her times, the declinists failed to grasp the dynamics of structural power and overlooked types of collective action that occur only when the United States chooses to proceed. Then, too, it was said that "the Pacific Century," with Tokyo at the forefront, would succeed "the American Century." But this narrative was soon overtaken when the Japanese economy came on hard times in the 1990s (M. Cox 2001). Indeed, it may be premature to bemoan or celebrate the decline of hyperpower. Just as the constraints on hyperpower are formidable, so do contenders for the helm have pronounced weaknesses. The policy blunders of a particular administration in Washington in the run-up to a worldwide economic slump do not necessarily signify the displacement of hyperpower or obviate the possibility of a resurgence of the lead state under more adept leadership. As compelling as the short-term events are, it would be an error to mistake what may be a diversion as the main path of future world order (see Epilogue).

Whatever the strategies, tactics, and resources of power agents, state and nonstate actors alike face the enduring issue of climate change. Additionally, there are accidents of history that shape the outcome of contending scenarios. It is worth recalling that the bubonic plague and ancillary maladies together killed almost 40 percent of Europeans, contributed importantly to the fall of Western feudalism, and allowed for the rise of capitalism. And the Spanish influenza in 1918–19 infected 28 percent of U.S. citizens (including President Woodrow Wilson) and hampered economic growth after World War I. In short, pandemics and natural catastrophes impinge profoundly on the course of history. Even so, the tsunamis of our era are subject to human redress. This intervention can be aided by timely and bracing warnings as well as political vision. But how to rouse intelligent responses to deal with the cataclysms visited on humankind not only by disease and nature but also warring parties?

IMPLICATIONS

Toward this end, security planners may flat-out ask, What are the policy "solutions"? Is this book on hyperconflict too abstract and overly generalized? Does it lack concrete proposals?

The rejoinder is that these questions miss the point of basic research. Such policy-driven queries themselves raise prior issues, namely, What is the problem? What assumptions are brought to bear in perceiving and analyzing the problem? Who defines the problem? And when a problem is securitized, in whose interests? Furthermore, what is a solution? Is it a blueprint? A manual with how-to-do-it instructions?

If the answers to these questions are unclear, there cannot be solutions. Hence, in the previous chapters, I have sought to sharply define what is at stake and what particular understandings of it convey.

Although the objective in this book is not to proffer "solutions" to predefined problems, I take comfort in the belief that basic research should precede policy recommendations. That said, principles for the formulation of policy can flow from theoretical knowledge. In other words, basic and applied research are not watertight compartments. There may be a blending, not a split, between them so that they are mutually enriching. Besides, the here-and-now genre of inquiry becomes most incisive when it is situated within an appreciation of how a configuration of power came to be and is changing. When mainstream research has produced limited results, then critical reflections that extend its parameters may be the more fruitful strategy.

Explaining why analysts should reorient existing knowledge, Hirschman cut to the heart of the matter: "Such reformulations will not leave things exactly as they were: occasionally they will make us see the forces at work as well as possible options and outcomes in a new light" (Hirschman 1981, 284). To the extent that rethinking the links between globalization and security or, rather, insecurity disturbs the reigning agenda and opens original questions, while sensitizing researchers to enduring themes, the payoff would seem to be eminently worthwhile. And what could be more practical than looking at issues in a new way, elucidating their meanings and discovering possibilities that have eluded policymakers?

There is much to commend Hirschman's call for "trespassing" intellectual borders and offering different perspectives (1981). In this spirit, I have tilted against convention and have argued that standard knowledge about peace and security is highly specialized and segmented. It lacks a holistic perspective and has not caught hyperconflict and the ways in which this macro condition is directly or indirectly tethered to micro conflicts. Accordingly, four major episodes in the course of globalization examined here show the contours of the route.

Viewing insecurity through this prism, one gains clarity about hypercompetition and hyperpower as the systemic drivers of hyperconflict. For the sake of conflict resolution and peacemaking, the task is to restructure this system. Efforts to do so are cramped by short-termism when long-run perspective is needed. Moreover, discordance is due to prevalent forms of line-drawing: imagining "we" and "they," conjuring absolutist notions of good and evil, and thereby deepening cleavages between insiders and outsiders. Lately, outwitting demons, the Other who does not accept "our" way of life and respect "our" laws, is on offer as how to cope with what is framed as the great threat to civilized nations.

Another frame is mapping the path of hyperconflict and conveying that it is not an inescapable condition. Hyperconflict is hardly for once and all. A "long war" or permanent wars do not have to be. This perspective departs from wishful thinking to the extent that it resonates with a clientele that resolutely embraces an alternative narrative. Then there would be grounds for cautious optimism about solving proximate problems.

As warranted, the instigators of untoward acts would be criminalized. Emotive metaphors about battles and war would be set aside. Too often, they train thinking on violent responses and beget idioms of the same order as from the groups targeted. The emotional rhetoric is galvanizing but also provokes more graphic language. This cycle revs up fear and provides selling points for aggressive policies, serving the mutual interests of protagonists seeking to mobilize constituencies. It deflects attention from getting to the bottom of problems.

The proposed refocusing would address the question of how to create a new "us," which is an alternative to identifying states and peoples as friends or foes. Setting aside ingrained beliefs about being "one" would be an initial step toward achieving ontological security.

Of course, beliefs about these matters vary from one part of the world to another and within the same zone. In impoverished countries lacking power at a world level, discourses often center on the "terror of globalization." Discourses in Africa and elsewhere feature marginalization and globalization as two sides of the same coin. More politely, policymakers and officials talk about broadening inclusion in globalization and the pitfalls of exclusion from its benefits. These narratives are based on the failure of globalization to bring prosperity to large swaths of people, the lack of opportunities in terms of life chances, and the indignities visited upon the poor and powerless, some of them by their own rulers.

It used to be that marginalized countries and regions were seen as being the least secure. Now, insecurity may be understood more expansively in light of factors such as the lack of protection from global climate change, pandemics, the depletion of natural resources, as well as outright attacks. In fact, the wealthiest and most powerful states themselves are among the sources of these forms of insecurity and are also exposed to their harms. To defend citizens against such risks, Europeans have started to regionalize sovereignty, or aspects of it, in a common union. And elsewhere, including in the United States, sovereignty is qualified, regardless of whether policymakers acknowledge or deny this shift.

States cannot abdicate their responsibility for physical security. But peace-planning involves broadening the sources from which security can be derived. Successful defense means credibly making and keeping peace. This approach would entail breaking away from archaic practices, some of them vestiges of the Cold War and inappropriate for the third millennium. Winning peace is a matter of transforming the political and economic environment and changing mind-sets. Inasmuch as globalization is a multiscalar phenomenon, the places to control violence and take positive steps toward peace are at all levels of behavior.

In the final analysis, hyperconflict eviscerates the prevailing configuration of order and orientation. Yet this need not be an apocalyptic vision. As well as a collage of patterns, hyperconflict is a domain of knowledge that provides early warning of a convergence of global shifts. Most notable is a disjunction between concentration and hierarchy over expanded space on the one hand, and the decline of neoliberal conservatism as a way to secure compliance on the other. In this breach, opportunities for viable alternatives arise. Analytically, the tools are available to come to grips with these processes. If this knowledge were implicated in power so as to summon political will to address hyperconflict, a rosy view of future world order would indeed be justified.

EPILOGUE

The preceding analysis points to the insecurity of the future. In the evolving world, increasing uncertainty has replaced the more durable order of a half century ago.

Although the social contract calls for sovereign actors to provide security, governments offer only limited protection from the ill effects of global shifts. This gap is partly due to the rise of financial globalization. Securitization (bundling thousands of loans and mortgages, repackaging them, and selling slices of these revalued debts) has brought insecurity, which is propagated among interlinked economies. The public becomes more and more vulnerable to forces over which it has little control. Subject to severe political and economic disturbances, the existing order is becoming a battleground for new ideas and alternative policies. Yet these patterns are too often viewed as short-term tendencies and chalked up to psychological motives, such as greed, shorn of structural moorings.

It is important to explore broad patterns and the conceptual apparatus for coming to grips with them. Explanations may be deepened by examining the ways in which the two forces behind growing insecurity—hyperpower and hypercompetition—converge after the events of 9/11. Simultaneous phenomena, they are perceptible in the wars in Afghanistan and Iraq and the downward spiral of a worldwide recession. Emanating from the United States, they are twin implosions in globalization. Joined together as a war economy, these symbiotic propensities are links in the chain of hyperconflict.

MANIFESTATIONS

In 2003, American billionaire investor and philanthropist Warren Buffett suggested that derivatives (a sophisticated technology for managing risks) are tantamount to "financial weapons of mass destruction." But his warning about heightened instability was taken lightly (Rich 2008). More than a turn of phrase, Buffett's formulation synthesized divergent sources of globalized insecurity and signaled peril. Nevertheless, it would be wrong to blur the distinctions between financial houses that offer incentives to minimize risks and military security apparatuses that seek to maximize them. Buffett's enticing metaphor should not lead to misspecifying the linkages between hyperpower and hypercompetition.

In the realm of military security, the United States' efforts to curb resurgent Taliban forces in Afghanistan coincided with escalating violence in postinvasion Iraq. Planned in 2006, a surge of armed forces entailed an adjustment in Washington's strategy to quell unrest in Iraq. Beginning in January 2007, the United States deployed an additional thirty thousand troops to this conflict zone. Implementation also meant building protective barriers, establishing more checkpoints, and augmenting funding for the war. In fact, since 2001, basic defense expenditure itself increased 40 percent in real postinflation dollars even before pouring in enormous supplemental budgets for the wars in Afghanistan and Iraq ("How to Pay for a 21st-Century Military" 2008).

In his 2007 lecture at Kansas State University, U.S. defense secretary Robert Gates gauged military spending as a percentage of GDP and below previous wartime periods (U.S. Department of Defense 2007). But in absolute terms, including the budgets for Afghanistan and Iraq, the figures for 2008 and 2009 are the highest since World War II, topping war funding for Korea and Vietnam (Center for Arms Control and Non-Proliferation 2008).

At the same time that critics highlighted the costs of military overreach, a surge in financial securitization led to bursting the mortgage and housing bubbles. It originated in the United States in late 2007 and fueled a globalizing credit crunch. There was little transparency about the pools of debt. The bundles took on more risks, and regulators were lax. Rating agencies like Moody's (supposedly secured in the United States by the Securities and Exchange Commission) acted as complicit, market-driven entities seeking to boost their own revenues garnered from the issuers themselves (Morgenson 2008). The group dynamic among the raters is to pursue profits by scoring major financial houses, a relationship that creates possible conflicts of interest.

In this environment, rampant speculation in instruments such as subprime mortgages, collateralized debt obligations, and other exotic products ballooned. The housing market started to deflate in 2006, and the number of defaults grew.

Based on years of increases in housing prices and high consumption patterns, household debt could not be sustained.

The stock market plunged. In the beginning of November 2008, the S&P 500 U.S. market index dropped 45 percent from its peak in 2007: a more pronounced fall than in 1981–82, which up to the 2008 crash was the worst slump since the worldwide depression in the 1930s (Altman 2009, 6). Major Wall Street investment banks and brokerages hemorrhaged in 2007 and 2008. And by early 2009, U.S. stocks declined to their lowest level since 1997, when the debacle in Asia rippled to markets in other parts of the world.

The downturn spread to the real economy of goods and services, causing alarm about the prospects of repeating the type of "lost decade" that Japan experienced in the 1990s. On the verge of bankruptcy, the automobile industry, long a symbol of the strength of the U.S. economy, appealed for a government rescue package. Inasmuch as this industry is linked to one of every ten jobs in the national economy, unemployment rates in different sectors mounted. Joblessness, in turn, further tamped down consumer spending and thus business investment, resulting in even more job losses and knock-on effects on home foreclosures. But the quandary of fixing the problem is that individual calculations on restraining spending and boosting savings are at odds with collective interests in increasing liquidity in the economy.

To rev up the economy, the U.S. government effectively took over the housing giants Fannie Mae and Freddie Mac as well as the American International Group (a U.S.-based insurance and financial services organization that operates in more than one hundred countries). The state also bailed out large lenders like Bear Stearns but allowed Lehman Brothers to fail. It pumped enormous amounts of cash into the economy, cut short-term interest rates, printed money, prosecuted corrupt traders, and temporarily shored up carmakers while calling on them to restructure. Yet the downsizing meant that unionized autoworkers would sacrifice wages and benefits or, critics alleged, be sent on the race to the bottom.

Although liquidity represented the immediate problem, solvency was a more arduous challenge that required greater government intervention. So as to avoid the ideological trappings of socialism, politicians coded what in effect amounted to the nationalization of certain enterprises with labels such as bridge loans. But stripped of this connotative cover, the shift was toward state capitalism. The irony of this move did not go unnoticed in developing countries such as Tanzania, which faced fierce opposition from the West in 1967 when its government intervened in the banking sector and sought to assert state control.

In the twenty-first century, global contagion effects are unambiguous. Wall Street lost $6.9 trillion in 2008. All together, the world's stocks were down 48 percent for the year ("Wall Street's Final '08 Toll: $6.9 Trillion Wiped Out" 2009). It bears emphasizing that the amount that had vanished represents money realized without adding value to a product. This is precisely the point in the opening pages of Smith's *Wealth of Nations*. In his story about the pin factory, specialization in the division of labor creates value before the products are worth swapping. Then a profit is made in exchange between buyers and sellers, as on today's stock market. A profit accrues to an individual or firm when an entrepreneur outsmarts competitors by buying cheap and selling dear. This activity occurs in the orbit of circulation and finance, circuits of capital expanded by contemporary globalization.

So in an era of speculative capitalism, the contraction in U.S. markets lessened demand for products from overseas. Developing countries experienced reduced exports, falling commodity prices, and the overall repercussions of U.S. policies to rein in financial leveraging. Meanwhile, this pullback establishes policy space for some states, such as China and the oil producers of the Persian Gulf, to exert greater influence in the global economy. But most countries, Russia included, suffered more than did the United States from the worldwide contraction.

Tethered to varying degrees to transnational flows of capital and labor, developed countries felt severe effects of the meltdown. Iceland is an extreme case in which the nation's banks had indulged in massive overseas speculation. As a result of large-scale losses, the authorities in Reykjavik had to adopt measures that require taxpayers to shoulder the burden of a significantly reduced standard of living. While deeply skeptical of conditionality, countries like Hungary, Belarus, and Ukraine had to approach the IMF, which had been increasingly sidelined owing to the availability of loans from China, India, and other sources of sovereign wealth funds.

CONFUSIONS

In assessing these phenomena, there are four confusions. The first one is to focus on proximate events without recognizing how these triggers fit into longer trends. Closely related, another error is to regard the episodes considered here as unprecedented. As indicated in previous chapters, other research findings puncture the myth that spending on wars revs up an economy. And Chapter 5, on the Asian debacle, notes precedents of the consequences of deregulated markets and crony capitalism. Like the turmoil in the opening decade of the 2000s, the 1997–98 turbulence that rocked Asia and other regions involved a property boom, a lack of transparency in banking, easy money, unchecked short-selling, and mismanagement, culminating in large-scale restructuring. Still, according to *The Economist*'s calculations, the scope of the twenty-first century contraction is even broader, the speed faster, than the 1997–98 debacle ("Asia's Suffering" 2009, 13).

Third, the oft-mentioned notion of decoupling suggests that economies are neatly separated into national units and that volatility in American markets could be detached from the rest of the world. On the contrary, globalizing processes are superimposed on territorial jurisdictions.

A fourth mistake is failing to discern the interactions between fallout in the geostrategic and geoeconomic spheres. Indeed, policymakers and financiers becloud efforts to probe the combined results of the U.S. war efforts, including fluctuations in oil prices, and America's macroeconomic policies, such as tax cuts for the wealthy that did not bolster the economy. High-ranking officials have emphasized the sheer complexity of myriad pathways and claim that they are too difficult to understand. As former Federal Reserve Board Chairman Greenspan put it, "Markets have become too huge, complex, and fast-moving to be subject to twentieth-century supervision and regulation. No wonder this globalized behemoth stretches beyond the full comprehension of even the most sophisticated market participants" (Greenspan 2007, 489). Yes, the markets are chaotic; but bewilderment is another matter. The trouble with Greenspan's way of thinking is that it can serve as an excuse for deficient oversight and inept leadership. It also fogs analysis of underlying forces. Clearly, these elements have been taking shape for several decades or, according to some accounts, far longer.

ROOTS

During the Great Depression, John Maynard Keynes cautioned about the tendency of enterprise to become "the bubble on a whirlpool of speculation" (Keynes 1936, 159). He also noted that capitalist development can be like the activities of a casino in that Wall Street's sense of its social mission is to channel new investment into the most profitable future yields. A half century on, Susan Strange's books *Casino Capitalism* (1986) and *Mad Money* (1998) identi fied specific ways in which financial entrepreneurs could take advantage of the weaknesses in the American regulatory system. With an eye on the Wall Street speculators, Strange underlined the power of financial markets and innovations in banking that largely started in the United States and spread worldwide. Linking money markets to steep defense spending, which makes governments poorer and less able to satisfy the welfare needs of their citizens, she called for a historical perspective on the driving forces behind financial innovation (1998, 28, 135). As Strange put it, "History, including economic history, is the essential corrective for intellectual hubris. Economists, please note" (1998, 20).

But how deep are the roots of the setback in the global political economy that emerged in the initial decade of the twenty-first century? Commentators such as Roger Altman, a former U.S. deputy treasury secretary and CEO of Evercore Partners (an investment firm that provides advisory services for TNCs), traces the underlying cause of the tribulations to the combination of "very low interest rates and unprecedented levels of liquidity" (Altman 2009, 4). This time span approximates what I have called "manifestations," a moment early in the third millennium.

Other observers look at a period of about twenty-five to thirty years. For example, *Financial Times* columnist Martin Wolf (2008) finds parallels in a succession of upheavals, including in Asia in 1997–98 and Mexico in 1982, when the government could not service its debt and jeopardized the viability of moneylenders in New York and London. Wolf notes the effects of low interest rates at times of rapid economic growth on a world scale: "Cheap money encouraged an orgy of financial innovation, borrowing and spending" (Wolf 2008, 9).

Economists have also focused on antecedents before the 1980s' global hike in debt and defaults, or the 1930s' spike that began in the United States and had worldwide repercussions in financial markets. Examples include the shock stemming from London in 1825, the German and Austrian stock market collapse in 1873, and the Baring Bank run leading to insolvency in 1890 (Reinhart and Rogoff 2008, 35). In fact, a National Bureau of Economic Research survey of eight centuries of financial downturns identifies a "striking correlation between free capital mobility and the incidence of banking crises" (2008, 7). Mindful that financial collapses differ from one another, the authors report an overarching pattern: "Periods of high international capital mobility have repeatedly produced international banking crises, not only famously as they did in the 1990s, but historically" (2008, 7).

This broad historical perspective complements a structural interpretation that stresses the disjunction between economic globalization and the political order. That is to say, economic globalization entails an acceleration of cross-border flows—among them, finance capital and services—that slice across territorial states. However, according to the Westphalian, territorial model of political organization, sovereign states seek to control these transactions and affirm the logic of the interstate system. The horizontal interconnections forged in the world economy and the vertical dimensions of state politics are two different vectors of social order, with the latter seeking to adjust to changing global structures (Mittelman 2000, 238).

This dynamic system provides incentives for the economically powerful to beat competitors, but global markets lack accountability. When the logics of markets and democracy clashed in the first part of the twenty-first century, the United States sought to strengthen its coercive quotient in the mix of instruments at its disposal.

THE COERCIVE COMPONENT

In this vein, it is well to recall Melman's concept of a war economy. He cautioned about a kind of "military Keynesianism" in which the wrong lesson is drawn from the experience of World War II, namely, that it pulled the United States out of the Great Depression. On the contrary, he argued that war diverts resources into pursuits that neither meet consumer demand nor produce capital goods for human needs:

> From the economic standpoint the main characteristic of war economy is that its products do not yield ordinary economic use-value: usefulness for the level of living (consumer goods and services); or usefulness for further production (as in machinery or tools being used to make other articles). [Melman (1974) 1985, 19]

In painstaking detail, Melman's data on misdirected resources showed the ways in which the U.S. defense industry wastes investment in the American educational system by employing graduates in a nonproductive field and concentrates resources on military contractors as part of a huge public-private bureaucracy. Drawing on his expertise in industrial engineering, Melman counseled that defense spending represented an opportunity loss for public sector expenditure on physical infrastructure, such as mass transit, bridges, energy supply, and thus the development of new technologies. In the 1980s, he cited the deterioration of U.S. automakers in Detroit as an instance of industrial inefficiency in the context of a complex of defective conditions. His thesis is that prolonged war channeled technical capacity away from civilian industries and has "highly destructive effects on the rest of economy and society" (Melman [1974] 1985, 21). The upshot, Melman warned, is "a large network of depleted industries and a flight of capital from the country" ([1974] 1985, 68).

Although Melman's 1974 book *The Permanent War Economy* focuses more on the real economy than on financial markets, one can extrapolate from his analysis of the ways in which military spending is related to the fundamental dynamics of a political economy. His findings leave no doubt that blame for a war economy's opportunity costs cannot be assigned to a single U.S. president or congress. From the onset of the Cold War, all of them are implicated (Melman 2003). Melman also sends an unambiguous message about how sustaining wars can squander economic power.

The war economy has evolved from Melman's day. In the twenty-first century, it is a complex of (1) energy issues, (2) multiplier effects of expenditure reallocations, (3) the crowding out of productive and infrastructure investment, and (4) shifts in R&D spending:

1. President George W. Bush called the American public's attention to its "addiction to oil." As a way to deal with it, his administration claimed that Iraqi oil would cover the cost of the Iraq War and reconstruction. In fact, this venture reduced oil supplies below the level that would have obtained had there not been military intervention. Rather than secure cheap oil, the Iraq War, in conjunction with factors that extend beyond resource endowments, drove up energy prices.

2. Stiglitz and Bilmes (2008) point out that the short-run costs of war are eclipsed by the full macroeconomic sum spent over the long term on items like veterans' health care, debt payments for reequipping the armed forces, and high fees paid to military-contractor CEOs. Their research demonstrates that monetary policies (the Federal Reserve's low interest rates and other measures to encourage increased household consumption) along with tax policies that favor upper-income brackets assigned the burden of financing the Iraq War to future generations. Specifically, the impact of spending on armed conflict is evident in productivity, where needs for plant and equipment have been neglected, and thus potential output suffers. It is also apparent in "expenditure switching" (Stiglitz and Bilmes 2008, 115, 120). War expenditure on items like overseas contractors hired in Iraq does not stimulate the economy in the same

way as would domestic investment in, say, schools. In other words, the multiplier effects differ.

3. In a closely related argument, Stiglitz and Bilmes (2008, 121) maintain that in effect, public money for the Iraq War is a reallocation of funds. It "crowds out" private investment and leads to larger deficits accruing from overseas financing for the shortfalls: an increase of 50 percent in the national debt in merely eight years, nearly one trillion dollars of which is attributable to the Iraq War (Stiglitz 2008). Under these conditions, financing the war on credit from abroad involves heightened competition between the U.S. private sector and government, with some American private investors getting pushed out (Stiglitz and Bilmes 2008, 123). In this hypercompetition between the public and private sectors, the conundrum is that with government spending substituting for private expenditure, the rate of turnover of capital can fail to increase. The velocity of accumulation is of course a basic feature of the dynamics of a capitalist economy. The combination of uncertainty about this geoeconomic process and, in the domain of geopolitics, continuing threats of terror means not more security but greater insecurity.

4. Uncertainty about the future is associated with the physical and social infrastructure in the United States. Upgrading and maintaining infrastructure reflect the priorities that strengthen or weaken a people's well-being. This is notable in innovation in science and technology, which is sustained by R&D. In the United States, beginning with fiscal 2005 and allowing for inflation, the federal allocation for R&D has not trended up. The United States still spends more than any other country on R&D and about one-third of global R&D, but only 2.6 to 2.8 percent of GDP per annum, less in percentage terms than for some countries, such as Japan and South Korea. In fact, certain Asian nations, including China and South Korea, are augmenting their government research investments by 10 percent or more per year (Koizumi 2008, 26, citing American Association for the Advancement of Science data for the period from 1976 to estimates for 2009). Meanwhile, basic research in corporate facilities like Bell Laboratories in Murray Hill, New Jersey, which produced six Nobel Prizes, is diminished. In fact, a number of leading R&D laboratories in the United States have been shut down (Organisation for Economic Cooperation and Development [OECD] 2002, 105), signifying a lower rate of reinvestment in vital aspects of science and technology. The shift is to bottom-line profit (Spotts 2008).

The latter point is telling in terms of the nexus of hypercompetition and hyperpower, and warrants elaboration. In a highly competitive environment, corporations in the OECD area have increasingly emphasized development activities rather than underlying research. Facing more competition from new entrants into the market, established business enterprises have moved closer to commercialization, which directly links scientific knowledge to near-term outcomes. Accentuating development activities means the application of knowledge to definite marketable products. At the other end of the spectrum, basic research seeks to make discoveries and expand science, but its spin-offs for practical use may be decades away (S. Campbell 2007, 10). In this restructuring, globalization has influenced the shift from early-stage research. Greater globalization of R&D entails intensifying specialization of firms and regions in the drive for profit as they look to external sources of knowledge and innovation (OECD 2002, 107).

At the sites of technological innovation, firms are impelled to get their products quickly to market. Yet the security risk is leakage of certain technologies abroad, especially when advanced weaponry is a highly valued product. The overall trend is toward military R&D, which supports the security strategy of the "war on terror." The United States alone is responsible for more than 80 percent of government spending in the industrialized world on military R&D (2006 figures cited in Parkinson 2008, 7–8, which draws on OECD and International Energy Agency documents). In a sustained period from 1976, when nondefense spending has remained flat, the most recent figures reflect large increases in federal support for weapons systems development (Koizumi 2008, 22).[1]

Consequently, military influence over R&D squeezes out R&D that could address root issues such as poverty, environmental harms, and poor health, all of which may fuel conflict. Allocations for war fighting displace resources for use in matters of human security and conflict prevention.

GOVERNANCE

As intimated in Chapter 8, hyperpower contains a paradox. In a contradictory manner, it tamps down some conflicts, but the asymmetries inherent in this condition bring structural conflict. To examine this phenomenon in our turbulent times, it is instructive to recall the foremost writing on the 1929 global depression and learn from historical experience.

In his seminal work, Charles Kindleberger ([1973] 1986) contends that the Great Depression surpassed a typical business downturn due to geopolitical reasons. After World War I, the United Kingdom was unable to bear the short-term costs of maintaining an open market for goods and for providing countercyclical lending, and the United States was unwilling to do so ([1973] 1986, 289). In other words, a single, strong leader—a hegemon—did not avert instability. The absence of a stabilizer impaired both public and private interests. With the onset of depression, an upswing in competition, such as with aggressive exchange depreciation, and more chaotic behavior prevailed ([1973] 1986, 293). Nonetheless, in the interwar years, the United States remained uncertain of its international role and was loath to commit to a stabilization program for the world economy.

In comparison to Kindleberger's analysis, Galbraith's classic volume ([1955] 1972) on the Great Depression is more focused on the stock market crash and domestic factors. Yet he too underlines power holders' lack of will to exercise effective leadership, the tendency to protect short-term interests, and like Stiglitz and Bilmes on securities in a later era, the role of new types of instruments that enable speculation. A counterpart to Kindleberger's international perspective, Galbraith's work centers on inadequate efforts in the United States to take responsibility for checking excessive speculation, a lack of transparency, and growing fear of risky markets.

All in all, national governments responded to the Great Depression to varying degrees with their own monetary and fiscal measures. The post-1945 order then ushered in new international institutions to avoid repetition of the dire conditions that marked the interwar period. The launch of the United Nations and the Bretton Woods institutions was supposed to put in place a more comprehensive range of mechanisms to avert this type of trauma. These arrangements are an acknowledgment that state responsibilities need to be supplemented by additional layers of governance.

Yet the complex of global governance agencies is still groping for security in the face of rising anxieties about instability in the twenty-first century. The IMF and other international organizations are not equipped to regulate national institutions or quasi-governmental instruments such as sovereign wealth funds. Moreover, the leaders of countries such as China and India have expressed their displeasure with institutions in which their weight is not commensurate with the size of their populations and burgeoning roles in the global economy.

In this century, market turmoil has provoked added protectionism, as with the U.S. rescue package for the Big Three carmakers. This action has triggered similar measures elsewhere (for example, the Canadian government's assistance for its automobile manufacturers), thereby slowing world trade. During the 1930s, too, governments sought to protect domestic industries. A global trade war followed and worsened the world depression. In the contemporary period, similar prospects are within the WTO's purview, especially given that the Doha Round of trade talks stalled in 2001 and remains uncertain.

The barriers to new agreements toughen during hard times. In the G-8, the United States under the George W. Bush presidency balked at European calls for a new international regulatory agency and refused proposals for major re- structuring of the Bretton Woods institutions. In 2008, the Group of Twenty (G-20) summit of major and emerging economies pledged to refrain from pro- tectionist measures and to reach a global trade deal that would lower tariffs on various exports. However, at the time of writing (August 2009), these promises are unfulfilled. Still on the table is the G-20's process for realizing a "Bretton Woods II" architecture of institutional reform. Yet, by all indications, it barely touches on the deeper issues of regulation, the ideas and norms being institu- tionalized, and the conundrum of who governs globalization. These matters are at the core of world order. They are tied to underlying causes of hyperconflict, including poverty, maldevelopment, energy scarcity, environmental damage, and distributive injustice.

In the absence of reworking rules in these spheres, policies are piecemeal. Sufficient international cooperation to mitigate the deleterious effects of hy- percompetition is conspicuously lacking. Not only the means but also the po- litical resolve is deficient. Leaving aside authorities' rhetorical flourishes about curbing abuses, market-driven organizations and pro-market ideas attendant to maximizing revenues continue to prevail along with paltry regulatory mea- sures. In this atmosphere, many investors, government officials, and consumers express anger at the reckless behavior of firms. Public distrust grows. In some cases, as in Greece in 2008–9, workers and youth mount vehement protests over the self-seeking behavior of their antiheroes: corrupt politicians, dishonest bureaucrats, and the very rich who maintain the dominant ideology and profit from deregulated market economies.

IDEOLOGY

The policy failures are indeed partly in the realm of ideology. In the United States after 9/11, commentators have complained about the intelligence agen- cies' blind-sighted assessments of Iraq, decision-makers' refusal to heed warnings about the pitfalls of military intervention in the Persian Gulf region, and enduring faith in free-market solutions. Time and again, standard-bearers such as President George W. Bush, Treasury Secretary Hank Paulson, Federal Reserve Board Chairman Alan Greenspan, and the latter's successor, Ben Bernanke, affirmed their conviction that left to their own devices, markets self-correct.

Yet free-market orthodoxy, a cornerstone of neoliberal conservatism, could not accommodate glaring discrepancies with its tenets. Patently, the lack of fit came to the fore when, in a Schmittian manner, the American head of state had to decide on the exception in applying extraordinary measures. As Schmitt put it, "Sovereign is he who decides on the exception" ([1922] 1985, 5). Thus, when the constitutional order required the president to respond swiftly to the events of September 11, 2001, George W. Bush aimed to normalize behavior. Referring to himself, not the three branches of government, as "the decider," President Bush told the American public to go shopping (Bush 2006). His reflex was to buoy markets. Citizenship is thus defined as a matter of patriotic consumption. In this optic, citizens ought to optimize their individual interests by means of market transactions.

Increasingly, the market is a modus operandi for national security. The armed forces are jobbed by outsourced private military contractors along with voluntary recruits, some of them impelled by rising unemployment in the United States (Jensen 2008). Additionally, deficit spending at home and borrowing from abroad has sustained the wars in Afghanistan and Iraq.

In 2007–8, when the war economy entered a slump, U.S. policymakers abrogated key positions that they had brandished in international negotiations for twenty or more years. In an emblematic move, Washington had demanded that American firms be treated by counterpart countries within their territorial domains according to the same provisions as they apply to local companies. This is the concept of "national treatment" that the United States promoted in the MAI treaty (Chapter 4). However, the American government then reversed course by assisting auto manufacturers at home without bolstering overseas corporations, such as Toyota and BMW, that built factories in the United States, employed American workers, and paid benefits to them (Sanger 2008).

Reckoning with such vast changes in globalizing capitalism, Greenspan distills his experience and worldview in *The Age of Turbulence* (2007), a book that offers insight into how ideology and power are interconnected. In his eighteen-and-a-half years at the helm of the Federal Reserve and as a senior advisor to heads of state, Greenspan vigorously defended free markets, but he was also responsible for the Fed's regulatory apparatus. Steadfast in his belief that competition is "the primary driver of economic growth and standards of living in the United States," Greenspan acknowledges that he staunchly opposed most regulation (2007, 249, 373): "Economic reregulation would be a distinct step backward in our quest for a prosperous future" (2007, 468). The only wise policy, he counsels, is to rely on the invisible hand: "maintain maximum market flexibility—freedom of action for key market participants such as hedge funds, private equity funds, and investment banks" (2007, 489). Greenspan insists that although economic shocks are bound to occur, "human nature does not change" (2007, 490–91).

Yet less than three years after stepping down as Fed chairman, Greenspan admitted that his faith in the self-correcting mechanisms of free markets failed to anticipate the self-destructive power of mortgage lending, leading him to "a state of shocked disbelief" ("Looking Back in Disbelief" 2008). Questioned by Congressman Henry Waxman, head of the U.S. House Committee on Oversight and Government Reform, in 2008, Greenspan said that he made a mistake in presuming that self-interested organizations could best protect their shareholders (U.S. Congress. . . . 2008, 33). He testified that "a conceptual framework is . . . the way people deal with reality. Everyone has one. You have to. To exist, you need an ideology" (2008, 36). However, Greenspan found that his ideology defining how the world operates "contained a flaw" (2008, 37). "I was shocked, because I had been going for 40 years or more with very considerable evidence that it was working exceptionally well" (2008, 37). Unfortunately, a multitude of citizens must pay the price for these grave errors.

In this changing political milieu, public intellectuals have provided perspective on the predicaments of the United States. In a cogent account, *Bad Money* (2008), political commentator and former Republican Party strategist Kevin Phillips cautions about "ideological doctrine" clouding perception of financialization and a debt mentality (Phillips 2008, 40). Phillips also links military hubris and policymakers' incompetence to trends in political economy, mainly during the quarter century beginning in the 1980s. He traces the expansion of debt and serial scandals: the collapse of savings and loan (S&L) associations leading to federal relief, the Federal Reserve–coordinated rescue of New York's Citibank, and the Federal Reserve's bailout of junk (high-yielding) bonds in the 1990s. These problems in the financial sector spilled over to the deregulated energy and telecommunications sectors, typified by the problems of Enron, WorldCom, and Global Crossing. The high tech and stock market bubbles popped during the Clinton years in office (2008, 47). A converging financial triangulation—a vulnerable dollar, the housing bubble, and the credit crisis—followed (2008, 52). This came amid energy scarcity and global climate change.

Phillips's narrative is valuable in that it delves beneath prime-time stories. But it does not reach deeply enough for the basic transformations in capitalism, another and more global type of convergence. As argued throughout this book, shifts in competition and the means of hyperpower form an arc of hyperconflict. But other analysts seek to tell the backstory of this turmoil in a different manner.

Like Phillips, Niall Ferguson, a financial historian at Harvard and Oxford universities (also a writer and presenter of television documentaries), wants to look behind proximate shocks roiling the global political economy. Compared to Phillips's script, Ferguson's *The Ascent of Money* (2008) offers a longer view. In fact, he searches for the origins of moneylending and then extends this story to the present day.

Ferguson (2003, 2006) is attuned to the power dynamics of empire and imperialism. He is unabashedly nostalgic for the security that hegemony has provided. And edging close to the concept of hypercompetition, Ferguson employs Joseph Schumpeter's notion of "creative destruction" (Schumpeter [1942] 1947, 82–83) to explain the annihilation of firms that cannot adapt in the financial sphere. Schumpeter underscored the "distinct rushes" in technology, business models, and markets that "incessantly revolutionize[ ]" capitalism; the tendency toward stagnation is a major strength because it brings impulses for radical improvements ([1942] 1947, 83). Highlighting the extent of this kind of destruction in a modern economy, Ferguson indicates that about one of every ten U.S. companies fails each year. In finance, the mortality rate is even higher in troubled times: 20 percent in the District of Columbia at the peak of the S&L collapse in 1989 (Ferguson 2008, 349, citing Ormerod 2005, 180ff). His grand historical tour shows the nexus between great power and sound finance.

Drawing lessons from the past, Ferguson cautions about the risks of financial overstretch. The United States has become part of a symbiotic relationship with China that he dubs "the dual country of Chimerica." To keep its financial system afloat, America has relied on overseas capital. Ferguson observes that "for a time it seemed like a marriage made in heaven. The East Chimericans did the saving. The West Chimericans did the spending" (Ferguson 2008, 335). From the mid-1990s, China enjoyed strong export growth, amassed large savings, and recycled a portion of its trade earnings in the United States. It invested heavily in American government bonds and government-supported mortgage debt, thereby lowering interest rates, helping fuel consumption, adding to the U.S. trade deficit, and swelling the housing bubble. For Ferguson, Chimerica is the "underlying reason" for the spike in bank lending, the explosion of new derivatives and hedge funds, and the high level of cash flushed through the U.S. mortgage market by 2006 (2008, 336). But then came a rash of mortgage defaults in the United States in 2007 and a cave-in of financial giants and Wall Street investment houses. "Maybe," Ferguson conjectures, "Chimerica is nothing more than a chimera" (2008, 339).

In other words, Ferguson contends that the weakness in finance lies in the synergy between China and the United States. Surely, his cautionary tales provide important lessons about the ways in which financial capital can bring insecurity. But is Chimerica really the source of the shocks that are shaking the contemporary order? Do the upheavals come down to this issue? And the conclusion that the long-term "trajectory" of finance is uneven but "unquestionably upwards" (2008, 358) seems fanciful given the pattern of self-destructive behavior (Hirsh 2008, 10). Ferguson, in effect, expresses a rosy ideological outlook on these tumultuous times.

Also, a shortcoming in Ferguson's frame is the omission of arguments that spring from competing paradigms. He blithely engages celebrity economists like W. W. Rostow, Hernando de Soto, Paul Krugman, Joseph Stiglitz, and Muhammad Yunus. These savants include Nobel Prize winners with high-level policy experience. While not of one mind, they are all liberals who ply the neoclassical tools of their trade. But Ferguson silences critics of the conventional paradigm itself, such as Samir Amin, Walden Bello, Jomo K.S., and Martin Khor. The point is that Ferguson's analysis suffers from a problem of voice. While the worldviews of pundits like Ferguson court controversies, they could further expand the possibilities for sparking new ideas and efforts to reorganize world order.

THE UNFINISHED BUSINESS IN WORLD ORDER

In summary, a basic facet of world order is a double surge of interrelated buildups in major conflicts and financial speculation. These stem from multiple causes. Some of the self-destructive behavior, such as the machinations of neoconservative hawks, the U.S. addiction to foreign creditors for financing consumption, and record government spending, is homegrown. These malfunctions are tunneled more deeply than the ill-conceived policies of particular administrations in Washington.

Indeed, the twin implosions that mark the course of hyperconflict are linked to coercive globalization in three ways. First, they undermine the credibility of the policy framework of deregulation, privatization, and liberalization. Second, the war economy engenders multiple resistances. Finally, the dominant ideology is being reworked, with alternative proposals for curbing militarism and reembedding footloose capital.

If the future is ever to see the chain of hyperconflict broken, dramatic steps must be taken. On this score, it is important to hazard priorities. The key ones are cutting defense spending, closing military bases, detaching globalization from a neoliberal framework, and linking economic reform to social policy.

Taken together, these measures offer an opportunity to step up and reshape the kinds of societies we will live in after the wars and bailouts of the early part of this millennium. After all, what are those efforts really for? To return to prior ways of political and economic life? Or are they an occasion to help reorient world order? Certainly, broad issues of global governance, distributive justice, and environmental sustainability can be reenvisaged. This potential could either be wasted or used to bend hyperconflict into democratic globalization and durable peace.

NOTES

Chapter 1

1. The WEF is a private, not-for-profit foundation based in Geneva. Each year, it brings together CEOs of the one thousand largest corporations in the world, central bankers, presidents, prime ministers, journalists, and some scholars, usually in Davos, Switzerland. As a counterpoint, the World Social Forum debates strategies of resistance to market globalization (Reitan 2006; Teivainen 2009).

2. For this point, I am grateful to Jacob Stump (2006).

3. Like Chua, political scientist Stanley Hoffman (2002, 113) thinks of American preponderance in terms of "hyperpower."

4. There are of course different theories of the state; Weber's definition is a foundation for realism and a touchstone for other definitions. In an oft-cited passage, Weber submits, "A compulsory political organization with continuous operations will be called a 'state' insofar as its administrative staff successfully upholds the claim to the monopoly of the legitimate use of physical force in the enforcement of its order" (1978, 54–56). For a slight inflection in this conceptualization, drawn from a translation of another book by Weber, see Chapter 2, p. 46.

5. Preliminary attempts to fill this void are Ripsman and Paul (2005); Barkawi (2006); Kahler and Walter (2006); Kirshner (2006); Patomäki (2007); Bigo and Tsoukala (2008); Brooks and Wohlforth (2008); and Grenfell and James (2008). The stony silence is discussed in Chapter 2.

Chapter 2

1. The designations "security studies" and "conflict analysis" are frequently used interchangeably, and I will follow this convention.

2. For this point on production for the home market, I am indebted to John Willoughby (personal communication with the author, 4 November 2007).

3. For reviews of the burgeoning literature on democratic peace, see James Ray (1995) and Steve Chan (1997).

4. The 2008 Brookings Institution's *Index of State Weakness in the Developing World* (Rice and Patrick 2008) is one attempt to establish criteria for identifying failed or weak states and to rank them. In this research, described as "a new tool for policymakers," the "Failed State Index" delimits "critically weak states." Somalia, Afghanistan, the DRC, and Iraq are assigned the worst scores among 141 states (Rice and Patrick 2008, 10, 17). Brookings 2008 similarly identifies lower numbers with more weakness, but its findings differ markedly from *Foreign Policy*'s "Failed States Index" ("Failed State Index 2008," 2008), prepared in collaboration with the Fund for Peace. For instance, Brookings puts Iran at 66; Egypt, 78; and Kenya, 50. By comparison, on the *Foreign Policy* Index for the same year, Iran is 49; Egypt, 40; and Kenya, 26. Arguably, methodological disagreements may account for the divergence in ratings. But how to decide which global scorekeeper is correct? Who is really going to dig into all the ways in which the statistical detail is tallied? And how to treat anomalies like Belgium, which a German newspaper called the "most successful failed state," whose per capita income is greater than that of Germany and where the consensus between French-speaking Wallonia and Dutch-speaking Flanders has broken down to the point of talk about "linguistic cleansing" (Kimmelman 2008).

5. In subsequent work, Reno (n.d.) contributed an impressive paper to the Social Science Research Council (SSRC)'s (n.d.) "Project on Globalization and Conflict." In contrast to my own attempt to develop a political-economy approach to the study of globalization and insecurity, the SSRC project allows boundaries between the study of politics and of economics, as at its April 2004 conference "The Economic Analysis of Conflict: Problems and Prospects."

6. The new-wars approach intersects with the emphasis in feminist security studies on the ways in which women are implicated (Elshtain 1987; Enloe 2000); the Copenhagen school on who securitizes what and for whom (Buzan, Waever, and de Wilde 1998); and, more broadly, critical security studies on community, identity, and emancipation (Booth 1991; Krause and Williams 1997; R. Jones 1999; Booth 2005; C.A.S.E. Collective 2006).

7. For my account of the Finnish civil war, I owe a debt of gratitude to Timo Pankakoski (2004) for stellar assistance.

8. Similar findings are reported in Stathis Kalyvas's analysis (2001) of "old" and "new" civil wars as well as Mats Berdal's study of "new" wars and economic globalization (2003).

Chapter 3

1. Although it is widely held that Strauss's authoritarian persuasions, including approval of Plato's "noble lies," had great influence on the neoconservative movement that flourished early in the twenty-first century (e.g., Schlesinger 2004), some observers take issue with the notion that a political philosopher focused on the classical works could give impetus to the hawks who shaped foreign policy during the presidency of George W. Bush (S. Smith 2006).

2. Manfred B. Steger (2006, 2008) has advanced my thinking on neoconservatism.

3. Updating this formulation, Shaw (2005) added the sociology of risk management to issues of war: with increasingly potent military technologies, risk-transfer war is a way to extend the nature of life-risks away from the architects of armed conflict and their agents and transmit them to the enemy.

4. I am indebted to Jan Aart Scholte for raising this issue in response to my presentation at the University of Warwick, Coventry, U.K., 20 October 2004.

5. I owe this point to Raimo Väyrynen, conversation with the author, Helsinki, Finland, 23 November 2004.

6. Jacob Stump (2006) kindly alerted me to this aspect of Foucault's writings. Before Foucault made this point, Orwell ([1949] 1950) presented the critical view that "war is peace."

7. For drawing my attention to the writings of Carl Schmitt, I am grateful to Mika Ojakangas. Today, the Schmittian revival includes left-wing Schmittians, attracted to the German scholar's ideas because of the ways in which they skewer liberal democracy and incorporate a structural perspective on power, and right-wing Schmittians, who want to bolster sovereignty and who criticize neoconservatives for drifting too far from their philosophical moorings. Balakrishnan (2002) provides Schmitt's intellectual biography and explores his concept of enemy.

8. Among the authors who later found nuance in the friend/enemy distinction and developed the Self/Other notion are Edward Said (1979), David Campbell (1992), R.B.J. Walker (1993), Christine Sylvester (1994), Naeem Inayatullah and David Blaney (2004), and Michel Foucault (2005).

9. Mindful that the term "foreign" is the convention, but fraught, I use it advisedly in this book.

10. Randolph Persaud (2007) drew my attention to this danger in employing the Self/Other distinction.

Chapter 4

1. The relationship between trade and investment is less than straightforward. From the standpoint of macroeconomics, FDI and investment are not identical (Vocke 1997).

2. Estimates of the number of BITs in any year vary. These agreements differ in many respects, and analysts count them at diverse stages of ratification.

Chapter 5

1. This section builds on Mittelman and Pasha (1997, 130–53), which details the strategies of the Asian NICs.

2. For an annotated list of sources on recovery strategies, see Lim, Ching, and Villeges (online).

3. It is important to note, too, that by 2000, most Asian countries increased their

foreign exchange reserves and signed the Chiang Mai Initiative, a bilateral swap arrangement among thirteen countries, wherein they would help one another if global capital flows adversely impinged on their economies.

4. Reports by international organizations, including the ILO and the International Organization for Migration, draw on national statistics, the reliability of which, especially for undocumented migrants, is often questionable.

5. I am grateful to Pek Koon Heng for bringing RELA to my attention and sharing research material.

6. The arrest of activist Irene Fernandez, director of Tenaganita, drew substantial attention to the demands of these organizations. Charged with "maliciously publishing false news" and criminal defamation in 1996, Fernandez was found guilty and sentenced to prison in 2003. Two years later, she received Sweden's prestigious Right Livelihood Award for her work to stop violence against women and maltreatment of migrant workers.

Chapter 6

1. In Britain, the Battle of Seattle terminology appeared in venues spanning the tabloid press to standard regional and national newspapers (e.g., "Colin Putts in Bid" 1998; "Cool Monty Relishes the Battle in Seattle" 1998; "Westwood Misses His First Cut of the Season" 1998).

2. In this context, swarms, unlike waves (in traditional warfare), employed the tactic of striking from several directions and in many ways. Both protestors and the RAND National Defense Research Institute (Arquilla and Ronfeldt 2001) use this language. Earlier, the concept may be found in Foucault (1978).

3. For a popular rendering of the flat-world concept and an account that disapproves of social criticism formulated at the Battles of Seattle, see Friedman (2005, esp. 384–86; cf. N. Smith 2005 and Steger 2008), a book published after the WTO Third Ministerial that made the best-seller lists.

Chapter 7

1. Even after the British government dropped the "war" title, the George W. Bush administration equivocated about this metaphor. Senior officials in Washington referred to "the global war against [variously on] terrorism," omitted the "global" modifier, sometimes referenced the "long war," and occasionally termed it "persistent conflict." Throughout this book, the metaphors "global war on terror" and, without the adjective, simply "war on terror" are used interchangeably. For us, however, the word "global" calls to mind both the metaphor (without an endorsement of the idea of a worldwide movement of terrorists) and the compression of time and space, which, as stated, is a core feature of contemporary globalization.

2. To illustrate the material impact of this dispute, between February and June 2006

total Danish exports fell by 15.5 percent and Denmark's trade with the Middle East declined by half ("Cartoon Row Hits Danish Exports" 2006).

3. President George W. Bush declared that the United States is "at war with Islamic fascists who will use any means to destroy those of us who love freedom, to hurt our nation" ("President Bush Discusses Terror Plot upon Arrival in Wisconsin" 2006). Viewing the phrases "Islamo fascists" and "Islamic fascists" as epithets, U.S. Muslims complained about political officials who use these terms ("Bush's Language Angers U.S. Muslims" 2006).

4. Juergensmeyer notes that he uses the term "guys" because "it evokes the camaraderie of young males slightly on the edge of social acceptance" (Juergensmeyer 2003, 201).

5. Critics assailed this icon-of-war story about an endangered heroine rescued by courageous special forces. It is alleged that although local doctors had arranged to deliver her by ambulance from a hospital that the Iraqi military had fled, U.S. soldiers charged into the facility for the sake of news coverage by embedded reporters and the production of a Hollywood-style film clip that could be used to garner support for the occupation (Kampfner 2003).

Chapter 8

1. In preparing this section on "the rosy view," I received valuable research assistance from Carl Anders Härdig (2007).

2. Building on a dataset prepared at the Center for International Development and Conflict Management at the University of Maryland in 1994, the PITF's work is undertaken in cooperation with research at the Center for Systemic Peace at George Mason University.

3. Chapter 5 in Beck ([2004] 2006), entitled "War Is Peace: On Postnational War," informs my thinking about postnational security.

4. Randolph Persaud (2008) shared this observation; I have greatly benefited from his meticulous comments on this chapter.

5. My discussion of political fear borrows from Robin (2004).

6. In line with the point that security is a multifaceted concept surrounding the uncertainties of risk (Chapter 1), "securitization," as it is known in the bank-investment industry, developed in the United States starting in the 1970s. Bankers mobilized capital from mortgages, used the funds to issue bonds, and bundled them for trading in other sectors. This way of doing business with "collateralized debt obligations" (repackaged products) and its attendant risks rapidly spread to other world regions. The volume of U.S. mortgage lending financed in this manner escalated. It resulted in toxic assets and exceeded the infrastructure of an unregulated market. This instability linked to leveraged loan securitization ramified widely in global markets.

7. The passages on China that follow are based on Mittelman (2006) and incorpo-

rate findings from research visits to China (1985, 1988, 2000, 2002, and 2005) and Japan (2000).

8. Among world-systems theorists, sociologists such as Immanuel Wallerstein (1974) and Christopher Chase-Dunn (Chase-Dunn and Hall 1997) track long waves but not security per se. In this scholarly tradition, political scientists, including George Modelski (1987) and William Thompson (Gills and Thompson 2006), examine power and leadership cycles. Joined to these very long perspectives is critical thinking on empire (Hardt and Negri 2000), changing structures of global capitalism (W. Robinson 2004), and "new imperialism" (Harvey 2005). More broad-gauged in their time frames than my analysis, they inform the research undertaken in this book.

Epilogue

1. At 57.1 percent, the defense share of government-financed R&D for the United States far exceeded that of other countries: 13.5 percent for fifteen EU countries tallied together; 4.0 percent for Japan; and 13.3 percent for South Korea (S. Campbell 2007, 5, using 2005 figures). Data for China are not available.

REFERENCES

Abbott, Chris, Paul Rogers, and John Sloboda. 2006. *Global Response to Global Threats: Sustainable Security for the 21st Century*. Oxford, UK: Oxford Research Group.

Abdul Kadir Jasin and Syed Nazri. 1997. "No Choice but to Accept Globalisation." *New Straits Times* (Kuala Lumpur), 25 October.

Abdul Rahman Embong. 2002. *State-Led Modernization and the New Middle Class in Malaysia*. New York: Palgrave Macmillan.

Abella, Manolo I. 2004. "Labour Migration in East Asian Economies." Paper presented at the Annual Bank Conference on Development Economics—Europe. Brussels, Belgium, 10–11 May. Unpublished.

ACME Collective. 2002. "N30 Black Bloc Communiqué." In *The Battle of Seattle: The New Challenge to Capitalist Globalization*, ed. Eddie Yuen, George Katsiaficas, and Daniel Burton Rose, 115–19. New York: Soft Skull Press.

Adams, Jason. n.d. Interview by Jeremy Simer, 16 March 2000. Center for Labor Studies. http://depts.washington.edu/wtohist/interviews/Adams.pdf (accessed 22 December 2006).

Addison, Tony, and S. Mansoob Murshed. 2003. "Explaining Violent Conflict: Going beyond Greed versus Grievance." *Journal of International Development* 15, no. 4 (May): 391–96.

Adhikari, Gautam. 2004. "The End of the Unipolar Myth: American Power." *International Herald Tribune*, 27 September.

Agamben, Giorgio. 1998. *Homo Sacer: Sovereign Power and Bare Life*. Trans. Daniel Heller-Roazen. Stanford, CA: Stanford University Press.

———. 1999. *Potentialities: Collected Essays in Philosophy*. Ed. and trans. Daniel Heller-Roazen. Stanford, CA: Stanford University Press.

———. 2005. *State of Exception*. Trans. Kevin Attell. Chicago: University of Chicago Press.

Ahmed, Tofail. 1999. *Statement to the Conference Plenary*. http://www.wto.org/english/thewto_e/minist_e/min99_e/english/state_e/d5199e.pdf (accessed 18 February 2007).

Akamatsu, Kaname. 1962. "A Historical Pattern of Economic Growth in Developing Countries." *The Developing Economies* 1, no. 1 (March–August): 3–25.

Al-Qaeda. 2000. *The al-Qaeda Manual*. http://www.fas.org/irp/world/para/manual-part1_1.pdf (accessed 7 September 2006).

Altman, Roger C. 2009. "The Great Crash, 2008." *Foreign Affairs* 88, no. 1 (November): 2–14.

American Association for the Advancement of Science. 2006. http://www.aaas.org/spp/rd/guiintl.htm (accessed 21 February 2006).

Amsden, Alice. 1989. *Asia's Next Giant: South Korea and Late Industrialization*. New York: Oxford University Press.

Anderson, Benedict. 1991. *Imagined Communities: Reflections on the Origin and Spread of Nationalism*. London and New York: Verso.

"Another Item on the Fed Worry List: Inequality." 2006. *Wall Street Journal*, 7 November. http://blogs.wsj.com/washwire/2006/11/07/another-item-on-the-fed-worry-list-in-equality/ (accessed 30 June 2008).

Appadurai, Arjun. 2006. *Fear of Small Numbers: An Essay on the Geography of Anger*. Durham, NC: Duke University Press.

Aron, Raymond. 1966. *Peace and War: A Theory of International Relations*. Trans. Richard Howard and Annette Baker Fox. Garden City, NY: Doubleday.

Arquilla, John, and David Ronfeldt. 2001. "The Advent of Netwar (Revisited)." In *Networks and Netwars: The Future of Terror, Crime and Militancy*, ed. John Arquilla and David Ronfeldt, 1–25. Santa Monica, CA: RAND.

Arrighi, Giovanni. 2005. "Globalization in World-Systems Perspectives." In *Critical Globalization Studies*, ed. Richard P. Appelbaum and William I. Robinson, 33–44. New York: Routledge.

Asian Development Bank. 2007. *Beyond the Crisis: Emerging Trends and Challenges*. Manila: ADB.

"Asia's Suffering." 2009. *The Economist* (London), 31 January.

A. T. Kearney, Inc. 2007. "The Globalization Index." *Foreign Policy* 163 (November–December): 68–76. http://www.foreignpolicy.com/story/cms.php?story_id=3995 (accessed 17 February 2008).

Atlas, James. 2003. "The Nation: Leo-Cons; A Classicist's Legacy: New Empire Builders." *New York Times*, 4 May.

Authers, John. 2006. "After the Nation State, Say Goodbye to National Indices." *Financial Times*, 28–29 October.

Avant, Deborah D. 2005. *The Market for Force: The Consequences of Privatizing Security*. New York: Cambridge University Press.

Balakrishnan, Gopal. 2002. *The Enemy: An Intellectual Portrait of Carl Schmitt*. London: Verso.

Ballentine, Karen, and Jake Sherman, eds. 2003. *The Political Economy of Armed Conflict.* Boulder, CO: Lynne Rienner Publishers.

Barbieri, Katherine, and Gerald Schneider. 1999. "Globalization and Peace: Assessing New Directions in the Study of Trade and Conflict." *Journal of Peace Research* Special Issue on Trade and Conflict 36, no. 4 (July): 387–404.

Barkawi, Tarak. 2006. *Globalization and War.* Lanham, MD: Rowman and Littlefield.

Barlow, Maude, and Tony Clarke. 1998. *MAI: The Multilateral Agreement and the Threat to American Freedom.* New York: Stoddart.

Barnes, Henry Elmer, ed. 1953. *Perpetual War for Perpetual Peace: A Critical Examination of the Foreign Policy of Franklin Delano Roosevelt and Its Aftermath.* Caldwell, ID: Caxton.

Barnett, Thomas P.M. 2004. *The Pentagon's New Map: War and Peace in the Twenty-first Century.* New York: G. P. Putnam's Sons.

"The Battle of Seattle." 1892. *New York Times,* 18 July.

"Battle of Seattle." 1906. *Los Angeles Times,* 29 April.

Beard, Charles. 1946. *American Foreign Policy in the Making 1932–1940: A Study in Responsibilities.* New Haven, CT: Yale University Press.

———. 1948. *President Roosevelt and the Coming of the War, 1941: A Study in Appearances and Realities.* New Haven, CT: Yale University Press.

Beck, Ulrich. 1999. *World Risk Society.* Cambridge, UK: Polity Press.

———. [2004] 2006. *The Cosmopolitan Vision.* Trans. Ciaran Cronin. Cambridge, UK: Polity Press.

Berdal, Mats. 2003. "How 'New' Are 'New' Wars? Global Economic Change and the Study of Civil War." *Global Governance* 9, no. 4 (October–December): 477–502.

Berdal, Mats, and David M. Malone, eds. 2000. *Greed and Grievance: Economic Agendas in Civil Wars.* Boulder, CO: Lynne Rienner Publishers.

Bernasek, Anna. 2006. "The State of Research Isn't All That Grand." *New York Times,* 3 September.

Bernstein, Richard. 2004. "Germany's Challenge on Muslim Integration." *International Herald Tribune,* 10 December.

Bhagwati, Jagdish. 2004. *In Defense of Globalization.* New York: Oxford University Press.

Bigo, Didier, and Anastassia Tsoukala, eds. 2008. *Terror, Insecurity and Liberty: Illiberal Practices of Liberal Regimes after 9/11.* New York: Routledge.

Blank, Stephen J. 1999. "East Asia in Crisis: The Security Implications of the Collapse of Economic Institutions." Carlisle, PA: Strategic Studies Institute, U.S. Army War College. Unpublished.

Bloom, Allan. 1987. *The Closing of the American Mind.* New York: Simon and Schuster.

Bob, Clifford. 2005. *Marketing the Rebellion: Insurgents, Media, and International Activism.* Cambridge, UK: Cambridge University Press.

Bobbitt, Philip. 2002. *The Shield of Achilles: War, Peace, and the Course of History*. New York: Alfred A. Knopf.

Booth, Ken, ed. 1991. *New Thinking about Strategy and International Security*. London: HarperCollins.

——, ed. 2005. *Critical Security Studies and World Politics*. Boulder, CO: Lynne Rienner Publishers.

Bradsher, Keith. 2007. "Asia's Long Road Back." *New York Times*, 28 June.

Braudel, Fernand. 1980. *On History*. Trans. Sarah Matthews. Chicago: University of Chicago Press.

Broad, William J. 2004. "U.S. Is Losing Its Dominance in the Sciences." *New York Times*, 3 May.

Brooks, Stephen G. 2005. *Producing Security: Multinational Corporations, Globalization, and the Changing Calculus of Conflict*. Princeton, NJ: Princeton University Press.

Brooks, Stephen G., and William C. Wohlforth. 2008. *World Out of Balance: International Relations and the Challenge of American Primacy*. Princeton, NJ: Princeton University Press.

Brun, Ellen, and Jacques Hersh. 2008. "The Danish Disease: A Political Culture of Islamophobia." *Monthly Review* 60, no. 2 (June): 11–22.

Brzezinski, Zbigniew. 1997. *The Grand Chessboard: American Primacy and Its Geostrategic Imperatives*. New York: Basic Books.

Brzoska, Michael. 2004. "'New Wars' Discourse in Germany." *Journal of Peace Research* 41, no. 1 (January): 107–17.

Bull, Hedley. 1977. *The Anarchical Society: A Study of Order in World Politics*. New York: Columbia University Press.

Bush, George W. 2006. "Press Conference on the Nominations of Rob Portman as OMB Director and Susan Schwab for USTR." 18 April. http://www.whitehouse.gov/news/releases/2006/04/20060418-1.html (accessed 15 January 2009).

"Bush's Language Angers U.S. Muslims." 2006. BBC News Online, 12 August. http://news.bbc.co.uk/2/hi/americas/4785065.stm (accessed 19 September 2006).

Butler, Judith. 2004. *Precarious Life: The Powers of Mourning and Violence*. London and New York: Verso.

——. 2005. *Giving an Account of Oneself*. New York: Fordham University Press.

Buzan, Barry, and Ole Waever. 2004. *Regions and Powers: The Structure of International Security*. Cambridge, UK: Cambridge University Press.

Buzan, Barry, Ole Waever, and Jaap de Wilde. 1998. *Security: A New Framework for Analysis*. Boulder, CO: Lynne Rienner Publishers.

Camdessus, Michel, James D. Wolfensohn, and Mike Moore. 1999. *Joint Statement by the Heads of the International Monetary Fund, the World Bank, and the World Trade Organization*. http://www.wto.org/English/news_e/pres99_e/pr153_e.htm (accessed 18 February 2007).

Campbell, David. 1992. *Writing Security: United States Foreign Policy and the Politics of Identity*. Minneapolis: University of Minnesota Press.

Campbell, Sheila. 2007. *Federal Support for R&D*. U.S. Congressional Budget Office. http://www.cbo.gov/ftpdocs/82xx/doc8221/06-18-Research.pdf (accessed 16 January 2009).

"Cartoon Row Hits Danish Exports." 2006. BBC News Online, 9 September. http://news.bbc.co.uk/2/hi/europe/5329642.stm (accessed 10 September 2006).

C.A.S.E. Collective. 2006. "Critical Approaches to Security in Europe: A Networked Manifesto." *Security Dialogue* 37, no. 4 (December): 443–87.

Center for Arms Control and Non-Proliferation. 2008. http://www.armscontrolcenter.org/policy/securityspending/articles/current_spending_vs_historical_highs/ (accessed 22 December 2008).

Cha, Victor D. 2000. "Globalization and the Study of International Security." *Journal of Peace Research* 37, no. 3 (May): 391–403.

Chan, Steve. 1997. "In Search of Democratic Peace." *Mershon International Studies Review* 41, no. 1 (May): 59–91.

Chase-Dunn, Christopher, and Thomas D. Hall. 1997. *Comparing World-Systems*. Boulder, CO: Westview Press.

Chenoy, Anuradha M. 2004. "Gender and International Politics: The Intersections of Patriarchy and Militarisation." *Indian Journal of Gender Studies* 11, no. 1 (January–April): 27–42.

Chin, Christine B.N. 1998. *In Service and Servitude: Foreign Female Domestic Workers and the Malaysian "Modernity" Project*. New York: Columbia University Press.

Chossudovsky, Michel. 1999. "Fighting MAIgalomania: Canadian Citizens Sue Their Government." *The Ecologist* 29, no. 8 (December): 449–51.

Chua, Amy. 2004. *World on Fire: How Exporting Free Market Democracy Breeds Ethnic Hatred and Global Instability*. Westminster, MD: Knopf Publishing Group.

———. 2007. *Day of Empire: How Hyperpowers Rise to Global Dominance—And Why They Fall*. New York: Doubleday.

Clarke, Tony, and Maude Barlow. 1997. "The War on Cultural Rights." *Canadian Forum* 76, no. 865 (December): 20–24.

Clausewitz, Carl von. [1832] 1968. *On War*. Trans. J. J. Graham and ed. with an introduction by Anatol Rapoport. London: Penguin.

Clinton, Bill. 1999a. "Clinton Addresses the WTO." PBS Online NewsHour with Jim Lehrer. 1 December. http://www.pbs.org/newshour/bb/international/wto/clinton_wto_12-1.html (accessed 18 February 2007).

———. 1999b. "Remarks by the President to Farmers, Students from the Seattle-Tacoma Area Who Study Trade, and Area Officials." 1 December. *The White House Office of the Press Secretary*. http://clinton4.nara.gov/WH/New/WTO-Conf-1999/remarks/19991201-1237.html (accessed 22 December 2006).

————. 1999c. "Remarks by the President in Telephone Interview with Seattle Post-Intelligencer Newspaper." 30 November. *The White House Office of the Press Secretary.* http://clinton4.nara.gov/WH/New/WTO-Conf-1999/remarks/19991130-1650.html (accessed 22 December 2006).

"Colin Putts in Bid." 1998. *Evening News* (Edinburgh, UK), 15 August.

Collier, Paul. 2007. *The Bottom Billion: Why the Poorest Countries Are Failing and What Can Be Done About It.* New York: Oxford University Press, 2007.

Collier, Paul, and Anke Hoeffler. 2001. "Greed and Grievance in Civil War." http://econ. worldbank.org/programs/conflict/library/doc?id=12205 (accessed 19 November 2004).

"A Conversation with David Harvey." 2006. *Logos* 5, no. 1 (Winter). http://www.logos-journal.com/issue_5.1/harvey.html (accessed 13 October 2006).

"Cool Monty Relishes the Battle in Seattle." 1998. *Sunday Mirror* (UK), 16 August.

Cooley, Alexander, and James Ron. 2002. "The NGO Scramble: Organizational Insecurity and the Political Economy of Transnational Action." *International Security* 27, no. 1 (Summer): 5–39.

Cooper, Denise. n.d. Interview by Monica Ghosh. *Center for Labor Studies.* http://depts. washington.edu/wtohist/interviews/Cooper-Ghosh.pdf (accessed 22 December 2006).

Cooper, Robert. 2003. *The Breaking of Nations: Order and Chaos in the Twenty-first Century.* New York: Atlantic Monthly Press.

Correlates of War (project). online. http://cow2.la.psu.edu (accessed 22 February 2006).

Cox, Michael. 2001. "Whatever Happened to American Decline? International Relations and the New United States Hegemony." *New Political Economy* 6, no. 3 (November): 311–40.

Cox, Robert W. 1996. *Approaches to World Order.* With Timothy J. Sinclair. Cambridge, UK: Cambridge University Press.

Crumpton, Henry A. 2006. "Testimony on Improving Interagency Coordination for the Global War on Terror and Beyond." 4 April. http://www.globalsecurity.org/security/ library/congress/2006_h/060404-crumpton.pdf (accessed 29 May 2007).

Daniel, Caroline. 2006. "Anxious Agenda: Bush Will Battle to Turn His Stumbling Second Term into a Legacy of Reform." *Financial Times*, 31 January.

D'Aveni, Richard. 1994. *Hypercompetition: Managing the Dynamics of Strategic Maneuvering.* With Robert Gunther. New York: Free Press.

————. 1995. *Hypercompetitive Rivalries: Competing in Highly Dynamic Environments.* With Robert Gunther. New York: Free Press.

Dawood, Abdul Razak. 1999. *Statement to the Conference Plenary.* http://www.wto.org/ english/thewto_e/minist_e/min99_e/english/state_e/d5203e.pdf (accessed 18 February 2007).

Decalo, Samuel. 1976. *Coups and Army Rule in Africa: Studies in Military Rule.* New Haven, CT: Yale University Press.

Deng Yong, and Thomas G. Moore. 2004. "China Views Globalization: Toward a New Great-Power Politics." *Washington Quarterly* 27, no. 3 (Summer): 117–36.

Denny, Emily Inez. circa 1890. "Battle of Seattle." Painting of 1856 battle; photographed 6 August 1986. *University of Washington Libraries Digital Collections.* http://content.lib.washington.edu/cgi-bin/viewer.exe?CISOROOT=/imlsmohai&CISOPTR=3119&CISORESTMP=&CISOVIEWTMP= (accessed 22 December 2006).

Der Derian, James. 1987. *On Diplomacy: A Genealogy of Western Estrangement.* Oxford, UK: Basil Blackwell.

Deyo, Frederick C., ed. 1987. *The Political Economy of the New Asian Industrialism.* Ithaca, NY: Cornell University Press.

Dhar, Biswajit, and Sachin Chaturvedi. 1998. "Multilateral Agreement on Investment: An Analysis." *Economic and Political Weekly* 33, no. 15 (11 April): 837–49.

Dicken, Peter. 2003. *Global Shift: Reshaping the Global Economic Map in the 21st Century.* 4th ed. New York: Guilford Press.

Divine, Robert A. 2000. *Perpetual War Through Perpetual Peace.* College Station: Texas A&M University Press.

Dixit, Priya. 2004a. "Research Note," 7 September. Unpublished.

———. 2004b. "Research Note," 21 September. Unpublished.

———. 2005. "Research Note," 30 March. Unpublished.

Doyle, Michael W. 1983a. "Kant, Liberal Legacies and Foreign Affairs," Part I. *Philosophy and Public Affairs* 12, no. 3 (Summer): 205–35.

———. 1983b. "Kant, Liberal Legacies and Foreign Affairs," Part II. *Philosophy and Public Affairs* 12, no. 4 (Fall): 323–53.

Drinnon, Richard. 1997. *Facing West: The Metaphysics of Indian-Hating and Empire Building.* Norman: University of Oklahoma Press.

Duffield, Mark. 2001. *Global Governance and the New Wars: The Merging of Development and Security.* London: Zed Books.

———. 2007. *Development, Security and Unending War: Governing the World of Peoples.* Cambridge, UK: Polity Press.

Duke, Simon. 2003. "The Hyperpower and the Hype: Reassessing Transatlantic Relations in the Iraqi Context." Working Paper No. 2003/W/1. Maastricht, Netherlands: European Institute of Public Administration.

Dyer, Braven. 1951. "Sports Parade." *Los Angeles Times,* 9 October.

Economy, Elizabeth. 2008. "Leadership Gap in China." *Washington Post,* 1 December.

Edkins, Jenny. 2000. "Sovereign Power, Zones of Indistinction, and the Camp." *Alternatives: Social Transformation and Humane Governance* 25, no. 1 (January–March): 3–25.

Egan, Daniel. 2001. "The Limits of Internationalization: A Neo-Gramscian Analysis of the Multilateral Agreement on Investment." *Critical Sociology* 27, no. 3: 74–97.

Elshtain, Jean. 1987. *Women and War*. New York: Basic Books.

Enloe, Cynthia. 2000. *Maneuvers: The International Politics of Militarizing Women's Lives*. Berkeley: University of California Press.

———. 2003. "Masculinity as a Foreign Policy Issue." In *After Shock: Global Feminist Perspectives on September 11, 2001*, ed. Susan Hawthorne and Bronwyn Winter, 284–89. Vancouver, Canada: Raincoast Books.

"The Failed State Index 2008." 2008. *Foreign Policy* 167 (July–August): 64–73.

Falk, Richard. 1997. "The Critical Realist Tradition and the Demystification of Interstate Power: E. H. Carr, Hedley Bull and Robert W. Cox." In *Innovation and Transformation in International Studies*, ed. Stephen Gill and James H. Mittelman, 39–55. Cambridge, UK: Cambridge University Press.

———. 2004. *The Declining World Order: America's Imperial Geopolitics*. New York: Routledge.

Fanon, Frantz. 1965. *Studies in a Dying Colonialism*. Trans. Haakon Chevalier. New York: Monthly Review Press.

Faux, Jeff. 2006. "The Party of Davos." *The Nation* 282, no. 6 (13 February): 18–22.

Fauza Ab. Ghaffar. 2003. "Globalisation and Malaysia's Policies on Migrant Labour." In *The State, Economic Development and Ethnic Co-existence in Malaysia and New Zealand*, ed. Edmund Terence Gomez and Robert Stephens, 274–96. Kuala Lumpur: Centre for Economic Development and Ethnic Relations, University of Malaya.

Ferguson, Niall. 2003. *Empire: The Rise and Demise of the British World and the Lessons for Global Power*. New York: Basic Books.

———. 2006. *The War of the World: Twentieth-Century Conflict and the Descent of the West*. New York: Penguin.

———. 2008. *The Ascent of Money: A Financial History of the World*. New York: Penguin.

Fischer, Stanley. 1998a. "In Defense of the IMF." *Foreign Affairs* 77, no. 4 (July/August): 103–6.

———. 1998b. "The IMF and the Asian Crisis." In "Resource Materials: International Workshop on International Studies in the Era of Globalization: States, Markets, Values." Institute of Malaysian and International Studies at the National University of Malaysia, the Program for International Studies in Asia, and the Carnegie Council on Ethics and International Affairs, 1–18. Bangi, Malaysia: Universiti Kebangsaan Malaysia.

Fleshman, Michael. 1999. "WTO Impasse in Seattle Spotlights Inequities of Global Trading System." *Africa Recovery* 13, no. 4 (December): 1, 30–34.

Foucault, Michel. 1978. *History of Sexuality*, Vol. 1. Trans. Robert Hurley. New York: Pantheon.

———. 2003. *"Society Must Be Defended": Lectures at the Collège de France, 1975–1976*. Trans. David Macey. New York: Picador.

———. 2005. *The Hermeneutics of the Subject: Lectures at the Collège de France, 1981–1982.* Trans. Graham Burchell. New York: Picador.

Friedman, Thomas L. 1999. *The Lexus and the Olive Tree.* New York: Farrar, Straus and Giroux.

———. 2005. *The World Is Flat: A Brief History of the Twenty-first Century.* New York: Farrar, Straus and Giroux.

Frost, Ellen L. 2001. "Globalization and National Security: A Strategic Agenda." In *The Global Century: Globalization and National Security,* ed. Richard L. Kugler and Ellen L. Frost, Vol. 1, 35–74. Washington, DC: National Defense University Press.

Fukuyama, Francis. 1989. "The End of History?" *The National Interest* 16 (Summer): 3–16.

———. 2006. *America at the Crossroads: Democracy, Power, and the Neoconservative Legacy.* New Haven, CT: Yale University Press.

Furedi, Frank. 2002. *Culture of Fear: Risk-Taking and the Morality of Low Expectation.* London: Continuum.

Galbraith, John Kenneth. [1955] 1972. *The Great Crash, 1929.* Boston: Houghton Mifflin.

Galtung, Johan. 1967. *Theory and Methods of Social Research.* New York: Columbia University Press.

George Mason University Molecular and Microbiology Department. online. http://www.gmu.edu/departments/mmb/biodefense/acad_phdprg.html (accessed 20 October 2006).

Giddens, Anthony. 1991. *Modernity and Self-Identity: Self and Society in the Late Modern Age.* Cambridge, UK: Polity Press.

Giddens, Anthony, and Christopher Pierson. 1998. *Conversations with Anthony Giddens: Making Sense of Modernity.* Stanford, CA: Stanford University Press.

Giles, Chris. 2007. "Poll Reveals Backlash in Wealthy Countries Against Globalisation." *Financial Times,* 23 July.

Gill, Ranjit. 1998. *Asia under Siege: How the Asian Miracle Went Wrong.* Singapore: Epic Management Services Pte Ltd.

Gills, Barry K., and William R. Thompson. 2006. *Globalization and Global History.* New York: Routledge.

Gilpin, Robert. 2002. *The Challenge of Global Capitalism: The World Economy in the 21st Century.* Princeton, NJ: Princeton University Press.

Gleditsch, Nils Petter. 2007. "The Decline of War—Will It Continue?" Paper presented at the annual meeting of the International Studies Association, Chicago, 28 February–3 March.

Glickman, Daniel. 1999. *Statement to the Conference Plenary.* http://www.wto.org/english/thewto_e/minist_e/min99_e/english/state_e/d5245e.pdf (accessed 18 February 2007).

Gomez, Edmund Terence, and Jomo K. S. 1997. *Malaysia's Political Economy: Politics, Patronage and Profits.* Cambridge, UK: Cambridge University Press.

Goodman, James, and Patricia Ranald, eds. 2000. *Stopping the Juggernaut: Public Interest versus the Multilateral Agreement on Investment.* Annandale, New South Wales, Australia: Pluto Press.

Gorlick, Arthur C. 1998. "City Sized Up for High Power Meeting: WTO Checks Out Seattle Bid for 1999." *Seattle Post-Intelligencer,* 1 October.

Gramsci, Antonio. 1971. *Selections from the Prison Notebooks.* Trans. and ed. Quintin Hoare and Geoffrey Nowell Smith. London: Lawrence and Wishart.

Greenspan, Alan. 2007. *The Age of Turbulence: Adventures in a New World.* New York: Penguin.

Grenfell, Damian, and Paul James, eds. 2008. *Rethinking Insecurity, War and Violence: Beyond Savage Globalization?* London: Routledge.

Grimaldi, James V., and Ross Anderson. 1999. "Clinton Will Use Protests in Talks—Demonstrations Give Him Leverage." *Seattle Times,* 29 November.

Gurowitz, Amy. 2000. "Migrant Rights and Activism in Malaysia: Opportunities and Constraints." *Journal of Asian Studies* 50, no. 4 (November): 863–88.

Gurr, Ted Robert. 2000. *Peoples versus States: Minorities at Risk in the New Century.* Washington, DC: United States Institute of Peace Press.

Habermas, Jürgen. 1973. *Legitimation Crisis.* Trans. Thomas McCarthy. Boston: Beacon Press.

Halliday, Fred. 2001. "No Man Is an Island." *Observer* (London), 16 September.

Hamilton, Gary. 1999. "Asian Business Networks in Transition or What Alan Greenspan Does Not Know about the Asian Business Crisis." In *The Politics of the Asian Economic Crisis,* ed. T. J. Pempel, 45–61. Ithaca, NY: Cornell University Press.

Hamilton-Hart, Natasha. 2000. "Thailand and Globalization." In *East Asia and Globalization,* ed. Samuel S. Kim, 187–207. Lanham, MD: Rowman and Littlefield.

Harbom, Lotta, Stina Högbladh, and Peter Wallensteen. 2006. "Armed Conflict and Peace Agreements." *Journal of Peace Research* 43, no. 5 (September): 617–31.

Härdig, Carl Anders. 2007. "Research Note," 31 May. Unpublished.

Hardt, Michael, and Antonio Negri. 2000. *Empire.* Cambridge, MA: Harvard University Press.

———. 2004. *Multitude: War and Democracy in the Age of Empire.* London: Penguin.

Harsch, Ernest. 1998. "Africa Tenses for Asian Aftershocks." *Africa Recovery* 12, no. 2 (November). http://www.un.org/ecosocdev/geninfo/afrec/subjindx/122asia5.thm (accessed 13 November 2006).

Harvey, David. 2005. *The New Imperialism.* New York: Oxford University Press.

Hawthorne, Susan, and Bronwyn Winter, eds. 2003. *After Shock: Global Feminist Perspectives on September 11, 2001.* Vancouver, Canada: Raincoast Books.

Hearden, Patrick J. 2008. *The Tragedy of Vietnam.* New York: Pearson Longman.

Heisler, Mark. 1984. "Hoyas, Wildcats: It May Get Down to Push and Shove." *Los Angeles Times,* 31 May.

Held, David. 2004. *Global Covenant: The Social Democratic Alternative to the Washington Consensus*. Cambridge, UK: Polity Press.

Henderson, David. 2000. *The MAI Affair: A Story and Its Lessons*. London: Royal Institute of International Affairs.

Herbert, Bob. 2005. "The Mobility Myth." *New York Times*, 6 June.

Hettne, Björn, András Inotai, and Osvaldo Sunkel, eds. 1999. *Globalism and the New Regionalism*. London: Macmillan, and New York: St. Martin's.

Hirschman, Albert O. 1981. *Essays in Trespassing: Economics to Politics and Beyond*. Cambridge, UK: Cambridge University Press.

Hirsh, Michael. 2008. "Follow the Money." *New York Times*, 28 December.

Hobsbawn, Eric. 2002. "The Future of War and Peace." *CounterPunch*, 27 February.

Hoffman, Stanley. 1978. *Primacy or World Order: American Foreign Policy since the Cold War*. New York: McGraw-Hill.

———. 2002. "Clash of Globalizations." *Foreign Affairs* 81, no. 4 (July–August): 104–15.

Holsti, Kal J. 1996. *The State, War, and the State of War*. Cambridge, UK: Cambridge University Press.

Homer-Dixon, Thomas F. 1999. *Environment, Scarcity, and Violence*. Princeton, NJ: Princeton University Press.

Hough, Peter. 2004. *Understanding Global Security*. New York: Routledge.

"How to Pay for a 21st-Century Military." 2008. *New York Times*, 21 December.

Hunt, Krista, and Kim Rygiel, eds. 2006. *(En)Gendering the War on Terror: War Stories and Camouflaged Politics*. Aldershot, Hampshire, UK: Ashgate.

Huntington, Samuel P. 1996. *The Clash of Civilizations and the Remaking of World Order*. New York: Simon and Schuster.

———. 1999. "The Lonely Superpower." *Foreign Affairs* 78, no. 2 (March/April): 35–49.

———. 2004. *Who Are We? The Challenges to America's National Identity*. New York: Simon and Schuster.

Hussain, Mohammed Nureldin, Kupukile Mlambo, and Temitope Oshikoya. 1999. "Global Financial Crisis: An African Perspective." African Development Bank, Research Paper 42. http://www.afdb.org/pls/portal/docs/PAGE/ADB_ADMIN_PG/DOCUMENTS/ECONOMICSANDRESEARCH/ERP-42.PDF (accessed 13 November 2006).

Ikenberry, G. John. 2001. *After Victory: Institutions, Strategic Restraint, and the Rebuilding of Order after Major Wars*. Princeton, NJ: Princeton University Press.

Inayatullah, Naeem, and David Blaney. 2004. *International Relations and the Problem of Difference*. New York: Routledge.

Institute for National Security and Counterterrorism. online. http://inst.syr.edu (accessed 29 May 2007).

International Labor Organization. 1998. "The Social Impact of the Asian Financial Crisis." 22–24 April. Bangkok: ILO.

International Monetary Fund (IMF). 1997. *International Monetary Fund Annual Report 1997*. Washington, DC: IMF.

———. 1998. *International Monetary Fund Annual Report 1998*. Washington, DC: IMF.

———. 2003. *IMF and Recent Capital Account Crises: Indonesia, Korea, Brazil*. Washington, DC: IMF.

"Is It Doing More Harm or Has the IMF Cured Asia?" 1998. *New Straits Times* (Kuala Lumpur), 26 April.

Ishak Shari. 1998. "Asian Financial and Economic Crisis and Implications on Poverty and Income Inequality in Malaysia: A Preliminary Observation." Bangi, Malaysia: Institute of Malaysian and International Studies, Universiti Kebangsaan Malaysia. Unpublished.

———. n.d. "Economic Growth and Income Inequality in Malaysia." Bangi, Malaysia: Institute of Malaysian and International Studies, Universiti Kebangsaan Malaysia. Unpublished.

Jackson, Robert H. 1990. *Quasi-States: Sovereignty, International Relations and the Third World*. Cambridge, UK: Cambridge University Press.

Jensen, Benjamin. 2008. Personal correspondence with the author. 6 December.

"The Jobs of War: As Conflicts Stretch Armed Forces Worldwide, the Private Sector Is Seizing Its Chance to Profit." 2003. *Financial Times*, 11 August.

Johnson, Chalmers A. 1982. *MITI and the Japanese Miracle: The Growth of Industrial Policy, 1925–1975*. Stanford, CA: Stanford University Press.

———. 2006. *Nemesis: The Last Days of the American Republic*. New York: Metropolitan Books.

Jomo K. S., ed. 1998. *Tigers in Trouble: Financial Governance, Liberalisation and Crises in East Asia*. London: Zed Books.

Jones, Adam, and Elizabeth Rigby. 2006. "Carrefour Gets Competitive: The New Head of the French Hypermarket Is Increasing Market Share by Cutting Prices." *Financial Times*, 30 March.

Jones, Richard Wyn. 1999. *Strategy, Security, Critical Theory*. Boulder, CO: Lynne Rienner Publishers.

Jones, Sidney. 1998. "Social Cost of Asian Crisis." *Financial Times*, 26 January.

Juergensmeyer, Mark. 2003. *Terror in the Mind of God: The Global Rise of Religious Violence*. Berkeley: University of California Press.

Jung, Dietrich. 2003. "A Political Economy of Intra-state War: Confronting a Paradox." In *Shadow Globalization, Ethnic Conflicts and New Wars: A Political Economy of Intrastate War*, ed. Dietrich Jung, 9–26. New York: Routledge.

Kahler, Miles, and Barbara F. Walter, eds. 2006. *Territoriality and Conflict in an Era of Globalization*. Cambridge, UK: Cambridge University Press.

Kaldor, Mary. 1999. *New and Old Wars: Organized Violence in a Global Era*. Stanford, CA: Stanford University Press.

———. 2000. "Cosmopolitanism and Organised Violence." First Press. http://www.the-globalsite.ac.uk (accessed 27 November 2004).

———. 2003. *Global Civil Society: An Answer to War*. Cambridge, UK: Polity Press.

Kalyvas, Stathis N. 2001. "'New' and 'Old' Civil Wars: A Valid Distinction?" *World Politics* 54, no. 1 (October): 99–118.

Kampfner, John. 2003. "The Truth about Jessica." *Guardian* (London), 15 May. http://www.guardian.co.uk/world/2003/may/15/iraq.usa2 (accessed 22 January 2009).

Kanapathy, Vijayakumari. 2004. "Malaysia: Country Paper. "International Migration and Labour Market Developments in Asia: Economic Recovery, The Labour Market and Migrant Workers in Malaysia." Paper presented at the 2004 Workshop on International Migration and Labour Markets in Asia, 5–6 February.

Kant, Immanuel. [1795] 1948. *Perpetual Peace: A Philosophical Essay*. Trans. M. Campbell Smith. New York: Liberal Arts Press.

Keck, Margaret E., and Kathryn Sikkink. 1998. *Activists beyond Borders: Advocacy Networks in International Politics*. Ithaca, NY: Cornell University Press.

Kennedy, Paul M. 1987. *The Rise and Fall of the Great Powers: Economic Change and Military Conflict from 1500 to 2000*. New York: Random House.

Keohane, Robert O. 1984. *After Hegemony: Cooperation and Discord in the World Political Economy*. Princeton, NJ: Princeton University Press.

———. 1989. *International Institutions and State Power: Essays in International Relations Theory*. Boulder, CO: Westview Press.

Keynes, John Maynard. 1936. *The General Theory of Employment, Interest and Money*. New York: Harcourt, Brace, and World.

Khan, Haider A. 2004. *Global Markets and Financial Crises in Asia: Towards a Theory for the 21st Century*. New York: Palgrave Macmillan.

Khor, Martin. 1998. "NGOs Mount Protests Against MAI." *Third World Resurgence* 90/91 (February–March). http://www.ngos/net.mai.html#ngos (accessed 23 February 2006).

Kimmelman, Michael. 2008. "With Flemish Nationalism on the Rise, Belgium Teeters on the Edge." *New York Times*, 4 August.

Kindleberger, Charles P. [1973] 1986. *The World in Depression, 1929–1939*. Berkeley: University of California Press.

Kirshner, Jonathan, ed. 2006. *Globalization and National Security*. New York: Routledge.

Klare, Michael T. 2001. *Resource Wars: The New Landscape of Global Conflict*. New York: Henry Holt.

Klein, Naomi. 2000. "The Vision Thing." *The Nation* 271, no. 2 (10 July).

Kobrin, Stephen J. 1998. "The MAI and the Clash of Globalizations." *Foreign Policy* 112 (Fall): 97–109.

Koizumi, Kei. 2008. "Historical Trends in Federal R&D." In *AAAS Report XXXIII: Re-*

search and Development FY 2009. American Association for the Advancement of Science Industry Working Group. http://www.aaas.org/spp/rd/rd09main.htm (accessed 18 January 2009).

Kolko, Gabriel. 2006. *The Age of War: The United States Confronts the World*. Boulder, CO: Lynne Rienner Publishers.

Kono, Yohei. 1999. *Statement to the Conference Plenary*. http://www.wto.org/english/thewto_e/minist_e/min99_e/english/state_e/d5224e.pdf (accessed 18 February 2007).

Koppel, Ted. 2006. "Will Fight for Oil." *New York Times*, 24 February.

Krasner, Stephen D. 1999. *Sovereignty: Organized Hypocrisy*. Princeton, NJ: Princeton University Press.

Krause, Keith, and Michael Williams, eds. 1997. *Critical Security Studies: Concepts and Cases*. Minneapolis: University of Minnesota Press.

Kregel, J. A. 1998. "East Asia Is Not Mexico: The Difference Between Balance of Payments Crises and Debt Deflation." In *Tigers in Trouble: Financial Governance, Liberalisation and Crises in East Asia*, ed. Jomo K. S., 44–62. London: Zed Books.

Krill, Jennifer. 2000. Interview by Miguel Bocangere, Center for Labor Studies. http://depts.washington.edu/wtohist/interviews/Krill.pdf (accessed 22 December 2006).

Kristof, Nicholas D. 2007. "Our Gas Guzzlers, Their Lives." *New York Times*, 28 June.

Krugman, Paul. 1994. "The Myth of Asia's Miracle." *Foreign Affairs* 73, no. 6 (November/December): 62–78.

———. 1998. "Will Asia Bounce Back?" Speech for Credit Suisse First Boston, Hong Kong, March. Reprinted in "Resource Materials: International Workshop on International Studies in the Era of Globalization: States, Markets, Values." Institute of Malaysian and International Studies, Program for International Studies in Asia, and Carnegie Council on Ethics and International Affairs, 1–6. Bangi, Malaysia: Universiti Kebangsaan Malaysia.

Kugler, Richard L., and Ellen L. Frost, eds. 2001. *The Global Century: Globalization and National Security*, 2 vols. Washington, DC: National Defense University Press.

Kumanoff, Nicolas. 2004. "What Is *Leitkultur*?" *Atlantic Times* (Washington, DC), December.

Lacina, Bethany, and Nils Petter Gleditsch. 2005. "Monitoring Trends in Global Combat: A New Dataset of Battle Deaths." *European Journal of Population* 1, nos. 2–3 (June): 145–66.

Lacina, Bethany, Nils Petter Gleditsch, and Bruce Russett. 2006. "The Declining Risk of Death in Battle." *International Studies Quarterly* 50, no. 3 (September): 673–80.

Lake, David A., and Donald Rothchild. 1998. "Spreading Fear: The Genesis of Transnational Ethnic Conflict." In *The International Spread of Ethnic Conflict: Fear, Diffusion, and Escalation*, ed. David A. Lake and Donald Rothchild, 3–32. Princeton, NJ: Princeton University Press.

Lampreia, Luiz Felipe. 1999. *Statement to the Conference Plenary*. http://www.wto.org/english/thewto_e/minist_e/min99_e/english/state_e/d5243e.pdf (accessed 18 February 2007).

Lamy, Pascal. 1999. *Statement to the Conference Plenary*. http://www.wto.org/english/thewto_e/minist_e/min99_e/english/state_e/d5196e.pdf (accessed 18 February 2007).

Larson, Alan. 1998. "The Multilateral Agreement on Investment: A Work in Progress." *U.S. Department of State Dispatch* 9, no. 3 (April): 30–33.

Levy, Jack S. 1983. *War in the Modern Great Power System*. Lexington: University of Kentucky Press.

Lichbach, Mark Irving. 2002. "Global Order and Local Resistance: Structure, Culture, and Rationality in the Battle of Seattle." Unpublished.

Lim, Joseph Y. 1998. "The Philippines and the East Asian Economic Turmoil." In *Tigers in Trouble: Financial Governance, Liberalisation and Crises in East Asia*, ed. Jomo K. S., 199–221. London: Zed Books.

Lim, Linda Y.C. 1997. "The Southeast Asian Currency Crisis and Its Aftermath." *Journal of Asian Business* 13, no. 1: 65–83.

———. 1998. "Economic Crisis and Conspiracy Theory in Asia." In "Resource Materials: International Workshop on International Studies in the Era of Globalization: States, Markets, Values." Institute of Malaysian and International Studies, Program for International Studies in Asia, and Carnegie Council on Ethics and International Affairs, 1–20. Bangi, Malaysia: Universiti Kebangsaan Malaysia.

Lim, Linda Y.C., Frank Ching, and Bernardo M. Villeges. online. "East and Southeast Asia: An Annotated Directory of Internet Resources. The Asian Financial Crisis and Recovery." http://newton.uor.edu/Departments&Programs/AsianStudiesDept/general-crisis.html (accessed 30 September 2006).

Lipscy, Philip Y. 2003. "Japan's Asian Monetary Fund Proposal." *Stanford Journal of East Asian Affairs* 3, no. 1 (Spring): 93–104.

"Looking Back in Disbelief." 2008. *New York Times*, 24 October.

Lukauskas, Arvid John, and Francisco L. Rivera-Batiz. 2001. "Introduction: The Political Economy of the East Asian Crisis." In *The Political Economy of the East Asian Financial Crisis and Its Aftermath*, ed. Arvid John Lukauskas and Francisco L. Rivera-Batiz, 1–27. Cheltenham, UK: Edgar Algar.

Mabey, Nick. 1999. "Defending the Legacy of Rio: The Civil Society Campaign Against the MAI." In *Regulating International Business: Beyond Liberalization*, ed. Sol Picciotto and Ruth Mayne, 60–81. Houndmills, Basingstoke, UK: Macmillan, and New York: St. Martin's.

Mack, Andrew, ed. 2006. *The Human Security Report 2005: War and Peace in the 21st Century*. Oxford, UK: Oxford University Press.

MacKinnon, Catherine A. 2003. "State of Emergency." In *After Shock: Global Feminist*

Perspectives on September 11, 2001, ed. Susan Hawthorne and Bronwyn Winter, 467–73. Vancouver, Canada: Raincoast Books.

———. 2006. "Women's September 11th: Rethinking the International Law of Conflict." *Harvard International Law Journal* 47, no. 1 (Winter): 1–31.

MacMillan, John. 2003. "Beyond the Separate Democratic Peace." *Journal of Peace Research* 40, no. 2 (March): 233–43.

Magnus, Kathy Dow. 2006. "The Unaccountable Subject: Judith Butler and the Social Conditions of Intersubjective Agency." *Hypatia* 21, no. 1 (Winter): 81–103. http://www.humansecurityreport.info/ (accessed 7 February 2006).

Mahathir Mohamad. 2000. *Islam and the Muslim Ummah: Selected Speeches of Dr. Mahathir Mohamad,* ed. Hashim Makaaruddin. Kuala Lumpur: Pelanduk Publications (M) Sdn Bhd.

Mamdani, Mahmood. 2004a. *Good Muslim, Bad Muslim: America, the Cold War, and the Roots of Terror.* New York: Pantheon Books.

———. 2004b. *"Good Muslim, Bad Muslim:* An Interview with Mahmood Mamdani." By Nermeen Shaikh. *CODESRIA Bulletin,* nos. 3 and 4: 6–11.

Mandel, Michael J. 2004. "How to Sharpen the Innovation Edge." *Business Week* 3903 (11 October): 225.

Mansfield, Edward D., and Jon C. Pevehouse. 2003. "Institutions, Interdependence, and International Conflict." In *Globalization and Armed Conflict,* ed. Gerald Schneider, Katherine Barbieri, and Nils Petter Gleditsch, 233–50. Lanham, MD: Rowman and Littlefield.

Mansfield, Edward D., and Jack Snyder. 2005. *Why Emerging Democracies Go to War.* Boston: MIT Press.

Maran, Murasoli. 1999. *Statement to the Conference Plenary.* http://www.wto.org/english/thewto_e/minist_e/min99_e/english/state_e/d5194e.pdf (accessed 18 February 2007).

Marshall, Monty G., and Jack Goldstone. 2007. "Global Report on Conflict, Governance, and State Fragility 2007: Gauging System Performance and Fragility in the Globalization Era." *Foreign Policy* 17, no. 1 (Winter): 3–21.

Marshall, Monty G., and Ted Robert Gurr. 2005. *Peace and Conflict 2005: A Global Survey of Armed Conflicts, Self-Determination Movements, and Democracy.* College Park: Center for International Development and Conflict Management, University of Maryland. http://www.cidcm.umd.edu/ (accessed 15 February 2006).

Marshall, Monty G., Ted Robert Gurr, and Barbara Harff. 2001. "PITF Problem Set Codebook." January revision. http://globalpolicy.gmu.edu/pitf/pitfcode.htm (accessed 20 February 2007).

Marshall, Monty G., Keith Jaggers, and Ted Robert Gurr. n.d. "Polity IV Project: Political Regime Characteristics and Transitions, 1800–2002." http://www.cidcm.umd.edu/polity/ (accessed 18 July 2007).

Martinez, Elizabeth. 2000. "Where Was the Color in Seattle? Looking for Reasons Why the Great Battle Was So White." In *Globalize This!*, ed. Kevin Danaher and Roger Burbach, 74–81. Monroe, ME: Common Courage Press. http://www.cidcm.umd.edu/ (accessed 4 December 2004).

McDermott, Terry. 1992. "Battle of Seattle: Why Is Baseball Afraid of Japan, Land of the Rising Sum?" *Calgary Herald*, 2 February.

McDonald, Patrick J. 2004. "Peace Through Trade or Free Trade?" *Journal of Conflict Resolution* 48, no. 4 (August): 547–72.

Melloan, George. 1998. "Crony Capitalist Will Cheer Seattle Zanies." *Wall Street Journal*, 8 November.

Melman, Seymour. 1970. *Pentagon Capitalism: The Political Economy of War*. New York: McGraw-Hill.

———. 1971. *The War Economy of the United States: Readings on Military Industry and Economy*. New York: St. Martin's.

———. [1974] 1985. *The Permanent War Economy: American Capitalism in Decline*. New York: Simon and Schuster.

———. 2003. "In the Grip of a Permanent War Economy." *Swans*. http://www.swans.com/library/art9/melman01.html (accessed 26 November 2008).

Migdal, Joel S. 1988. *Strong Societies and Weak States: State-Society Relations and State Capability in the Third World*. Princeton, NJ: Princeton University Press.

Mittelman, James H. 1975. *Ideology and Politics in Uganda: From Obote to Amin*. Ithaca, NY: Cornell University Press.

———. 1981. *Underdevelopment and the Transition to Socialism: Mozambique and Tanzania*. New York: Harcourt Brace Jovanovich/Academic Press.

———, ed. 1996. *Globalization: Critical Reflections*. Boulder, CO: Lynne Rienner Publishers.

———. 2000. *The Globalization Syndrome: Transformation and Resistance*. Princeton, NJ: Princeton University Press.

———. 2004a. Feature Review of Joseph E. Stiglitz, *Globalization and Its Discontents*. *New Political Economy* 9, no. 1 (March): 129–33.

———. 2004b. *Whither Globalization? The Vortex of Knowledge and Ideology*. New York: Routledge.

———. 2006. "Globalization and Development: Learning from Debates in China." *Globalizations* 3, no. 3 (September): 377–91.

———. 2008. "Beyond Impoverished Antipoverty Paradigms." *Third World Quarterly* 29, no. 8 (December): 1639–52.

———. 2009. "The Valence of Iraq? Globalization and the State," *Globalizations* 6, no. 1 (March): 111–16.

Mittelman, James H., and Norani Othman, eds. 20001. *Capturing Globalization*. New York: Routledge.

Mittelman, James H., and Mustapha Kamal Pasha. 1997. *Out from Underdevelopment Revisited: Changing Global Structures and the Remaking of the Third World.* London: Macmillan, and New York: St. Martin's.

Modelski, George. 1987. *Long Cycles in World Politics.* Seattle: University of Washington Press.

Moore, Mike. 1999a. "Director-General's Press Statement." *World Trade Organization,* 30 November. http://www.wto.org/english/thewto_e/minist_e/min99_e/english/press_e/pres157_e.htm (accessed 22 December 2006).

———. 1999b. "Labour Issue Is 'False Debate,' Obscures Underlying Consensus, WTO Chief Mike Moore Tells Unions." *World Trade Organization,* 28 November. http://www.wto.org/english/thewto_e/minist_e/min99_e/english/press_e/pres152_e.htm (accessed 22 December 2006).

———. 1999c. "Moore Cites Role of Legislators in WTO." *World Trade Organization,* 2 December. http://www.wto.org/english/thewto_e/minist_e/min99_e/english/press_e/pres159_e.htm (accessed 22 December 2006).

Morgenson, Gretchen. 2008. "Debt Watchdogs: Tamed or Caught Napping?" *New York Times,* 7 December.

Murshed, S. Mansoob. 2002. "Conflict, Civil War and Underdevelopment: An Introduction." *Journal of Peace Research* Special Issue on Civil War in Developing Countries 39, no. 4 (July): 387–93.

Mustapa Mohamed. 2000. "Globalisation: A Malaysian View." In *The Economic and Financial Imperatives of Globalisation: An Islamic Response,* ed. Nik Mustapha, Nik Hassan, and Mazilan Musa, 3–12. Kuala Lumpur: Institute of Islamic Understanding.

Mydans, Seth. 2007. "A Growing Source of Fear for Migrants in Malaysia." *New York Times,* 10 December.

Nafziger, E. Wayne, and Juha Auvinen. 2003. *Economic Development, Inequality, and War: Humanitarian Emergencies in Developing Countries.* Houndmills, Basingstoke, UK: Palgrave Macmillan.

Naim, Moisés. 2003. "The Five Wars of Globalization." *Foreign Policy* 134 (January/February): 28–37.

National Consortium for the Study of Terrorism and Responses to Terrorism (START). online. http://www.start.umd.edu/ (accessed 16 October 2006).

Nau, Henry. 2004/2005. "No Enemies on the Right: Conservative Foreign Policy Factions beyond Iraq." *National Interest* 78 (Winter): 19–28.

Naylor, R. T. 2002. *Wages of Crime: Black Markets, Illegal Finance, and the Underworld Economy.* Ithaca, NY: Cornell University Press.

Nederveen Pieterse, Jan. 2003. "Hyperpower Exceptionalism: Globalisation the American Way." *New Political Economy* 8, no. 3 (November): 299–319.

Nidets, Steve. 1976. "Henry Tries 'Diplomacy' at Olympics." *Chicago Tribune,* 15 February.

Nobel Foundation. online. http://nobelprize.org (accessed 6 August 2009).

Noble, Gregory W., and John Ravenhill. 2000. "Causes and Consequences of the Asian Financial Crisis." In *The Asian Financial Crisis and the Architecture of Global Finance*, ed. Gregory W. Noble and John Ravenhill, 1–35. Cambridge, UK: Cambridge University Press.

Nossal, Kim Richard. 1999. "Lonely Superpower or Unapologetic Hyperpower? Analyzing American Power in the Post-Cold War Era." Paper presented at the South African Political Studies Association. Saldanha, Western Cape, South Africa, 29 June–2 July.

Nye, Joseph S., Jr. 1990. *Bound to Lead: The Changing Nature of American Power*. New York: Basic Books.

———. 2001. "Military Deglobalization?" *Foreign Policy* 122 (January/February): 82–83.

Ohio State University Program for International and Homeland Security. online. http://homelandsecurity.osu.edu/ (accessed 9 October 2006).

Ojakangas, Mika. 2003. "Carl Schmitt's Real Enemy: The Citizen of the Non-exclusive Democratic Community?" *The European Legacy* 8, no. 4 (August): 411–24.

———. 2004. *A Philosophy of Concrete Life: Carl Schmitt and the Political Thought of Late Modernity*. Jyväskylä, Finland: SoPhi 77.

Oneal, John R. 2003. "Measuring Interdependence and Its Pacific Benefits: A Reply to Gartzke & Li." *Journal of Peace Research* 40, no. 6 (November): 721–25.

Oneal, John R., Bruce Russett, and Michael L. Berbaum. 2003. "*Causes* of Peace: Democracy, Interdependence, and International Organizations, 1885–1992." *International Studies Quarterly* 47, no. 3 (September): 371–94.

Opertti, Didier. 1999. *Statement to the Conference Plenary*. http://www.wto.org/english/thewto_e/minist_e/min99_e/english/state_e/d5240e.pdf (accessed 18 February 2007).

Organisation for Economic Cooperation and Development. 1998a. "The MAI Negotiating Text (as of 24 April 1998)." Paris: OECD.

———. 1998b. "Commentary to the MAI Negotiating Text (as of 24 April 1998)." Paris: OECD.

———. 2002. *Science, Technology and Industry Outlook 2002*. http://lysander.sourceoecd.org/vl+6464985/cl=28/nw=1/rsvp/~6681/v2002n12/s1/p11 (accessed 28 January 2009).

———. 2004. Programme for International Student Assessment Survey. http://www.oecd.org/document/28/0,2340,en_2649_201185_34010524_1_1_1_1,00.html (accessed 9 March 2006).

———. 2006. *Main Science and Technology Indicators* 2006, no. 2: 1–102.

Organisation for Economic Cooperation and Development, Negotiating Group on the Multilateral Treaty on Investment (MAI). 1998. "Main Features of the Multilateral Agreement on Investment." DAFE/MAI(98)4, 5 February.

Orwell, George. [1949] 1950. *Nineteen Eighty-Four*. London: Secker and Warburg.

Pankakoski, Timo. 2004. "Research Note," 15 December. Unpublished.

Parkinson, Stuart. 2008. "Military R&D 85 Times Larger Than Renewable Energy R&D." *INES Newsletter*. 28 April. International Network of Engineers and Scientists for Global Responsibility. http://www.inesglobal.com/_Publications/inesBooks/NewsletterGeneva.pdf. (accessed 14 January 2009).

Patomäki, Heikki. 2007. *The Political Economy of Global Security: War, Future Crises and Changes in Global Governance*. New York: Routledge.

People's Volunteer Corps (RELA, or *Ikatan Relawan Rakyat Malaysia*). online. http://www.moha.gov.my/opencms/export/KHEDN/BhgJ2/index.html (accessed 20 October 2006).

Persaud, Randolph. 2007. Personal communication with the author. 15 October.

———. 2008. Personal communication with the author. 26 June.

Phelps, T. S. 1881. "Reminiscence of Seattle Washington Territory and the U.S. Sloop of War *Decatur* during the Indian War of 1855–56." *The United Service: A Monthly Review of Military and Naval Affairs* 5 (December): 669–706.

Phillips, Kevin. 2008. *Bad Money: Reckless Finance, Failed Politics, and the Global Crisis of American Capitalism*. New York: Penguin.

Picciotto, Sol. 1998. "Linkages in International Investment Regulation: The Antimonies of the Draft Multilateral Agreement on Investment." *University of Pennsylvania Journal of International Law* 19, no. 3 (Fall): 731–68.

Pin-Fat, Veronique, and Maria Stern. 2005. "The Scripting of Private Jessica Lynch: Biopolitics, Gender, and the 'Feminization' of the U.S. Military." *Alternatives: Global, Local, Political* 30, no. 1 (January–March): 25–53.

Polanyi, Karl. [1944] 1957. *The Great Transformation: The Political and Economic Origins of Our Time*. Boston: Beacon Press.

Porter, Bernard. 2006. *Empire and Superempire: Britain, America and the World*. New Haven, CT: Yale University Press.

Porter, Michael E. 1990. *The Competitive Advantage of Nations*. New York: Free Press.

"President Bush Discusses Terror Plot upon Arrival in Wisconsin." 2006. http://www.whitehouse.gov/news/releases/2006/08/20060810-3.html (accessed 13 September 2006).

"Princess Angeline Dies at Seattle." 1896. *Chicago Daily Tribune*, 1 June.

Putnam, Robert. 2000. *Bowling Alone: America's Social Capital*. New York: Simon and Schuster.

Raban, Jonathan. 2007. "Seattle Rising." *Financial Times*, 30 June–1 July.

Raghavan, Chakravarthi. 2000. "After Seattle, World Trade System Faces Uncertain Future." *International Review of Political Economy* 7, no. 3 (Autumn): 495–504.

Rajaram, Prem Kumar, and Carl Grundy-Warr. 2004. "The Irregular Migrant as Homo Sacer: Migration and Detention in Australia, Malaysia, and Thailand." *International Migration* 43, no. 1 (March): 33–63.

Ramo, Joshua Cooper. 2004. *The Beijing Consensus.* London: Foreign Policy Centre.

Rapoport, Anatol. 1968. "Introduction" to *On War* by Carl von Clausewitz, 11–80. London: Penguin.

Rasiah, Rajah. 1998. "Busting the Bubble: Causes of the Southeast Asian Financial Crisis." Bangi, Malaysia: Institute of Malaysian and International Studies, Universiti Kebangsaan Malaysia. Unpublished.

Rawls, John. 1993. *Political Liberalism.* New York: Columbia University Press.

Ray, James Earl. 1995. *Democracy and International Politics: An Evaluation of the Democratic Peace Proposition.* Columbia: University of South Carolina Press.

Reed, T. V. 2005. *The Art of Protest: Culture and Activism from the Civil Rights Movement to the Streets of Seattle.* Minneapolis: University of Minnesota Press.

Reinhart, Carmen M., and Kenneth S. Rogoff. 2008. "This Time Is Different: A Panoramic View of Eight Centuries of Financial Crises." National Bureau of Economic Research Working Paper 13882. http://www.nber.org/papers/w13882 (accessed 30 December 2008).

Reitan, Ruth. 2006. *Global Activism.* New York: Routledge.

"Relic of Battle of Seattle." 1906. *Atlanta Journal-Constitution,* 13 May.

Renner, Michael E. 2002. *The Anatomy of Resource Wars.* Worldwatch Paper 162, October. Washington, DC: Worldwide Institute.

Reno, William. 1998. *Warlord Politics and African States.* Boulder, CO: Lynne Rienner Publishers.

———. n.d. "The Empirical Challenge to Economic Analyses of Conflicts." http://www.ssrc.org/programs/gsc/publications/gsc_activities/globalization_conflict/reno (accessed 17 November 2004).

Rice, Susan E., and Stewart Patrick. 2008. *Index of State Weakness in the Developing World.* Washington, DC: Brookings Institution.

Rich, Frank. 2008. "Two Cheers for Rod Blagojevich." *New York Times,* 14 December.

Ripsman, Norrin M., and T. V. Paul. 2005. "Globalization and the National Security State: A Framework for Analysis." *International Studies Review* 7, no. 2 (June): 119–27.

Rivera-Batiz, Francisco L. 2001. "The East Asian Crisis and the Anatomy of Emerging Market Disease." In *The Political Economy of the East Asian Financial Crisis and Its Aftermath,* ed. Arvid John Lukauskas and Francisco L. Rivera-Batiz, 31–73. Cheltenham, UK: Edgar Algar.

Rivera-Batiz, Luis A., and Maria-Angels Oliva. 2001. "Revisiting the East Asian Crisis and Its Aftermath: A Political Economy Approach." In *The Political Economy of the East Asian Financial Crisis and Its Aftermath,* ed. Arvid John Lukauskas and Francisco L. Rivera-Batiz, 165–91. Cheltenham, UK: Edgar Algar.

Robb, John. 2007. *Brave New War: The Next Stage of Terrorism and the End of Globalization.* Hoboken, NJ: John Wiley and Sons.

Robin, Corey. 2004. *Fear: The History of an Idea.* New York: Oxford University Press.

Robinson, Eric. 2001. "Reading and Misreading the Ancient Evidence for Democratic Peace." *Journal of Peace Research* 38, no. 5 (September): 593–608.

Robinson, William I. 2004. *A Theory of Global Capitalism: Production, Class, and the State*. Baltimore: Johns Hopkins University Press.

Rosenau, James N. 1997. *Along the Domestic-Foreign Frontier: Exploring Governance in a Turbulent World*. Cambridge, UK: Cambridge University Press.

————. 2003. *Distant Proximities: Dynamics beyond Globalization*. Princeton, NJ: Princeton University Press.

Roth, Philip. 2004. *The Plot Against America*. New York: Random House.

Rothkopf, David J. 2008. *Superclass: The Global Power Elite and the World They Are Making*. New York: Farrar, Straus and Giroux.

Roy, Arundhati. 2004. *An Ordinary Person's Guide to Empire*. Cambridge, MA: South End Press.

Roy, Olivier. 2004. *Globalized Islam: The Search for a New Ummah*. New York: Columbia University Press.

Ruby, Jennie. 2003. "Is This a Feminist War?" In *After Shock: Global Feminist Perspectives on September 11, 2001*, ed. Susan Hawthorne and Bronwyn Winter, 177–79. Vancouver, Canada: Raincoast Books.

Rummel, Rudolph J. 1983. "Libertarianism and International Violence." *Journal of Conflict Resolution* 27, no. 1 (March): 27–71.

Russett, Bruce, and John R. Oneal. 2001. *Triangulating Peace: Democracy, Interdependence and International Organizations*. New York: W. W. Norton.

Sachs, Jeffrey. 1997. "Secretive Workings of the IMF Call for Reassessment." *New Straits Times*, 23 December.

Said, Edward. 1979. *Orientalism*. New York: Vintage.

Sandbrook, Richard, and David Romano. 2004. "Globalization, Extremism and Violence in Poor Countries." *Third World Quarterly: Journal of Emerging Areas* 25, no. 6 (January): 1007–31.

Sanger, David E. 2008. "Taking Risks Without Bailout." *New York Times*, 9 December.

Sarkees, Meredith Reid, and J. David Singer. 2001. "Armed Conflict Past & Future: A Master Typology?" Paper presented at the conference Identifying Wars: Systematic Conflict Research and Its Utility in Conflict Resolution and Prevention." Uppsala University, Uppsala, Sweden, 8–9 June.

Sarkees, Meredith Reid, Frank Whelon Wayman, and J. David Singer. 2003. "Inter-State, Intra-State, and Extra-State Wars: A Comprehensive Look at Their Distribution over Time, 1816–1997." *International Studies Quarterly* 47, no. 1 (March): 49–70.

Sassen, Saskia. 1996. *Losing Control? Sovereignty in an Age of Globalization*. New York: Columbia University Press.

Schlesinger, Arthur, Jr. 2004. "The Making of a Mess." *New York Review of Books* 51, no. 14 (23 September): 40–43.

Schmitt, Carl. [1922] 1985. *Political Theology: Four Chapters on the Concept of Sovereignty.* Trans. George Schwab. Cambridge, MA: MIT Press.

———. [1932] 1996. *The Concept of the Political.* Trans. George Schwab. Chicago: University of Chicago Press.

———. [1950] 2003. *The Nomos of the Earth in the International Law of the Jus Publicium Europaeum.* Trans. and annotated G. L. Ulmen. New York: Telos Press.

Schneider, Gerald, Katherine Barbieri, and Nils Petter Gleditsch. 2003. "Does Globalization Contribute to Peace? A Critical Survey of the Literature." In *Globalization and Armed Conflict*, ed. Gerald Schneider, Katherine Barbieri, and Nils Petter Gleditsch, 3–29. Lanham, MD: Rowman and Littlefield.

Scholte, Jan Aart. 2005. *Globalization: A Critical Introduction.* 2nd ed. New York: Palgrave Macmillan.

Schumpeter, Joseph A. [1942] 1947. *Capitalism, Socialism, and Democracy.* 2nd ed. New York: Harper and Brothers.

Segal, Adam. 2004. "Is America Losing Its Edge? Innovation in a Globalized World." *Foreign Affairs* 83, no. 6 (November/December): 2–8.

Sengupta, Somini. 2004. "Behind Sudan Killers, a Mass of Unknown." *International Herald Tribune*, 22 October.

Sennett, Richard. 2004. "The Age of Anxiety." *Guardian Review* (London), 23 October.

———. 2006. *The Culture of the New Capitalism.* New Haven, CT: Yale University Press.

Sforza-Roderick, Michelle, Scott Nova, and Mark Weisbrot. 1997. "Writing the Constitution of a Single Global Economy: A Concise Guide to the Multilateral Agreement on Investment." Washington, DC: Preamble Center Briefing Paper. December. http://www.globalpolicy.org/socecon/bwi-wto/sforza.htm (accessed 7 February 2006).

Shao Zhiqin. 2001. "Social Security and Women: Impact of Financial Crisis." In *Stability and Security of Socio-Economic Development in East Asia: Lessons from the Asian Financial Crisis*, ed. Zhang Yunling, 164–87. Beijing: China Social Sciences Press.

Shapiro, Michael J. 1989. "Representing World Politics: The Sport/War Intertext." In *International/Intertextual Relations: Postmodern Readings of World Politics*, ed. James Der Derian and Michael J. Shapiro, 69–96. New York: Lexington Books.

Shaw, Martin. 2000. *Theory of the Global State: Globality as an Unfinished Revolution.* Cambridge, UK: Cambridge University Press.

———. 2005. *The New Western Way of War: Risk Transfer War and Its Crisis in Iraq.* Cambridge, UK: Cambridge University Press.

Shepherd, Laura J. 2006. "Veiled References: Constructions of Gender in the Bush Administration Discourse on the Attacks on Afghanistan Post-9/11." *International Feminist Journal of Politics* 8, no. 1 (March): 19–41.

Sieg, Katrin. 2008. "Desiring the Global: Cinematic Family Affairs and International Relations." In *Choreographing the Global in the European Cinema and Theater*, ed. Katrin Sieg, 31–74. New York: Palgrave Macmillan.

Simpson, Erin. 2007. "Who Failed the World's 'Failed States'?" *Statesman* (Ghana), 23 June.

Singer, Max, and Aaron Wildavsky. 1993. *The Real World Order: Zones of Peace/Zones of Turmoil*. Chatham, NJ: Chatham House Publishers.

Singer, P. W. 2003. *Corporate Warriors: The Rise of the Privatized Military Industry*. Ithaca, NY: Cornell University Press.

Singer, Thomas, and Robert Stumberg. 1999. "A Multilateral Agreement on Investment: Would It Undermine Subnational Environmental Protection?" *Journal of Environment and Development* 8, no. 1 (March): 5–23.

"Six Nation Survey Finds Little Enthusiasm for Free Market Capitalism in Western Europe or the United States." 2007. 27 September. http://www.harrisinteractive.com/harris_poll/index.asp?PID=810 (accessed 30 June 2008).

Skeldon, Ronald. 1999. "Migration in Asia after the Economic Crisis: Patterns and Issues." *Asia-Pacific Population Journal* 14, no. 3 (1999): 3–24.

Skocpol, Theda. 2003. *Diminished Democracy: From Membership to Management in American Civic Life*. Norman: University of Oklahoma Press.

Slaughter, Anne-Marie. 2004. *A New World Order*. Princeton, NJ: Princeton University Press.

Smith, Adam. [1776] 1904. *An Inquiry into the Causes and the Wealth of Nations*. London: Methuen and Co.

Smith, Jackie. 2001. "Globalizing Resistance: The Battle of Seattle and the Future of Social Movements." *Mobilization: An International Journal* 6, no. 1 (Spring): 1–19.

Smith, Neil. 2005. "Neo-Critical Geography, Or, the Flat Pluralist World of Business Class." *Antipode* 37, no. 5 (November): 887–99.

Smith, Peter Jay, and Elizabeth Smythe. 2000. "Globalization, Citizenship and Technology: The MAI Meets the Internet." Paper presented at the annual meeting of the International Studies Association. Los Angeles, March.

Smith, Steven B. 2006. *Reading Leo Strauss: Politics, Philosophy, Judaism*. Chicago: University of Chicago Press.

Snyder, Scott, and Richard H. Solomon. 1998. "Beyond the Asian Financial Crisis: Challenges and Opportunities for U.S. Leadership," April. Reprinted in "Resource Materials: International Workshop on International Studies in the Era of Globalization: States, Markets, Values." Institute of Malaysian and International Studies, Program for International Studies in Asia, and Carnegie Council on Ethics and International Affairs, 1–20. Bangi, Malaysia: Universiti Kebangsaan Malaysia.

Social Science Research Council. n.d. "Project on Globalization & Conflict." http://www.ssrc.org/programs/gsc/publications/gsc_activities/globalization_conflict (accessed 17 November 2004).

Soros, George. 1998. *The Crisis of Global Capitalism: Open Society Endangered*. New York: Public Affairs.

———. 2002. *George Soros on Globalization*. New York: Public Affairs.

Spotts, Peter N. 2008. "Asia Trumping US on Science R&D." *Christian Science Monitor*, 9 October. http://features.csmonitor.com/innovation/2008/10/09/asia-trumping-us-on-science-rd/ (accessed 24 November 2008).

Steger, Manfred B., ed. 2003. *Rethinking Globalism*. Lanham, MD: Rowman and Littlefield.

———. 2005. *Globalism: Market Ideology Meets Terrorism*. 2nd ed. Lanham, MD: Rowman and Littlefield.

———. 2006. Comments at a roundtable on "Global Realignments" at the annual meeting of the International Studies Association. San Diego, March.

———. 2008. *The Rise of the Global Imaginary: Political Ideologies from the French Revolution to the Global War on Terror*. New York: Oxford University Press.

Stephanson, Anders. 1996. *Manifest Destiny: American Expansion and the Empire of Right*. New York: Hill and Wang.

Stiglitz, Joseph E. 2002. *Globalization and Its Discontents*. New York: W. W. Norton.

———. 2008. "America's War-Torn Economy." http://www.project-syndicate.org/commentary/stiglitz98 (accessed 24 November 2008).

Stiglitz, Joseph E., and Linda J. Bilmes. 2008. *The Three Trillion Dollar War: The True Cost of the Iraq Conflict*. New York: W. W. Norton.

Stockholm International Peace Research Institute (SIPRI). 2006. *SIPRI Yearbook: Armaments, Disarmament and International Security*. Oxford, UK: Oxford University Press.

———. 2008. *SIPRI Yearbook Armaments, Disarmament and International Security*. Oxford, UK: Oxford University Press.

———. n.d. http://www.sipri.org/contents/conflict/conflictdatasets.html#Anchor-Patterns-4783 (accessed 22 February 2006).

Strand, Håvard et al. 2005. "Armed Conflict Dataset Codebook." http:www.prio.no/cwp/armedconflict/current/Codebook_v3-2005.pdf (accessed 22 February 2006).

Strange, Susan. 1986. *Casino Capitalism*. Oxford, UK: Blackwell.

———. 1987. "The Persistent Myth of Lost Hegemony." *International Organization* 41, no. 4 (Autumn): 551–74.

———. 1996. *The Retreat of the State: The Diffusion of Power in the World Economy*. Cambridge, UK: Cambridge University Press.

———. 1998. *Mad Money: When Markets Outgrow Governments*. Ann Arbor: University of Michigan Press.

Strauss, Leo. 1964. *The City and Man*. Chicago: Rand McNally and Company.

Stubbs, Richard. 2005. *Rethinking Asia's Economic Miracle: The Political Economy of War, Prosperity and Crisis*. Houndmills, Basingstoke, Hampshire, UK: Palgrave Macmillan, New York: St. Martin's.

Stump, Jacob. 2006. Personal correspondence with the author. 13 March.

Syarisa Yanti Abubakar. 2002. "Migrant Labour in Malaysia: Impact and Implications of the Asian Financial Crisis." East Asian Development Network Regional Project on the Social Impact of the Asian Finanical Crisis (EADN RP1-5). Unpublished.

Sylvester, Christine. 1994. *Feminist Theory and International Relations Theory in a Postmodern Era*. Cambridge, UK: Cambridge University Press.

Tabb, William K. 2001. *The Amoral Elephant: Globalization and the Struggle for Social Justice in the Twenty-first Century*. New York: Monthly Review Press.

———. 2004. *Economic Governance in the Age of Globalization*. New York: Columbia University Press.

Tandon, Yash. 1999. "Transparency: A Casualty of Democratic and Ethical Deficit in WTO." *Southern and Eastern African Trade Information and Negotiations Institute*. 29 November. http://www.seatini.org/publications/articles/2002/transparency.html (accessed 25 April 2007).

Tarrow, Sidney. 2005. *The New Transnational Activism*. New York: Cambridge University Press.

Teivainen, Teivo. 2009. *Global Civil Society in Action?* New York: Routledge.

Tickner, J. Ann. 2002. "Feminist Perspectives on 9/11." *International Studies Perspectives* 3, no. 4: 333–50.

Tilly, Charles, ed. 1975. *The Formation of National States in Western Europe*. Princeton, NJ: Princeton University Press.

———. 1985. "War Making and State Making as Organized Crime." In *Bringing the State Back In*, ed. Peter B. Evans, Dietrich Rueschemeyer, and Theda Skocpol, 169–91. Cambridge, UK: Cambridge University Press.

———. 1986. *The Contentious French*. Cambridge, MA: Harvard University Press.

———. 1990. *Coercion, Capital, and European States, 990–1990*. Oxford, UK: Basil Blackwell Publishers.

———. 1993. *European Revolutions: 1492–1992*. Oxford, UK: Basil Blackwell Publishers.

———. 2002. *Stories, Identities and Political Change*. Oxford, UK: Rowman and Littlefield Publishers.

"Timeline." 2001. *The WTO History Project*. http://depts.washington.edu/wtohist/timeline.htm (accessed 22 December 2006).

"The Top 100 Public Intellectuals." 2008. *Foreign Policy* 166 (May/June): 58–61.

"Trade Expansion Remains the Engine of Growth." 1999. *Financial Times*, 29 November.

Tuomi, Krista. n.d. "Research Note." Unpublished.

United Nations Development Program. 1999. *Human Development Report*. New York: Oxford University Press.

U.S. Congress. House. Committee on Oversight and Government Reform. 2008. *The Financial Crisis and the Role of Federal Regulators*, 31–38. 110th Cong., 2nd sess., 23 October.

U.S. Department of Defense. 2007. http://www.defenselink.mil/speeches/speech.aspx?speechid=1199 (accessed 22 December 2008).

U.S. Department of Defense. 2008. Office of the Deputy Undersecretary of Defense (Installations and Environment). *Base Structure Report: FY 2008 Baseline.* Arlington, VA: U.S. Department of Defense. http://www.acq.osd.mil/ie/download/bsr/BSR2008Baseline.pdf (accessed 3 December 2008).

U.S. Department of Homeland Security. online. www.dhs.gov (accessed 29 May 2007).

U.S. Department of Homeland Security Office of University Programs. 2003. Fact Sheet 17, November. http://www.dhs.gov/xnews/releases/press_release_0296.shtm (accessed 29 May 2007).

U.S. National Counterterrorism Center. online. http://www.nctc.gov/about_us/about_nctc.html (accessed 20 September 2006).

U.S. National Intelligence Council. 2004. *Mapping the Global Future: Report of the National Intelligence Council's 2020 Project.* http://www.cia.gov/nic/NIC_2020_project.html (accessed 19 July 2005).

———. 2008. *Global Trends 2025: A Transformed World.* Washington, DC: U.S. Government Printing Office.

U.S. Office of the Coordinator for Counterterrorism. online. http://www.state.gov/s/ct/ (accessed 29 May 2007).

U.S. President. 2001. Address to a Joint Session of Congress and the American People. http://www.whitehouse.gov/news/releases/2001/09/20010920–8.html (accessed 23 June 2008).

———. 2002. *The National Security Strategy of the United States of America.* http://www.whitehouse.gov/nsc/nssintro.html (accessed 19 July 2005).

———. 2006. *The National Security Strategy of the United States of America.* http://www.whitehouse.gov/nsc/nss/2006/nss2006.pdf (accessed 13 September 2006).

Vaïsse, Justin. n.d. "L'hyper-puissance au défi de l'hyper-terrorisme." http://www.brookings.edu/dybdocroot/views/articles/fellows/20011023vaisse.pdf (accessed 28 March 2005).

Van Creveld, Martin. 1991. *The Transformation of War.* New York: Free Press.

Van Harten, Gus. 2007. *Investment Treaty Arbitration and Public Law.* New York: Oxford University Press.

Vandevelde, Kenneth J. 1998. "The Political Economy of a Bilateral Investment Treaty." *American Journal of International Law* 92, no. 4 (October): 621–41.

Väyrynen, Raimo. 1984. "Regional Conflict Formations: An Intractable Problem of International Relations." *Journal of Peace Research* 21, no. 4 (November): 337–59.

———. 2004. "Peace Research Between Idealism and Realism: Fragments of a Finnish Debate." In *Contemporary Security Analysis and Copenhagen Peace Research*, ed. Stefano Guzzini and Dietrich Jung, 27–39. London: Routledge.

Védrine, Hubert. 2001. *France in an Age of Globalization.* With Dominique Moisi. Trans. Philip Gordon. Washington, DC: Brookings Institution.

Vidal, Gore. 2002. *Perpetual War for Perpetual Peace: How We Got to Be So Hated*. New York: Thunder Mouth's Press/Nation Books.

Vision of Humanity. 2007. "Global Peace Index." http://www.visionofhumanity.com/rankings/ (accessed 6 June).

Vocke, Matthias. 1997. "Investment Implications of Selected WTO Agreements and the Proposed Multilateral Agreement on Investment." IMF Working Paper WP/97/60, Geneva.

Wade, Robert. 1998. "The Asian Crisis and the Global Economy: Causes, Consequences, and Cure." *Current History* 92, no. 622 (November): 361–73.

———. 2000. "Wheels within Wheels: Rethinking the Asian Crisis and the Asian Model." *American Review of Political Science* 3 (June): 85–115.

———. 2001. "The US Role in the Long Asian Crisis of 1990–2000." In *The Political Economy of the East Asian Financial Crisis and Its Aftermath*, ed. Arvid John Lukauskas and Francisco L. Rivera-Batiz, 195–226. Cheltenham, UK: Edgar Algar.

Walker, R.B.J. 1993. *Inside/Outside: International Relations as Political Theory*. Cambridge, UK: Cambridge University Press.

"Wall Street's Final '08 Toll: $6.9 Trillion Wiped Out." 2009. *Washington Post*, 1 January.

Wallensteen, Peter, and Margareta Sollenberg. 1998. "Armed Conflict and Regional Conflict Complexes, 1989–97." *Journal of Peace Research* 35, no. 5 (September): 621–34.

Wallerstein, Immanuel. 1974. *The Modern World System: Capitalist Agriculture and the Origins of the European World Economy in the Sixteenth Century*. New York: Academic Press.

Wapner, Paul. 1996. *Environmental Activism and World Civic Politics*. Albany: State University of New York Press.

Watal, Jayashree. 2000. "Developing Countries' Interests in a 'Development Round.'" In *The WTO After Seattle*, ed. Jeffrey J. Schott, 71–84. Washington, DC: Institute for International Economics.

Weart, Spencer R. 1998. *Never at War: Why Democracies Will Not Fight One Another*. New Haven, CT: Yale University Press.

Weber, Max. [1946] 1973. "Politics as a Vocation." In *From Max Weber: Essays in Sociology*. Trans. and ed. H. H. Gerth and C. Wright Mills, 77–129. New York: Oxford University Press.

———. [1947] 1969. *The Theory of Social and Economic Organization*. Trans. A. M. Henderson and Talcott Parsons. New York: Free Press.

———. 1978. *Economy and Society: An Outline of Interpretive Sociology*. Ed. Guenther Roth and Claus Wittich. Berkeley: University of California Press.

"Westwood Misses His First Cut of Season." 1998. *Nottingham Evening Post*, 15 August.

Willoughby, John. 2007. Personal communication with the author. 4 November.

Winslow, Deborah, and Michael D. Woost. 2004. "Articulations of Economy and Ethnic

Conflict in Sri Lanka." In *Economy, Culture, and Civil War in Sri Lanka*, ed. Deborah Winslow and Michael D. Woost, 1–27. Bloomington: Indiana University Press.

Winters, Jeffrey A. 1999. "The Determinant of Financial Crisis in Asia." In *The Politics of the Asian Economic Crisis*, ed. T. J. Pempel, 79–99. Ithaca, NY: Cornell University Press.

Witherell, William H. 1997. "Developing International Rules for Foreign Investment: OECD's Multilateral Agreement on Investment." *Business Economics* 32, no. 1 (January): 38–43.

Wolf, Martin. 2008. "Asia's Revenge." *Financial Times*, 9 October.

World Bank. 2007. Key Development Data and Statistics Web Page. http://web.world-bank.org/WBSITE/EXTERNAL/DATASTATISTICS/0, contentMDK:20535285~men uPK:1192694~pagePK:64133150~piPK:64133175~theSitePK:239419,00.html (accessed 2 May 2007).

———. 2008. "China Quarterly Update." http://web.worldbank.org/WBSITE/EXTERNAL/ COUNTRIES/EASTASIAPACIFICEXT/CHINAEXTN/0, contentMDK:21809859~page PK:1497618~piPK:217854~theSitePK:318950,00.html (accessed 28 June 2008).

World Bank. Independent Evaluation Group. 2006. *Engaging with Fragile States: An IEG Review of World Bank Support to Low-Income Countries under Stress*. Washington, DC: World Bank.

World Economic Forum. 2008. *The Global Competitiveness Report 2008–2009*. http://www.weforum.org/documents /GCR0809/index.html (accessed 25 February 2009).

Yip, Wei Kiat. 2001. "Prospects for Closer Economic Integration in East Asia." *Stanford Journal of East Asian Affairs* 1 (Spring): 106–11.

Youngs, Gillian. 2006. "Feminist International Relations in the Age of the War on Terror." *International Feminist Journal of Politics* 8, no. 1 (March): 3–18.

Zine, Jasmin. 2006. "Between Orientalism and Fundamentalism: Muslim Women and Feminist Engagement." In *(En)Gendering the War on Terror: War Stories and Camouflaged Politics*, ed. Krista Hunt and Kim Rygiel, 27–49. Aldershot, Hampshire, UK: Ashgate.

Zoll, Daniel. 1999. "NGOs Unwelcome at Forum." *World Trade Observer*, 30 November. http://www.globalpolicy.org/ngos/99deb/wto.htm (accessed 20 April 2007).

INDEX

Symbols: appropriation of, 39; legitimacy granted, 39; WTO as, 124, 126–27

Taiwan, 86, 92
Taliban, 151, 188
Tandon, Yash, 134–35
Tanzania, 189–90
Taxation, 79–80, 82, 168, 191, 194
Technological innovation: as factor in wars, 45; financial products, 45, 88; globalization of, 11–12; military use, 53; Revolution in Military Affairs, 56. *See also* Internet; Research and development spending
Territorial states, xix, xx, 63, 144, 160, 193
Territory: acquisition, 149; changes in spatial relations, 172; deterritorialization, 66, 144, 145; reterritorialization, 144, 149; sovereignty, 63
Terrorism: in Europe, 61; Islamic, 55–56, 61, 141, 143, 153; religious, 145; roots, 143; as threat, xix, 138; transnational networks, 2, 27, 55–56, 144, 167. *See also* Al Qaeda; Homeland security; September 11 attacks; "War on terror"
Thailand: central bank, 89; economic growth, 86, 88; financial crisis, 89, 90, 94; IMF loans, 92; migrant workers, 109, 110, 111, 112; political instability, 171
Theory, social, 59–61
Threats: climate change, 11, 164–65, 179, 182; nontraditional, 21, 164, 179, 184; Other as, 114, 151, 154–55, 183–84; transnational, 21–22, 27, 58. *See also* Enemies; Fear; Risk; Security; Terrorism
Tilly, Charles, 60–61
Time: compression, 4, 149; as factor in civil wars, 43; speed of, 18
TNCs, *see* Transnational corporations
Townsend, Stuart, 123
Trade: benefits, 129–30; disputes, 133, 198; hypercompetition, 136; liberalization, 45, 118, 169–70; peace and, 32–34; protectionism, 131, 197–98; volumes, 68. *See also* World Trade Organization
Trade unions, *see* Labor unions

Transformation, 20, 153, 156, 158. *See also* Globalization
Transnational corporations (TNCs): in developing countries, 79; expansion, 5; lobbying groups, 76, 81; power, 72; resource extraction, 44; support of MAI, 76. *See also* Business
Transnational identity, 123
Transnational networks: civil society, 76, 178–79; criminal, 2, 27, 45, 167; Internet use, 2, 76; security threats, 27; terrorist, 2, 27, 55–56, 144, 167
Treasury Department, U.S., 77, 108, 199
Treaties, *see* Bilateral investment treaties
Tribalism, 34–35
Trireme Partners, 55
Truman, Harry, 3
Turkish workers, in Germany, 61, 62

UCDP, *see* Uppsala Conflict Data Program
Uganda, 34–35, 40
Uhlman, Wes, 121
Ummah, 55–56, 111
UN, *see* United Nations
Uncertainty, *see* Insecurity; Risk; Threats
Unemployment: in Asia, 110, 111; in United States, 189, 199
Unilateralism, 56
Unions, *see* Labor unions
Unipolarity, 9
United Nations (UN): Charter, xvii; Charter of Economic Duties and Rights of States, 79; establishment, 197; peacekeepers, 45
United States: Afghanistan War, 38, 151, 188, 199; Asian financial crisis and, 85, 104–6, 107–8, 115–16, 169; competitiveness, 7; culture, 6, 140; debt, 10, 195, 201–2; defense spending, 4, 9, 162, 188, 193–94; economic policies, 191; economic stimulus and bailouts, 189–90, 197–98; education system, 10, 193; exceptionalism, 55, 80, 149; foreign policy, 88, 170; hegemony, 56, 181, 201; Helms-Burton legislation, 80; homeland security programs, 27, 139, 146–47, 155, 170;